The Red Thread

Leonard Yonkman

The Red Thread

© 2006 by Leonard Yonkman
All rights reserved. No part of this publication may be reproduced, stored in a retrieval system, or transmitted, in any form or by any means, electronic, mechanical, photocopying, recording, or otherwise, without the written prior permission of the author.

Layout by: Laurie Esposito Harley
Cover Design by: Jason Bacher
www.AardvarkWriting.com
Professional writing and design services

Published by Aardvark Publishers
www.AardvarkPublishers.com
Located in the USA
This book was published on-demand by Aardvark Publishers.
Book information and book sales:
Aardvark Publishers
www.AardvarkPublishers.com
orders@aardvarkpublishers.com

ISBN: 0-6151-3673-8
ISBN-13: 978-0-6151-3673-8

Contents

	Preface		...i
Ch 1	Genesis	The Promised Seed	...1
Ch 2	Exodus	Christ Our Passover	...9
Ch 3	Leviticus	The Sacrifice	...19
Ch 4	Numbers	A Star Out of Jacob	...29
Ch 5	Deuteronomy	The Rock	...35
Ch 6	Joshua	A Great Stone of Witness	...43
Ch 7	Judges	Our Saviour and Judge	...51
Ch 8	Ruth	The Kinsman Redeemer	...61
Ch 9	I Samuel	The Lord's Anointed	...67
Ch 10	II Samuel	My Son	...73
Ch 11	I Kings	A Man	...81
Ch 12	II Kings	The Resurrection	...89
Ch 13	I Chronicles	The Way	...95
Ch 14	II Chronicles	A Light	...101
Ch 15	Ezra	A Nail	...109
Ch 16	Nehemiah	The Door	...115
Ch 17	Esther	I Am	...121
Ch 18	Job	The Daysman	...129
Ch 19	Psalms	Thine Holy One	...137
Ch 20	Proverbs	The Wise Son	...145
Ch 21	Ecclesiastes	A Just Man	...153
Ch 22	The Song of Solomon	The Beloved	...161
Ch 23	Isaiah	God's Namesake	...169
Ch 24	Jeremiah	The Lord Our Righteousness	...177
Ch 25	Lamentations	The Comforter	...185
Ch 26	Ezekiel	The Son of Man	...191
Ch 27	Daniel	The Messiah	...199
Ch 28	Hosea	The Head	...211
Ch 29	Joel	The Vine	...219

Ch 30	Amos	The Lord Of Glory	227
Ch 31	Obadiah	The Judgment Of The Nations	235
Ch 32	Jonah	The Salvation Of The Lord	243
Ch 33	Micah	An Heir	251
Ch 34	Nahum	Our Peace	261
Ch 35	Habakkuk	His Faith	269
Ch 36	Zephaniah	The King Of Israel	279
Ch 37	Haggai	As A Signet	287
Ch 38	Zechariah	The Branch	293
Ch 39	Malachi	The Lord	303
	Appendix I		313
	Appendix II		327

Preface

Even in the Old Testament Jesus Christ is the underlying theme of the Bible, and this book discusses the prophesies of Jesus Christ throughout the Old Testament. In defining this study of the red thread it would be remiss of me not to share with you a little background on how the red thread came to be. From my understanding, Oral Roberts could have been the first one to coin the phrase "the red thread." He wanted to point out that Jesus Christ was found in every book of the Bible. It is Christ who holds the Word of God together similar to a thread woven throughout the scriptures. It is the blood of Christ which makes the thread red. The blood of Christ was shed to purge us of sin, and by his blood we are made white as snow. Oral Roberts is not the only one to have pointed out this wonderful truth. Others have also noted that Christ is inherent within the scriptures. E. W. Bullinger writes in his book *How to Enjoy the Bible* that the Word has one great subject. He goes on to say:

> Apart from Him, the natural eye of man sees only outward historical details and circumstances; some in themselves appearing to him trifling, others offensive, and pursued at a length which seems disproportionate to the whole; while things which "angels desire to look into" are passed over in a few words, or in silence. But once let "the spiritual mind" see Christ testified of "in Moses and the prophets," then all assumes a new aspect: trifles that seem hardly worth recording fill the whole vision and light up the written Word and make it to shine with the glory of the Divine presence.

I also was put on the trail of the red thread under the teaching of Dr. Victor Paul Wierwille, and I began to see Jesus Christ in my own study of the Old Testament records. The fruit of my labor is the joy of setting before you the one who has become affectionately known to me as "the red thread." Christ has always been God's plan for man's redemption. It is no wonder that you find him revealed in the Word even before he was born. The Old Testament holds a wealth of information regarding redemption and the redeemer. Jesus Christ himself testified to the truth of the red thread in his earthly ministry.

John 5:39
Search the scriptures; for in them ye think ye have eternal life: and they are they which testify of me.

In each book of the Bible there is one predominant theme, one thing which stands out above all the others, marking it as the red thread in that particular book of the Bible.

It is not only the attributes and characteristics found exemplified in Christ which make up the red thread, because those things can show up in others also. The study of the red thread contains those things that are peculiar to Christ, things that could only be fulfilled in him.

Luke 24:27 and 44- 47

And beginning at Moses and all the prophets, he expounded unto them in all the scriptures the things concerning himself.

And he said unto them, These *are* **the words which I spake unto you, while I was yet with you, that all things must be fulfilled, which were written in the law of Moses, and** *in* **the prophets, and** *in* **the psalms, concerning me.**

Then opened he their understanding, that they might understand the scriptures,

And said unto them, Thus it is written, and thus it behoved Christ to suffer, and to rise from the dead the third day:

And that repentance and remission of sins should be preached in his name among all nations, beginning at Jerusalem.

To have the understanding opened that we might understand the scriptures is a great thrill. To be able to look into the Word of God and see the red thread has been a tremendous blessing for me. I am thankful to have been put on the track of the red thread, and I trust it will hold the same blessing for you.

All scripture in this book is taken from the King James Version of the Bible. I have worked with the King James Version for many years and still prefer it today over other versions for many reasons. Perhaps two of the most notable would be the italicized words which the King James Version employs, and the fact that the King James interacts with the research materials I have. The italics found in the King James' Authorized Version show words which were added by the translators which were not in the Stephens Greek text or the Septuagint from which the Bible was translated. I have also grown accustomed to the old English and find it more exact than many of today's words and meanings. Language changes; words and their meanings are always under a constant state of change in use and definition. Therefore, any translation will never be quite current. Typically the meanings of words seem to degrade with change, making it even more difficult to communicate a thought or idea accurately. For example, the word 'create' has been degraded from its biblical usage. It has taken on a meaning in today's vernacular whereas anyone can create something. In the Bible, only God is ascribed to have the ability to start out with nothing and come up with something. In dealing with God's Word, I am concerned with communicating accurately the things which God had recorded for all of us to understand. Feel free to reference any version with which you are comfortable. However, you must remember that every version has to be looked at closely, and the Word has to be rightly divided in order to hold the true meaning.

The Promised Seed

Adam and Eve lived in paradise. They had it all. They only knew that which was right and good. When God formed man, He gave him a body and then He breathed soul life into him, and the man became alive, a living soul. God also created Adam and Eve in His own image, and God's image is spirit. God was then and is now a spirit being. He has no flesh and blood, no body and soul. But God's man was a three-part being, and the part which was created in God's image was lost; it was gone with the sin of Adam and Eve. Sin, by definition, is that which separates you from God. They could no longer commune with God, spirit to spirit. Their perception had changed; they could no longer define spiritual concepts. Their frequency band was now the "all senses network." The spirit allowed them to formulate thoughts which revealed the spirit and allowed them to see beyond the senses. Once the spirit was gone, the change became quite evident.

The Lord God planted a garden in Eden, and it was a perfect place to put a perfect couple. Out of the ground the Lord God made trees to grow, every tree that was pleasant to the eye and good for food, but also the tree of life and the tree of knowledge of good and evil. The tree of life and the tree of knowledge of good and evil were not physical trees but nonetheless their fruit could be picked and eaten by Adam and Eve. Adam and Eve had free will and were given a choice, which can be seen in the condition God placed on eating of the trees in the garden. God commanded them saying, "Of every tree of the garden thou mayest freely eat: but of the tree of the knowledge of good and evil, thou shalt not eat of it: for in the day that thou eatest thereof thou shalt surely die." When they ate the fruit of the tree of the knowledge of good and evil, they suffered a spiritual death, which left them with nothing more than their body and soul life. Adam and Eve left the Garden of Eden and were kept from eating of the tree of life. Man became known as a carnal man or a natural man. He was now a man of the senses, because by the five senses he now received his information. Therefore God devised a plan to restore the spirit to the senses man and for this He chose seed.

The idea of seed is something God had already introduced. In the plant kingdom, it is in the seed that you find the possibility for reproduction and the advancement of its kind. The seed carries the life of the plant to the next generation. There is an inherent spiritual source of life in all seeds. When looking at the animal kingdom and mankind, we see the soul life is also found in the seed. In humans, seed has been defined as sperm or semen.

Biblically the man is ascribed to having seed, not the woman. In the Bible, seed can also indicate an individual or a blood line. Seed can represent soul life as an entire category or an individual offspring or one's progeny. The promised seed, which is our study of the red thread in the book of Genesis, is Jesus Christ. Life starts with a seed. It would take Jesus Christ to restore the severed connection between God and man. It was Jesus himself who declared "I am come that they might have life and that they might have it more abundantly."

Genesis 3:14 and 15
And the LORD God said unto the serpent, Because thou hast done this, thou *art* cursed above all cattle, and above every beast of the field; upon thy belly shalt thou go, and dust shalt thou eat all the days of thy life:
And I will put enmity between thee and the woman, and between thy seed and her seed; it shall bruise thy head, and thou shalt bruise his heel.

There are two seeds identified here in Genesis 3:15: the seed of the serpent and the seed of the woman. When considering the seed of the serpent, you notice that the serpent refers to Satan or the Devil. Satan is a spirit being, one of the angels of heaven. The Devil and his angels have left their first estate and become evil, but nonetheless angels have no seed. They do not marry and reproduce like men or even as the beasts of the earth do. Yet God indicates there would be enmity or separation between the seed which Satan had and the seed of the woman. Through Adam's sin, he inadvertently handed over his dominion and authority to the Devil, God's archenemy. Adam was given dominion and authority over all soul life upon the earth when God put him in the Garden of Eden. God gave Adam every herb-bearing seed and every tree which has fruit-bearing seed. When Adam left the Garden of Eden, the ground was cursed for his sake, but perhaps more importantly soul life was now in the hands of the Devil. Once the Devil had control of this soul life, he chose to corrupt and kill it.

God stepped in to intercede with the seed of the woman. The woman has no seed, she produces the egg, but it remains unfertilized until the seed is introduced. A woman can conceive seed, but it is not hers to start with. This already indicates that God would have to do it. The supposition could be put forth claiming seed speaks of an offspring or the descendants of Adam and Eve. Yet Eve had respect for a seed coming from another place.

Genesis 4:1
And Adam knew Eve his wife; and she conceived, and bare Cain, and said, I have gotten a man from the LORD.

Eve thought that she had gotten a man from the Lord. Eve knew she and Adam had come together, yet she thought Cain was the man from the Lord. Cain was Adam and Eve's offspring, but he was not the seed of the woman. Cain never bruised Satan's head, but he did kill his brother Abel. Even though Eve obviously desired to have the man from the Lord, her seed in this instance was Cain. When Adam and Eve had another son, Eve's tone and expectations had changed a bit concerning the seed.

Genesis 4:25
And Adam knew his wife again; and she bare a son, and called his name Seth: For God, *said she*, hath appointed me another seed instead of Abel, whom Cain slew.

Every woman is made the same when it comes to how she conceives. In the annals of history, there is one woman who stands out from all others when it comes to how she conceived a child. In order for God to fulfill the promise He made back in Genesis 3:15 concerning the seed of the woman, He would have to become involved.

Matthew 1:18
Now the birth of Jesus Christ was on this wise: When as his mother Mary was espoused to Joseph, before they came together, she was found with child of [by] the Holy Ghost [*hagion pneuma*].

The use of the words 'Holy Ghost' may cause the reader to wonder just to whom this is referring. The Greek word *hagion* is holy and *pneuma* is spirit. When these words refer to God, it is because God is holy and God is spirit. The angel Gabriel came to Mary while she was still a virgin and told Mary she would conceive in her womb and bring forth a son. The soul life which is found in the sperm would be created and placed there by God, and this is how Mary would become pregnant.

Luke 1:34 and 35
Then said Mary unto the angel, How shall this be, seeing I know not a man?
And the angel answered and said unto her, The Holy Ghost [holy

spirit] **shall come upon thee, and the power of the Highest** [that would be God] **shall overshadow** [cover] **thee: therefore also that holy thing which shall be born of thee shall be called the Son** [son] **of God.**

I will build my point based on the idea that God has in His possession the spirit that was originally created and placed upon Adam and Eve while they were in the garden. God measured out holy spirit upon men and women of the Old Testament who were willing to work with Him. Moses had spirit upon him when he led the children of Israel out of Egypt. Others had spirit upon them, such as the prophets Elijah and Elisha, of whom it was said received a double portion of the spirit that was upon his predecessor. There were also others who received a portion of this spirit for a period of time in their lives, but the vast majority lived their whole life without the spirit of God. God places holy spirit upon people for a purpose. Since the loss of the spirit by Adam and Eve, men and women were not naturally equipped with holy spirit. Mary was given holy spirit to conceive seed and raise a son, God's son. God is not a man that he would have intercourse with Mary, but He placed the soul life, which would be the seed of the woman, in Mary and she conceived. God had a purpose for giving Jesus soul life which was separate from the soul life found in the blood of Adam and all his descendants. After Adam had forfeited the rights to his soul life, his seed became corrupted. Many of the people who had this corrupted soul life were doing a great deal of evil with their lives. Even those who desired to do good over evil were themselves saddled with Adam's sin. Jesus had soul life which did not fall under the jurisdiction of Adam's seed or of Adam's sin.

Hebrews 2:14- 16
Forasmuch then as the children are partakers of flesh and blood, he also himself likewise took part of the same; That through death he might destroy him that had the power of death, that is, the devil;
And deliver them who through fear of death were all their lifetime subject to bondage.
For verily he took not on *him the nature of* angels; but he took on *him* the seed of Abraham.

The children spoken of here in Hebrews 2:14 address all those who descended from Adam. All descendants of Adam partook of the flesh and blood of Adam and Eve. Mary was a descendant of Adam and Eve, partaking of flesh and blood, but Jesus only took part of the same. Jesus received the flesh from Mary but the blood which carries the soul life came from God. The purpose for this was that through death Jesus might destroy the Devil, who had the power of death. When Jesus' innocent blood was shed, his uncorrupted seed could then stand in the place of the corrupted seed of Adam. God could then offer life for death to everyone who would believe concerning that which Jesus had accomplished by his death. Jesus was holy in that he enjoyed purity in his soul life. Jesus did not take on the nature of angels, for his nature was that of a body and soul man. Jesus was marked out to be the seed of the woman but also took on the seed of Abraham.

Galatians 3:16
Now to Abraham and his seed were the promises made. He saith not, And to thy seeds, as of many; but as of one, And to thy seed, which is Christ.

God made promises concerning man's redemption. He made a promise concerning the seed of the woman. God was going to deliver us from the fear of death, which we were in bondage to all our lifetimes. Eve did not bring forth the seed God had promised. Mary did.
God also made promises regarding Abraham's seed, but again his seed referred to Christ. Jesus Christ, as the promised seed, truly would have a profound effect upon us all.

Genesis 15:5
And He [God] brought him [Abraham] forth abroad and said, Look now toward heaven, and tell the stars, if thou be able to number them: and He said unto him, So shall thy seed be. And he believed the LORD.

Abraham perceived what God was saying and believed. For this, Abraham became known as the father of all they that believe. Abraham's name was at the first Abram, which means *exalted father*. God changed his name to Abraham, which means *father of a multitude*.
God said, look now toward heaven and tell me how many stars there are and then He said, so shall thy seed be. How could this one seed be a multitude such as the stars for number? It is because that seed is Christ, and it is Christ in you the moment you are born again.

Colossians 1:27
To whom God would make known what *is* the riches of the glory of this mystery among the Gentiles; which is Christ in you, the hope of glory:

The mystery described in Colossians 1:27 shows the riches of God in the glory He has bestowed upon us in that promised seed which is Christ in you. There was something about this promised seed that had been kept secret. God had a plan of how to make this Christ in you more permanent than what anyone could have imagined.

II Corinthians 5:17
Therefore if any man *be* **in Christ,** *he is* **a new creature** [a new creature = a new creation]**: old things are passed away; behold, all things are become new.**

You are now, a new creation in Christ Jesus. Jesus Christ is the promised seed, and when this seed is in you, you are a new creation in Christ. God rarely uses the word create, but we are His workmanship created in Christ Jesus. Christ came into the world to reconcile the world unto God. Christ's blood was used to buy us back from the one who held us all in the fearful grip of death.

I Peter 1:18a, 19, 23
Forasmuch as ye know that ye were not redeemed [bought back]**, with corruptible things** *as* **silver and gold,**
But with the precious blood of Christ, as of a lamb without blemish and without spot:
Being born again, not of corruptible seed, but of incorruptible, by the word of God, which liveth and abideth forever.

This incorruptible seed, the seed which is Christ, is a spiritual seed. God's plan involved reuniting the man of body and soul with the spirit. For this God chose incorruptible seed. Being born again is a spiritual birth making this birth much more permanent than even our birth by corruptible seed. This new birth is a gift of God bringing life to each recipient. The seed is placed in each person once they have collected enough information to satisfy them, coming to a point of accepting the reconciliation Jesus Christ accomplished for them.

Galatians 3:14
That the blessing of Abraham might come on the Gentiles through [in] **Jesus Christ; that we might receive the promise of the spirit through faith** [believing]**.**

Jesus Christ made available a spiritual seed to all those who would accept the life of his physical seed as a substitute for the inevitable death of their own corrupted seed passed down from Adam. It is the Devil who kills at will, and no one could escape for he had dominion over the soul life of all mankind.

Romans 5:12
Wherefore, as by one man sin entered into the world, and death by sin; and so death passed upon all men, for that all have sinned.

This was the consequence of Adam's sin. When he became separated from God, this separation or sin was passed on to all of us, even at birth. All of us were left in a dire state of death in trespasses and sin, without God and without hope in this world. To be condemned by what Adam and Eve had done hardly seems fair.

Romans 5:18, 19
Therefore as by the offence of one *judgment came* **upon all men to condemnation; even so by the righteousness of one** *the free gift came* **upon all men unto justification of life.**
For as by one man's disobedience, [through disbelieving the Word] **many were made sinners, so by the obedience of one,** [by believing the Word] **shall many be made righteous.**

Jesus was given the opportunity to do that which Adam failed to do. Adam failed to believe when God told him not to eat of the tree of the knowledge of good and evil. Jesus Christ on the other hand did believe. Jesus Christ knew that righteousness and the justification of life were in his hands.

Romans 9:29
And as Esaias [Isaiah] **said before, Except the Lord of Sabaoth had left us a seed, we had been as Sodoma, and been made like unto Gomorrha.**

No one had a chance at life without Jesus Christ. It is now available to have our soul life covered by Jesus Christ's soul life, his in payment for each of ours. We now have the spirit returned to our lives in the form of seed. It is so exciting to see this blessing come upon all of us. Christ had no children by natural means, but he has produced a large family for the Father by being the seed which brings many sons to glory. The red thread in the book of Genesis is Jesus Christ, the promised seed. We may not be able to go back to not knowing evil like Adam and Eve in the beginning. But we have something far greater than Adam and Eve in that the spirit we have in Christ is seed. Adam and Eve had spirit on a condition. Our spirit is incorruptible in birth by the word of God which lives and abides forever.

Christ Our Passover

Out of all the children who were born in the generations of Adam, there was a linage which emerged distinct from the others. This ancestral line became identified as the sons of God because of an association with God. Once God had made known His plan to redeem man, the bloodline by which Christ would come came under attack. One of Satan's attempts to eliminate any hope of the coming seed came in the days of Noah when the earth was reduced to the eight souls of Noah and his family. In the book of Exodus, the attempt to do away with the seed and the bloodline was by Pharaoh's order to kill every son born of the Hebrew women. Out of the house of bondage God heard the cry of His people, whom He had named Israel.

The family plays an important role in God's design. Originally the family consisted of a group of people living under a patriarch. The father figure was responsible for the direction of the family unit. After the flood, in the generations of Noah, the family unit began to break up into many families and countries and nations. The linage which came out of Abraham, Isaac, and Jacob became identified as God's people. God was looking to build a family which would include the people living here upon the earth. God wanted His people to look to Him for direction and protection. God would like to be the ultimate father figure, and He set out to prove that to the children of Israel. God has a way of consummating His purpose and plan no matter who attempts to stop it, although men still retain their freedom of will.

Exodus 4:22
And thou shalt say unto Pharaoh, Thus saith the LORD, Israel *is* my son, *even* my firstborn:

The children of Israel set under a covenant with God; therefore by the rights of adoption, God declared Israel to be "My son, My firstborn." There are three ways to be a son: one is by association, two is by adoption, and the third is by seed. To be a son by association is the most rewarding and yet the most fickle, knowing you can walk away at any time. Adoption affords you certain rights and protection under the law, but it is still your free will which determines whether you choose to have a standing within the family. A son by seed is assured a place in the family, but the rights and protection are still only realized in the fellowship one chooses to keep with the Father. God's plan was to ensure a standing as a son while maintaining the freedom of a man's will to choose life over death, for God's desire has always been a more enduring association. The firstborn had certain rights of inheritance within the family. Typically the firstborn son would take on the responsibility of leading the family under his care. He was also given the resources of the family to be able to undertake the task.

By the time we get into the book of Exodus, Israel was in bondage. Jacob and his children had left the land of Canaan, entered into the land of Egypt, and dwelt in the country of Goshen. Joseph had found favor under Pharoah in Egypt, but as time passed, Joseph and all those of his generation died. The children of Israel were fruitful and increased abundantly. They multiplied in number, and they filled the land. But a new king arose over Egypt who did not know Joseph. The new king became concerned about the children of Israel. Pharaoh was afraid that the children of Israel were becoming too powerful and prosperous. The king was concerned about Israel's allegiance and began to tax and afflict them with many burdens. As they continued to lose their freedoms, Israel became enslaved under the heavy hand of Pharaoh. In spite of it all, Israel still continued to multiply and grow. It was then that Pharaoh set out to control the population by killing every son being born to the Hebrew women. This vicious attack did not go unnoticed by God. Israel was God's son, and God had a plan. Christ was to be born out of this bloodline. The true attack of God's adversary was aimed at the destruction of Christ our Passover. As things began to change for the children of Israel and the need for deliverance became evident, God called upon Moses to help. As the red thread, Christ shows up in the Passover in the book of Exodus, but later as our Passover. The Passover lamb was God's way of providing protection and the direction leading out of bondage. The Passover lamb proved to be of great benefit in Moses' day as well as today.

Exodus 12:3 and 4
Speak ye unto all the congregation of Israel, saying, In the tenth *day* of this month they shall take to them every man a lamb, according to the house of *their* fathers, a lamb for an house:
And if the household be too little for the lamb, let him and his neighbour next unto his house take *it* according to the number of the souls; every man according to his eating shall make your count for the lamb.

The whole family of Israel was given the direction of taking a lamb. Every man that wanted the protection afforded him by the lamb was to eat. As much or as little as you want, that was up to you. But without the lamb, there would be no protection against the destroyer. The idea of killing something and eating it was no longer a foreign notion. The concept of giving one's life for another was also recognized. This concept was noted by Abel when he offered a lamb in sacrifice to God. Then after the flood Noah offered sacrifice to the Lord and the eating of flesh was instituted. It was at this time that God said, "Every moving thing that lives shall be meat for you." Abraham learned that God Himself would provide a lamb for a burnt offering. All of this built toward the Passover. Even still the thought of eating something that has given its life for you seems disconcerting at times. Most people are not accustomed to raising or acquiring an animal, then killing, preparing, and eating it. Seeing the process helps to appreciate the life that was given. An innocent lamb paints quite a picture when it comes to the respect one has for the sacrifice that is given on your behalf.

Exodus 12:5- 11
Your lamb shall be without blemish, a male of the first year: ye shall take *it* out from the sheep, or from the goats:
And ye shall keep it up until the fourteenth day of the same month: and the whole assembly of the congregation of Israel shall kill it in the evening.
And they shall take of the blood, and strike *it* on the two side posts and on the upper door post of the houses, wherein they shall eat it.
And they shall eat the flesh in that night, roast with fire, and unleavened bread; *and* with bitter *herbs* they shall eat it.
Eat not of it raw, nor sodden at all with water, but roast *with* fire; his head with his legs, and with the purtenance thereof.
And ye shall let nothing of it remain until the morning; and that which remaineth of it until the morning ye shall burn with fire.
And thus shall ye eat it; *with* your loins girded, your shoes on your feet, and your staff in your hand; and ye shall eat it in haste: it *is* the LORD'S passover.

There were certain requirements placed upon the lamb, as well as to how the lamb was to be killed, prepared, and eaten. It was to be killed about three in the afternoon, because sunset was considered the start of a new day, and they needed time to roast the lamb before beginning to eat it at sunset. The blood was a covering for each soul that entered to eat. They were not to eat the lamb raw, nor boiled in water; it was to remain whole with the innards intact, roasted with fire. And if anything was left over in the morning, it was to be burned with fire. This is how they were to eat: fully dressed with their shoes on their feet while still holding their staff in hand.

They must eat in haste, for this is the Lord's Passover. The Lord's Passover, symbolized here but ultimately fulfilled in Christ.

I Peter 1:18a, 19
Forasmuch as ye know that ye were not redeemed with corruptible things, *as* silver and gold; But with the precious blood of Christ, as a lamb without blemish and without spot.

God redeemed us from our adversary, the Devil, with the blood of Christ, as of a lamb without blemish. The blood of the lamb covered the life of those that were under it, but the blood of Christ was used to redeem the lives of those who are covered by it. In the Lord's Passover the children of Israel were instructed to strike the blood, covering the place where they were to eat. Then concerning the flesh of the lamb it was said, "they shall eat it." When Jesus was speaking concerning himself, he said we were to eat his flesh and drink his blood.

John 6:53- 57
Then Jesus said unto them, Verily, verily, I say unto you, Except ye eat the flesh of the Son of man, and drink his blood, ye have no life in you.
Whoso eateth my flesh, and drinketh my blood, hath eternal life; and I will raise him up at the last day.
For my flesh is meat indeed, and my blood is drink indeed.
He that eateth my flesh, and drinketh my blood, dwelleth in me, and I in him.
As the living Father hath sent me, and I live by [because of] **the Father: so he that eateth me, even he shall live by** [because of] **me.**

Exodus says, "it is the Lord's Passover." I Corinthians 5:7 says, "Christ our Passover is sacrificed for us." Christ is our Passover and is sacrificed for us. As the red thread, he is the Lord's Passover in Exodus. Today Christ is our Passover; therefore, he becomes the Lamb of God, sacrificed for us. In I Corinthians, we find a record which should help us to understand the communion that we are to have with Christ in the Lord's supper.

I Corinthians 11:20- 31
When ye come together therefore into one place, *this* is not to eat the Lord's supper.
For in eating every one taketh before *other* his own supper: and one is hungry, and another is drunken.

What? have ye not houses to eat and to drink in? or despise ye the church of God, and shame them that have not? What shall I say to you? shall I praise you in this? I praise *you* not.

For I have received of the Lord that which also I delivered unto you, That the Lord Jesus the *same* night in which he was betrayed took bread:

And when he had given thanks, he brake *it*, and said, Take, eat: this is my body [this is a metaphor], which is broken [the word is "given," not "broken." Look at Luke 22:19] for you: this do in remembrance of me.

After the same manner also *he took* the cup, when he had supped, saying, This cup is the new testament [covenant] in my blood: this do ye, as oft as ye drink *it*, in remembrance of me.

For as often as ye eat this bread, and drink this cup, ye do show [examine the purpose of] the Lord's death till he come.

Wherefore whosoever shall eat this bread, and drink *this* cup of the Lord, unworthily [without knowing and accepting what Jesus has done and accomplished as our Passover], shall be guilty of the body and blood of the Lord.

But let a man examine himself [Look at where you are: Do you believe in Jesus Christ and what he has done? If so], let him eat of *that* bread, and drink of *that* cup. [For in eating and drinking we have life but if we deny him we have death.]

For he that eateth and drinketh unworthily, eateth and drinketh damnation [judgment] to himself, [and the judgment with which you judge yourself, is to be worthy of death], not discerning the Lord's body.

For this cause many *are* weak and sickly among you, and many sleep [are dead].

For if we would judge ourselves, [worthy, to be in the body] we should not be judged.

Paul wrote to the Corinthians concerning the Lord's supper. Paul wanted them to know that just because they all got together, it did not mean that they had to eat the Lord's supper. When thinking about Christ our Passover, there is a proper way to enjoy that communion. When we eat the Lord's supper, we should eat with the respect due the flesh and blood of the lamb. The Lord's supper is something to be revered. There is a respect due the solemnity of the occasion. The Corinthian church did not seem to be taking it seriously. The Lord's supper is not to be taken lightly. It is not done in jest, nor is it foolishness. When the communion service was instituted, it was Jesus himself that set the protocol. Paul said that he received his information from the Lord as to the procedure, meaning, and benefit of communion. There are two main elements dealing with communion: the body and the blood. The bread represents the body of Christ, and the wine represents the blood of Christ. The blood provides redemption, while the body offers health and wholeness. When we come together and eat of the bread and drink of the cup, it represents Christ's body and blood. The purpose is to keep Christ our Passover fresh in our minds. The benefit is life and strength and health to all those who judge themselves worthy.

There is life in the body if we care to eat. Since Adam chose death over life, not only was the spirit removed, but this then allowed for the corruption and untimely death of the soul life which kept the body alive. So it is now, when the spirit is returned in the new birth, man has eternal life, but the soul life still needs the health that only the body of Christ can provide. In the new birth, there is still a matter of routine maintenance and upkeep. Living in this world can wear on a body.

Returning now to the book of Exodus, we find the children of Israel were beginning to have second thoughts. When the children of Israel ate the Passover, they were instructed to be ready to go. And go they did. Pharaoh finally gave them leave. When they left, there was not one feeble person among them because of the Passover lamb which they had eaten. They left with much of the silver and gold of Egypt, which the Egyptians gladly gave them. They left under God's protection and guidance with a cloud for a covering and a pillar of fire to light the way. The children of Israel had all been caught up in the moment. They had witnessed the Passover and God's mighty hand. They were with Moses and saw the wonders and the parting of the Red Sea. But now they were faced with the reality of the wilderness and what to eat for breakfast.

Exodus 16:14 and 15
When the dew that lay was gone up, behold, upon the face of the wilderness *there lay* a small round thing, *as* small as the hoar frost on the ground.

And when the children of Israel saw *it*, they said one to another, It *is* manna: for they wist [knew] not what it *was*. [The word Manna means *What is it.*] **And Moses said unto them, This *is* the bread which the LORD hath given you to eat.**

This bread from heaven, which God gave them to eat everyday while they were in the wilderness, was to help them keep their mind off the wilderness and on the promise of their salvation. It is hard to see anything beyond the wilderness when you're living in it, yet God's hand can be clearly seen if we look for it. One day they were concerned about bread and the next concern was water, but did they ask to see God's plan? Did the children of Israel wonder why God had led them this way into the wilderness? No, instead they chose to murmur and chide with Moses.

Exodus 17:1- 6

And all the congregation of the children of Israel journeyed from the wilderness of Sin, after [according to] their journeys, according to the commandment of the LORD, and pitched in Rephidim: and *there was* no water for the people to drink.

Wherefore the people did chide with Moses, and said, Give us water that we may drink. And Moses said unto them, Why chide ye with me? wherefore do ye tempt the LORD?

And the people thirsted there for water; and the people murmured against Moses, and said, Wherefore *is* this *that* thou hast brought us up out of Egypt, to kill us and our children and our cattle with thirst?

And Moses cried unto the LORD, saying, What shall I do unto this people? they be almost ready to stone me.

And the LORD said unto Moses, Go on before the people, and take with thee of the elders of Israel; and thy rod, wherewith thou smotest the river, take in thine hand, and go.

Behold, I will stand before thee there upon the rock in Horeb; and thou shalt smite the rock, and there shall come water out of it, that the people may drink. And Moses did so in the sight of the elders of Israel.

The rock had to be smitten in order to give forth the water. Had the people not been so caught up in the murmuring, Moses would not have been so quick to strike the rock without first explaining to them the significance of the rock. The reason why it needed to be smitten is because Christ had to be smitten. Deuteronomy 32:51 and 52 explain that Moses did not enter the promised land with the children of Israel because of this incident. Moses failed to show the children of Israel God's purpose and plan.

Deuteronomy 32:51, 52

Because ye trespassed against me among the children of Israel at the waters of Meribah-Kadesh, in the wilderness of Zin; because ye sanctified me not in the midst of the children of Israel.

Yet thou shalt see the land before *thee*; but thou shalt not go thither unto the land which I give the children of Israel.

The rock is symbolic of Jesus Christ. As the red thread, Jesus Christ is all throughout the Word of God and we can see him if we can see the salvation that God has prepared for us.

Psalms 78:12- 22

Marvellous things did he in the sight of their fathers, in the land of Egypt, *in* the field of Zoan.

He divided the sea, and caused them to pass through; and he made the waters to stand as an heap.

In the daytime also he led them with a cloud, and all the night with a light of fire.

He clave the rocks in the wilderness, and gave *them* drink as *out of* the great depths.

He brought streams also out of the rock, and caused waters to run down like rivers.

And they sinned yet more against him by provoking the most High in the wilderness.

And they tempted God in their heart by asking meat for their lust.

Yea, they spake against God; they said, Can God furnish a table in the wilderness?

Behold, he smote the rock, that the waters gushed out, and the streams overflowed; can he give bread also? can he provide flesh for his people?

Therefore the LORD heard *this*, and was wroth: so a fire was kindled against Jacob, and anger also came up against Israel;

Because they believed not in God, and trusted not in his salvation:

If we choose to accept Jesus Christ our Passover, we can have salvation. The children of Israel saw many marvelous things in the wilderness, but many of them chose not to believe God and trusted not in His salvation. Jesus found the same thing in his day when he came to present salvation to the people. Believing in him has always been the challenge. God is not trying to make it hard, but He is working with people who no longer have spirit, which makes it all the more difficult. God is trying to communicate ideas to those who can only see the wilderness, even when He is so obviously present with them.

John 6:28- 36

Then said they unto him, What shall we do, that we might work the works of God?

Jesus answered and said unto them, This is the work of God, that ye believe on him whom he hath sent.

They said therefore unto him, What sign showest thou then, that we may see, and believe thee? what dost thou work? Our fathers did eat manna in the desert; as it is written, He gave them bread from heaven to eat.

Then Jesus said unto them, Verily, verily, I say unto you, Moses gave you not that bread from heaven; but my Father giveth you the true bread from heaven. For the bread of God is he which cometh down from heaven, and giveth life unto the world.

Then said they unto him, Lord, evermore give us this bread. And Jesus said unto them, I am the bread of life: he that cometh to me shall never hunger; and he that believeth on me shall never thirst. But I said unto you, That ye also have seen me, and believe not.

These people had Jesus Christ with them, and yet they were utterly confused. They had not learned what God had taught their fathers in the wilderness, and now it was obvious they were struggling with what Jesus was saying and just who this fellow was.

John 6:41, 42, 47- 51

The Jews then murmured at him, because he said, I am the bread which came down from heaven. And they said, Is not this Jesus, the son of Joseph, whose father and mother we know? how is it then that he saith, I came down from heaven?

Verily, verily, I say unto you, He that believeth on me hath everlasting life.

I am that bread of life.

Your fathers did eat manna in the wilderness, and are dead.

This is the bread which cometh down from heaven, that a man may eat thereof, and not die.

I am the living bread which came down from heaven: if any man eat of this bread, he shall live for ever: and the bread that I will give is my flesh, which I will give for the life of the world.

Is this too hard to believe? Consider who Jesus is and what it is that he came to do. There is life and wholeness in the body of Christ. Christ our Passover gives salvation and eternal life in the shed blood. As the lamb of God, Jesus Christ became what was only represented by the Passover of the Old Testament and is now and forever Christ our Passover. He is our bread of life as long as we are in this world.

The Red Thread of Exodus

The Sacrifice

The Book of Leviticus is about the sacrifice and sin and how to live and to stay alive as a natural man. The law in the Old Testament was instituted to keep man alive long enough for Christ to come and to offer the ultimate sacrifice for sin. One thing about the law seemed to work against the senses man: with the law came the knowledge of sin, for the law told man what not to do as well as what to do. Now, knowing the nature of the carnal man as well as we do, it is no wonder this proved to be a greater temptation than he could bear. The natural man cannot know the greater law and the things of the spirit. He cannot see the purpose of God and what is going on behind the scenes. So when God said, *don't do that*, the carnal mind gets to thinking, *why not? Now I'm intrigued and I can't let go of it until I try it for myself.* God still figured it was better to know and have the choice than to allow the natural man to stumble about blindly in his ignorance, blaming God for his own folly. The separation which existed between God and man could only be remedied by the sacrifice. As the red thread, Jesus Christ is the sacrifice. It was all fulfilled by the offering of himself and the sacrifice of his blood, redeeming man from sin.

Leviticus 1:1- 5
And the LORD called unto Moses, and spake unto him out of the tabernacle of the congregation, saying,
Speak unto the children of Israel, and say unto them, If any man of you bring an offering unto the LORD, ye shall bring your offering of the cattle, *even* of the herd, and of the flock.
If his offering *be* a burnt sacrifice of the herd, let him offer a male without blemish: he shall offer it of his own voluntary will at the door of the tabernacle of the congregation before the LORD.
And he shall put his hand upon the head of the burnt offering; and it shall be accepted for him to make atonement for him.
And he shall kill the bullock before the LORD: and the priests, Aaron's sons, shall bring the blood, and sprinkle the blood round about upon the altar that *is by* the door of the tabernacle of the congregation.

The burnt sacrifice was to be an offering made by the man's free will, and the offering had to be a male without blemish. In the book of Genesis we see Abel, who understood this very early on when he sought access to the Lord his God by offering a lamb and the fat thereof on the altar as a sacrifice acceptable to the Lord. Cain, on the other hand, did not like the idea of shedding blood; therefore, he looked for another way. Even after God told Cain what was needful and therefore acceptable as a sacrifice, he refused. Cain chose to blame Abel for giving God such an idea and said, *if it's blood you want, let's see how you like it*. So he slew his brother and spilled Abel's blood on the ground. In so doing, Cain proved not to be the sacrifice; he was not the lamb of God.

Genesis 4:1-10
And Adam knew Eve his wife; and she conceived, and bare Cain, and said, I have gotten a [the] **man from the LORD.**
And she again bare his brother Abel. And Abel was a keeper of sheep, but Cain was a tiller of the ground.
And in process of time it came to pass, that Cain brought of the fruit of the ground an offering unto the LORD.
And Abel, he also brought of the firstlings of his flock and of the fat thereof. And the LORD had respect unto Abel and to his offering:
But unto Cain and to his offering he had not respect. And Cain was very wroth, and his countenance fell.
And the LORD said unto Cain, Why art thou wroth? and why is thy countenance fallen?
If thou doest well, shalt thou not be accepted? and if thou doest not well, sin lieth at the door. And unto thee *shall be* **his desire, and thou shalt rule over him.**
And Cain talked with Abel his brother: and it came to pass, when they were in the field, that Cain rose up against Abel his brother, and slew him.
And the LORD said unto Cain, Where *is* **Abel thy brother? And he said, I know not:** *Am* **I my brother's keeper?**
And he said, What hast thou done? the voice of thy brother's blood crieth unto me from the ground.

Cain allowed sin to rule over him rather than believing God and accepting what God had proposed. God knew Cain was not the promised seed, nor would he be the willing sacrifice.

Hebrews 11:4
By faith [believing] **Abel offered unto God a more excellent sacrifice than Cain, by which he obtained witness that he was righteous** [right]**, God testifying of his gifts: and by it he**[Abel] **being dead yet speaketh.**

Cain chose not to believe, but Abel did believe. Could Cain's unbelief have been avoided had he not been wrongly taught? Eve thought she had gotten the man from the Lord. This idea had been passed on to Cain, and therefore he was under the misguided thinking that his blood had to be shed. Cain had the notion that he was the promised seed, but it became very clear that he was not the man from the Lord, as suggested by Eve. For it was indeed by his freedom of choice that he chose to kill rather than accept the idea of being killed. Jesus faced the same choice shortly before his crucifixion while praying in the garden. He asked if this cup could pass from him, if there was any other way for man's redemption to be accomplished. But in the end he said, *not my will but Thine be done.* And he went ahead and faced death for every man.

Matthew 26:39 and 42
And he [Jesus] went a little farther, and fell on his face, and prayed, saying, O my Father, if it be possible, let this cup pass from me: nevertheless not as I will, but as thou *wilt*.

He went away again the second time, and prayed, saying, O my Father, if this cup may not pass away from me, except I drink it, thy will be done.

In presenting Isaac as a burnt offering, Abraham proved to God where his believing was concerning what God had promised. Abraham also knew that God would provide a lamb for a burnt offering. Like Abel, Abraham was right in believing God concerning this sacrifice of the lamb. In Leviticus, God made provision for a burnt offering, a meal offering, a sin offering, a trespass offering, and the sacrifice of the peace offering. All of these were fulfilled in the offering of Jesus, the sacrifice of himself for every man.

Leviticus 7:37
This *is* the law of the burnt offering, of the meat [meal] offering, and of the sin offering, and of the trespass offering, and of the consecrations, and of the sacrifice of the peace offerings...

The Old Testament law and sacrifices offered only a covering for sin, while the sacrifice of Christ and the New Testament in his blood redeemed man from sin. When Adam and Eve sinned, they chose fig leaves for a covering. God also, saw the need for a covering, and He chose coats of skins and clothed them. The law of sacrifices brought in additional forms of coverings, but they all pointed to Christ.

Galatians 3:19, 21, 22
Wherefore then *serveth* the law? It was added because of transgressions, till the seed should come to whom the promise was made...
Is the law then against the promises of God? God forbid: for if there had been a law given which could have given life, verily righteousness should have been by the law. But the scripture hath concluded all under sin, that the promise by [proceeding from] **believing of Jesus Christ might be given to them that believe** [in Jesus Christ]**.**

Hebrews 7:19
For the law made nothing perfect, but the bringing in of a better hope *did*; by the which we draw nigh unto God.

Jesus Christ was the perfect sacrifice; for he was the lamb of God's choosing. Only he could fulfill all that the law foreshadowed of the good things to come.

John 1:29
The next day John seeth Jesus coming unto him, and saith, Behold the Lamb of God, which taketh away the sin of the world.

I Peter 1:18-20
Forasmuch as ye know that ye were not redeemed with corruptible things, *as* silver and gold, from your vain conversation *received* by tradition from your fathers;
But with the precious blood of Christ, as of a lamb without blemish and without spot:
Who verily was foreordained before the foundation of the world, but was manifest in these last times for you,

There are many offerings defined in Leviticus, and Jesus Christ is the epitome of all that is sacrificed. There are burnt offerings, sin offerings, offerings made by fire of a sweet savor unto the Lord. There are offerings of turtle doves, meal offerings, peace offerings, offerings of the first fruits, wave offerings, and heave offerings. The people gained access and audience before the Lord God with these gifts while looking for atonement and peace with God. I know that this is foreign to us today because our access is procured for us in Christ; but before Christ came, offerings were all that was available to people seeking atonement.

Hebrews 10:1
For the law having a shadow of good things to come, *and* not the very image of the things, can never with those sacrifices which they offered year by year continually make the comers thereunto perfect.

Today we come bearing the ultimate sacrifice, the sacrifice of Christ Jesus our Lord. We have available to us the perfect sacrifice, if only we believe.

Hebrews 9:24- 28
For Christ is not entered into the holy places made with hands, *which are* the figures of the true; but into heaven itself, now to appear in the presence of God for us:
Nor yet that he should offer himself often, as the high priest entereth into the holy place every year with blood of others;
For then must he often have suffered since the foundation of the world: but now once in the end of the world hath he appeared to put away sin by the sacrifice of himself.
And as it is appointed unto men once to die, but after this the judgment:
So Christ was once offered to bear the sins of many; and unto them that look for him shall he appear the second time without sin unto salvation.

We have the sacrifice of Christ to offer before God. We do not have need of any other. All that the law provided was taken away and replaced by the sacrifice of Christ, once and for all.

Hebrews 10:9- 18
Then said he, Lo, I come to do thy will, O God. He taketh away the first, that he may establish the second.
By the which will we are sanctified through the offering of the body of Jesus Christ once *for all*.
And every priest standeth daily ministering and offering oftentimes the same sacrifices, which can never take away sins:
But this man, after he had offered one sacrifice for sins for ever, sat down on the right hand of God;
From henceforth expecting till his enemies be made his footstool.
For by one offering he hath perfected for ever them that are sanctified.

Whereof **the Holy Ghost** [holy spirit] **also is a witness to us: for after that he had said before,**

This *is* the covenant that I will make with them after those days, saith the Lord, I will put my laws into their hearts, and in their minds will I write them;

And their sins and iniquities will I remember no more.

Now where remission of these *is, there is* no more offering for sin.

The sacrifice of Christ was so great that now the ultimate sacrifice is not to die for him but to live for him. Death has now been replaced with life. Let us therefore choose life.

Romans 12:1, 2
I beseech you therefore brethren by the mercies of God, that ye present your bodies a living sacrifice, holy, acceptable unto God, *which is* your reasonable service.

And be not conformed to this world: but be ye transformed by the renewing of your mind, that ye may prove what *is* that good and acceptable and perfect will of God.

Well, what is good and acceptable and perfect in God's will? You find the good in the physical order and setup of life when it is lived in accordance with God's will. You find that which is acceptable in the use of the spirit which God has given in the new birth, for in these things you serve Christ. Perfection today is only found in the Lord; and you, my friend, are in the Lord when you are living in the will of God and looking to the perfect hope that can only be found in Christ's return.

Ephesians 5:1, 2
Be ye therefore followers (imitators) **of God, as dear children; and walk in love as Christ also loved us and hath given himself for us an offering and a sacrifice to God for a sweet smelling savor.**

Jesus Christ shed his blood for us. Why blood? Because there is life in the blood. When we are dealing with the blood of Christ, we are dealing with more than just physical life. The blood of Christ atones for the soul in that it provides redemption and remission of sins.

Leviticus 17:11
For the life of the flesh is in the blood and *I* have given it to you upon the altar to make atonement for your souls: for *it is* the blood *that*

maketh an atonement for the soul.

Hebrews 9:12- 14
Neither by the blood of goats and calves, but by his own blood he entered in once into the holy place, having obtained eternal redemption *for us*.
For if the blood of bulls and of goats, and the ashes of an heifer sprinkling the unclean, sanctifieth to the purifying of the flesh:
How much more shall the blood of Christ, who through the eternal spirit offered himself without spot to God, purge your conscience from dead works to serve the living God?

Leviticus says, "the life of the flesh is in the blood." The blood of Christ carries with it life for all flesh. The blood of Christ clears the conscience of man. It not only puts us back in fellowship with God, but it keeps us in fellowship if we accept the sacrifice of God's son.

I John 1:7
But if we walk in the light, as he is in the light, we have fellowship one with another, and the blood of Jesus Christ his Son cleanseth us from all sin [broken fellowship].

The soul life is found in the blood, and it can be passed on from one generation to the next by way of the seed of the man. The Devil has been out to destroy man's seed ever since God made known the plan for the promised seed back in Genesis. The whole purpose of the Devil is to steal and to kill and to destroy; and with a blind fury, he has set out after the promised seed. The offering of blood was a key component in destroying him who had the power of death, which is the Devil. Most people today just pass it off as some barbaric obsession and ritual, not realizing just how important the offering of blood is. God made a covenant with Abraham concerning his seed, and as a token and sign that he believed, God had him circumcise himself and every male child who would believe and come under the same covenant for generations to come.

Genesis 17:4, 5, 7, 9- 11
As for me, behold, my covenant *is* with thee, and thou shalt be a father of many nations.
Neither shall thy name any more be called Abram, but thy name shall be Abraham; for a father of many nations have I made thee.
And I will establish my covenant between me and thee and thy

seed after thee in their generations for an everlasting covenant, to be a God unto thee, and to thy seed after thee.

And God said unto Abraham, Thou shalt keep my covenant therefore, thou, and thy seed after thee in their generations.

This *is* my covenant, which ye shall keep, between me and you and thy seed after thee; Every man child among you shall be circumcised.

And ye shall circumcise the flesh of your foreskin; and it shall be a token [and sign] of the covenant [pact] betwixt me and you.

Circumcision was given as a sign that they believed. The pact God made with Abraham was not only concerning Abraham's seed but also the promised seed, which is Christ. In the blood of the promised seed, there is life; and in believing in Christ, there would be bought for man a full redemption. With the blood of Christ came the return of the spirit as well as remission of the tainted soul life found in the blood of Adam. The significance of circumcision has been a point of contention through the years. Moses' wife thought him to be a bloody man because of the seemingly barbaric ritual.

Exodus 4:24-26

And it came to pass by the way [when they were returning to Egypt] **in the inn, that the LORD met him** [Moses] **and sought to kill him** [Moses' first born son]. **Then Zipporah** [Moses' wife] **took a sharp stone and cut off the foreskin of her son and cast** *it* **at his** [Moses'] **feet and said, "Surely a bloody husband** *art thou* **to me". So He** [God] **let him** [the son] **go: then she said, "A bloody husband** *thou art*, **because of the circumcision".**

The sign of circumcision was a precursor to the believing that is now available in Christ. You do not have to believe in Jesus Christ if you do not want to, but remember the choice you are making is the choice between life and death.

Galatians 3:6- 9, 13a and 14

Even as Abraham believed God, and it was accounted to him for righteousness.

Know ye therefore that they which are of faith, the same are the children of Abraham.

And the scripture, foreseeing that God would justify the heathen through faith, preached before the gospel unto Abraham, *saying*, **In thee shall all nations be blessed.**

So then they which be of faith are blessed with faithful Abraham.

Christ hath redeemed us from the curse of the law, being made a curse for us:

That the blessing of Abraham might come on the Gentiles through Jesus Christ; that we might receive the promise of the spirit through faith [believing].

If the blood of Christ affected only the soul life with no return of the spirit and no hope of eternal glory awaiting us upon his return, then we truly are of all men most miserable. The blood of Christ offers life unto all who will believe and are covered by 'the sacrifice' of the precious blood of the lamb. All that was offered or sacrificed in the book of Leviticus was fulfilled and brought to a close in those who believe in the sacrifice of the lamb of God, Jesus Christ. As the red thread, Jesus Christ is the sacrifice of the book of Leviticus.

The Red Thread of Leviticus

A Star Out of Jacob

The groupings of stars, called constellations, are set above us in the heavens. They are there for signs and for seasons and for days and for years. Each constellation carries a picture depicting something about God's plan for man's redemption. This is how God recorded His Word for man before there was the written text, the text we have come to know today as the Bible. Each of the twelve tribes of Israel was ascribed one of the twelve signs of the Zodiac. This was then the house in which they were to dwell, the house God gave them whose foundation was set in heaven. The children of Israel were given the charge of carrying this information and keeping it alive from one generation to the next, but it is recorded many times that Israel has been a rebellious house. Today we have very little accurate information concerning the stars, which should have been passed down through the years. Some reference is still made in the Word concerning their significance. It can be seen when considering the red thread in the book of Numbers, because the red thread is found in a star which shall come out of Jacob.

Numbers 2:1, 2, 34
And the LORD spake unto Moses and unto Aaron, saying, Every man of the children of Israel shall pitch by his own standard, with the ensign [the sign of the Zodiac] **of their father's house: far off about the tabernacle of the congregation shall they pitch.**
And the children of Israel did according to all that the LORD commanded Moses: so they pitched by their standards, and so they set forward, every one after their families, according to the house [constellation] **of their fathers.**

As this human drama unfolds, it becomes all too clear that even when men knew God, they glorified him not as God. Neither were they thankful, but became vain in their imaginations and their foolish heart was darkened. The children of Israel did not always retain God in their knowledge. Yet it is no secret that God always wanted to bless Israel. He wanted to put His name upon them. God wanted to give them His name and be associated with His children, Israel. Israel was not always a thankful recipient of this honor and blessing, but Moses proved many times to be a great intercessor between God and Israel.

Numbers 6:22- 27

And the LORD spake unto Moses, saying, Speak unto Aaron and unto his sons, saying, On this wise ye shall bless the children of Israel, saying unto them, The LORD bless thee, and keep thee: The LORD make his face shine upon thee, and be gracious unto thee: The LORD lift up his countenance upon thee, and give thee peace. And they shall put my name upon the children of Israel; and I will bless them.

Numbers 14:2- 5, 8- 21

And all the children of Israel murmured against Moses and against Aaron: and the whole congregation said unto them, Would God that we had died in the land of Egypt! or would God we had died in this wilderness! [The exhortation still applies, be careful what you ask as you just might get it.]

And wherefore hath the LORD brought us unto this land, to fall by the sword, that our wives and our children should be a prey? were it not better for us to return into Egypt?

And they said one to another, Let us make a captain, [At this point God was their captain] **and let us return into Egypt.**

Then Moses and Aaron fell on their faces before all the assembly of the congregation of the children of Israel. [Well, I can't imagine why, can you?]

If the LORD delight in us, then he will bring us into this land, and give it us; a land which floweth with milk and honey. Only rebel not ye against the LORD, neither fear ye the people of the land; for they *are* bread for us: their defence is departed from them, and the LORD *is* with us: fear them not.

But all the congregation bade stone them with stones. And the glory of the LORD appeared in the tabernacle of the congregation before all the children of Israel. And the LORD said unto Moses, How long will this people provoke me? and how long will it be ere they believe me, for all the signs which I have showed among them?

I will smite them with the pestilence, and disinherit them, and will make of thee a greater nation and mightier than they.

And Moses said unto the LORD, Then the Egyptians shall hear *it*, (for thou broughtest up this people in thy might from among them;) And they will tell *it* to the inhabitants of this land: *for* they have heard that thou LORD *art* among this people, that thou LORD art seen face to face, and *that* thy cloud standeth over them, and *that* thou goest before them, by day time in a pillar of a cloud, and in a pillar of fire by night.

Now *if* thou shalt kill *all* this people as one man, then the nations which have heard the fame of thee will speak, saying, Because the LORD was not able to bring this people into the land which he sware unto them, therefore he hath slain them in the wilderness.

And now, I beseech thee, let the power of my LORD be great, according as thou hast spoken, saying, The LORD *is* longsuffering, and of great mercy, forgiving iniquity and transgression, and by no means clearing *the guilty*, visiting the iniquity of the fathers upon the children unto the third and fourth *generation*. Pardon, I beseech thee, the iniquity of this people according unto the greatness of thy mercy, and as thou hast forgiven this people, from Egypt even until now.

And the LORD said, I have pardoned according to thy word:

But *as* truly *as* **I live, all the earth shall be filled with the glory of the LORD.**

God still wanted His glory to fill the earth. He still wanted His plan of redemption to be fulfilled for man. Now when Balak, the son of Zippor, who was king of the Moabites at the time, looked to hire a spiritualist named Balaam, the son of Beor, to curse Israel by means of divination, God again stepped in and blessed them. And this is where we find the red thread in the book of Numbers.

Numbers 24:14- 17

And now, behold, I [Balaam] go unto my people: come *therefore, and* I will advertise thee what this people shall do to thy [Balak's] people in the latter days.

And he took up his parable, and said, Balaam the son of Beor hath said, and the man whose eyes are open hath said: He hath said, which heard the words of God, and knew the knowledge of the most High, *which* saw the vision of the Almighty, falling *into a trance,* but having his eyes open:

I shall see him, but not now: I shall behold him, but not nigh: there shall come a Star out of Jacob, and a Sceptre shall rise out of Israel, and shall smite the corners of Moab, and destroy all the children of Sheth.

This star, which shall rise out of Jacob, and this scepter, which shall rise out of Israel, has to do with the Word that is written in the stars. Today we may not know all the names of the stars due to the failure of those to whom the names were entrusted. Although the names were not kept alive because of this failure, a few were preserved in the scriptures as well as some other writings. Let's follow this witness of the stars just a little through the Word to lay a foundation for our red thread in the book of Numbers.

Romans 1:19, 20
Because that which may be known of God is manifest in them; for God hath shewed [showed] *it* unto them.
For the invisible things of Him from the creation of the world are clearly seen, being understood by the things that are made, *even* His eternal power and Godhead; so that they are without excuse:

Romans 10:17, 18
So then faith [believing] *cometh* by hearing and hearing by the word of God.
But I say, have they not heard? Yes verily, their sound went out into all the earth and their words unto the ends of the world.

This is also a quote from the 19th Psalm. The word that comes from the stars may be inaudible but it speaks loudly to those who understand. Those to whom God showed it and taught it are without excuse, for they knew. But did they believe?

Psalm 19:1-4
The heavens declare the glory of God; and the firmament sheweth His handiwork. Day unto day uttereth speech, and night unto night sheweth knowledge. *There is* no speech nor language, *where* their voice is not heard.
Their line [In Romans the word *sound* is used rather than the word line] is gone out through all the earth and their words to the end of the world.

You can know their voice by knowing their names, for their names tell you of the knowledge they hold.

Psalm 147:4, 5
He telleth the number of the stars; He calleth them all by *their* names.
Great *is* our Lord and of great power: His understanding *is* infinite.

Now this star that shall come out of Jacob is witness to the birth of Jesus Christ. The wise men saw his star in the east which prompted them to seek him out and come and present him gifts when he was a young child.

Matthew 2:1-11
Now when Jesus was born in Bethlehem of Judaea in the days of Herod the king, behold, there came wise men from the east to Jerusalem, saying, Where is he that is born king of the Jews? For we have seen his star in the east, and are come to worship him.

When Herod the king had heard *these things*, he was troubled and all Jerusalem with him.

And when he had gathered all the chief priests and scribes of the people together, he demanded of them where Christ should be born.

And they said unto him, In Bethlehem of Judaea: for thus it is written by the prophet, And *thou* Bethlehem, in the land of Juda, art not the least among the princes of Juda: for out of thee shall come a governor, that shall rule My people Israel.

Then Herod, when he had privily called the wise men, enquired of them diligently what time the star appeared.

And he sent them to Bethlehem and said, Go and search diligently for the young child; and when ye have found *him*, bring me word again, that I may come and worship him also.

When they had heard the king, they departed; and lo, the star, which they saw in the east, went before them, till it came and stood over where the young child was.

When they saw the star, they rejoiced with exceeding great joy. And when they were come into the house, they saw the young child with Mary his mother and they fell down and worshiped him: and when they had opened their treasures, they presented unto him gifts; gold, and frankincense and myrrh.

The wise men were aware of what God had written in the stars. The wise men had knowledge of the stars and the activity of the astrological conjunctions and movements that told them the king had been born. The one who was written of in the stars had come, born of Mary, and come with the scepter of a kingdom from heaven. The Word that is written in the stars is not made up of cunningly devised fables, but it attests to the truth of the day star that shall arise in our hearts.

II Peter 1:16-19
For we have not followed cunningly devised fables, when we made known unto you the power and coming of our Lord Jesus Christ, but were eyewitnesses of *his* majesty.

For he received from God the Father honour and glory, when there came such a voice to him from the excellent glory, This is My beloved son, in whom I am well pleased.

And this voice which came from heaven *we* **heard, when we were with him in the holy mount.**

We have also a more sure word of prophecy; whereunto ye do well that ye take heed, as unto a light that shineth in a dark place, until the day dawn and the day star arise in your hearts:

Jesus Christ is like a light from heaven, enlightening those who let him shine in their heart. Jesus Christ is the star that shall come out of Jacob, the red thread in the book of Numbers.

Revelation 22:16
I Jesus have sent mine angel to testify unto you these things in the churches. I am the root and the offspring of David, *and* **the bright and morning star.**

The Rock

"Behold, I set before you this day a blessing and a curse." "See, I have set before thee this day life and good, and death and evil." The book of Deuteronomy contains some very defining statements. God lays it out very clearly. In the book of Deuteronomy, God gives a rock upon which to build a firm foundation where one can find refuge and security. Moses declared this Word of God to the children of Israel before they went into the land which the Lord promised unto their fathers, even Abraham, Isaac, and Jacob. Moses set this Word of God to give unto the children of Israel and to their seed after them. This rock could prove to be a perfect place to build, but also a devastating blow if you were to break yourself against it, for this rock is an immovable object. As the red thread, Jesus Christ is The Rock in the book of Deuteronomy.

Deuteronomy 11:18- 28
Therefore shall ye lay up these My words in your heart and in your soul, and bind *them* for a sign upon your hand, that they may be as frontlets between your eyes.
And ye shall teach *them* your children, speaking of them when thou sittest in thine house, and when thou walkest by the way, when thou liest down, and when thou risest up.
And thou shalt write them upon the door posts of thine house, and upon thy gates:
That your days may be multiplied, and the days of your children, in the land which the LORD sware unto your fathers to give them, as the days of heaven upon the earth.
For if ye shall diligently keep all these commandments which I command *you*, to do them, to love the LORD your God, to walk in all his ways, and to cleave unto him;
Then will the LORD drive out all these nations from before you, and ye shall possess greater nations and mightier than yourselves.
Every place whereon the soles of your feet shall tread shall be yours: from the wilderness and Lebanon, from the river, the river Euphrates, even unto the uttermost sea shall your coast be.
There shall no man be able to stand before you: *for* the LORD your God shall lay the fear of you and the dread of you upon all the land that ye shall tread upon, as he hath said unto you.

Behold, I set before you this day a blessing and a curse;

A blessing, if ye obey the commandments of the LORD your God, which I command *you* this day:
And a curse, if ye will not obey the commandments of the LORD your God, but turn aside out of the way which I command you this day, to go after other gods, which ye have not known.

Yes, a blessing and a curse; there is always a choice. You must choose to accept God's blessing in your life, for He will not force His will upon you. The alternative, although, is no less drastic than death.

Deuteronomy 30:11- 19
For this commandment which I command thee this day, *it is* not hidden from thee, neither *is it* far off.
***It is* not in heaven, that thou shouldest say, Who shall go up for us to heaven, and bring it unto us, that we may hear *it*, and do it?**
Neither *is it* beyond the sea, that thou shouldest say, Who shall go over the sea for us, and bring it unto us, that we may hear *it*, and do it?
But the word *is* very nigh unto thee, in thy mouth, and in thy heart, that thou mayest do it.

See, I have set before thee this day life and good, and death and evil;

In that I command thee this day to love the LORD thy God, to walk in his ways, and to keep his commandments and his statutes and his judgments, that thou mayest live and multiply: and the LORD thy God shall bless thee in the land whither *thou* goest to possess it.
But if thine heart turn away, so that thou wilt not hear, but shalt be drawn away, and worship other gods, and serve them;
I denounce unto you this day, that ye shall surely perish, *and that* ye shall not prolong *your* days upon the land, whither thou passest over Jordan to go to possess it.
I call heaven and earth to record this day against you, *that* I have set before you life and death, blessing and cursing: therefore choose life, that both *thou* and thy seed may live:

If you take God to heart and allow His word to dwell within you, there is life. Believing what God has said can bring one thing to your life and that is the good which God has always intended for life to produce. We do not have to be blown about by every foul wind that blows our way, for we have a firm foundation and safe anchorage upon The Rock.

Deuteronomy 32:1-4
Give ear, O ye heavens, and I will speak; and hear, O earth, the words of my mouth.
My doctrine shall drop as the rain, my speech shall distil as the dew, as the small rain upon the tender herb, and as the showers upon the grass:
Because I will publish the name of the LORD: ascribe ye greatness unto our God.

He is **the Rock, His work** *is* **perfect:** [Take out the italics and read; The Rock, His work perfect.] **for all his ways are judgment: a God of truth and without iniquity, just and right** *is he.*

The Rock is His perfect work. Once you remove the italicized words, you have the truth of the Word here in Deuteronomy. The Rock is God's perfect work. This Rock is the red thread in the book of Deuteronomy.

Deuteronomy 32:5, 6
They have corrupted themselves, their spot *is* **not** *the spot* **of his children:** *they are* **a perverse and crooked generation.**
Do ye thus requite [repay] the LORD, O foolish people and unwise? *is* **not** *he* **thy father** *that* **hath bought thee? hath he not made thee, and established thee?**

Is this how you repay the Lord for His perfect work? That's the question. Is this how you requite Him? All God wanted was a people to love Him. All He wanted was a family with children that He could call His own, a people who would take His name.

Deuteronomy 32:9-13
For the LORD'S portion *is* **His people; Jacob** *is* **the lot of his inheritance.**
He found him in a desert land, and in the waste howling wilderness; He led him about, He instructed him, He kept him as the apple of His eye.
As an eagle stirreth up her nest, fluttereth over her young, spreadeth abroad her wings, taketh them, beareth them on her wings:

So the LORD alone did lead him, and *there was* no strange god with him.

He made him ride on the high places of the earth, that he might eat the increase of the fields; and He made him to suck honey out of the rock, and oil out of the flinty rock;

He made Jacob suck honey out of the rock and oil out of the flinty rock. When God uses words in a figurative way like this, He does it for emphasis. He is showing the love and sweetness that are in the perfect work of the rock. The oil represents the blessing and abundance of prosperity found in the rock. Honey is set for that which is pure and sweet and good. Just look at the love and blessing God declared on His people back in chapter seven.

Deuteronomy 7:6- 15
For *thou art* an holy people unto the LORD thy God: the LORD thy God hath chosen thee to be a special people unto himself, above all people that *are* upon the face of the earth.

The LORD did not set his love upon you, nor choose you, because ye were more in number than any people; for *ye were* the fewest of all people:

But because the LORD loved *you* [God did it because He loved you], and because he would keep the oath which he had sworn unto your fathers, hath the LORD brought you out with a mighty hand, and redeemed you out of the house of bondmen, from the hand of Pharaoh king of Egypt.

Know therefore that the LORD thy God, *he is* God, the faithful God, which keepeth covenant and mercy with them that love him and keep his commandments to a thousand generations;

And repayeth them that hate him to their face, to destroy them: he will not be slack to him that hateth him, he will repay him to his face.

Thou shalt therefore keep the commandments, and the statutes, and the judgments, which I command thee this day, to do them.

Wherefore it shall come to pass, if ye hearken to these judgments, and keep, and do *them*, that the LORD thy God shall keep unto thee the covenant and the mercy which He sware unto thy fathers:

And He will love thee, and bless thee, and multiply thee: He will also bless the fruit of thy womb, and the fruit of thy land, thy corn, and thy wine, and thine oil, the increase of thy kine [cows], and the flocks of thy sheep, in the land which He sware unto thy fathers to give thee.

Thou shalt be blessed above all people: there shall not be male or female barren among you, or among your cattle.

And the LORD will take away from thee all sickness, and will put none of the evil diseases of Egypt, which thou knowest, upon thee; but will lay them upon all *them* that hate thee.

What a declaration of God's love and blessing! But did you also see the stark reality of what awaits those who hate God? It is a repayment of God, face to face, to destroy them. I don't want God in my face. I would much rather have God's love and blessing.

Deuteronomy 32:15, 16
But Jeshurun [the upright one, put by a figure for the ideal Israel] **waxed fat, and kicked** [trampled under foot]: **thou art waxen fat, thou art grown thick, thou art covered *with fatness*; then he forsook God *which* made him, and lightly esteemed the Rock of his salvation.**

They provoked Him to jealousy with strange *gods*, with abominations provoked they Him to anger.

They lightly esteemed the Rock. Israel found the Rock of their salvation to be offensive; they spurned the love which God showed in His perfect work.

Romans 9:33
For they stumbled at that stumblingstone;
As it is written, Behold, I lay in Sion a stumblingstone and rock of offence: and whosoever believeth on him shall not be ashamed [disappointed].

You will be disappointed if you see him as an offensive rock, for you will crumble under the weight of that decision. For this rock is Jesus Christ, the son of the living God.

Matthew 16:15- 18
He saith unto them, But whom say ye that I am?
And Simon Peter answered and said, Thou art the Christ, the Son of the living God.
And Jesus answered and said unto him, Blessed art thou, Simon Barjona: for flesh and blood hath not revealed *it* unto thee, but my Father which is in heaven.
And I say also unto thee, That thou art Peter [*petros*]**, and upon**

this rock [*petra*] I will build my church; and the gates of hell [*hades* = the grave] shall not prevail against it.**

Jesus told Peter that he was *petros*, a Greek word meaning a little stone or tiny grain of sand which could be blown about with every wind that blew. Look at Peter's life sometime. He was a tremendous man, but he blew hot for God one minute and the next you couldn't see him for dust. In contrast, Jesus pointed to himself when he said, "upon this rock I will build my church." Jesus is *petra*, a rock, immovable. Even the grave cannot prevail against it. Upon which rock would you like to build?

Matthew 7:24- 27
Therefore whosoever heareth these sayings of mine, and doeth them, I will liken him unto a wise man, which built his house upon a rock:
And the rain descended, and the floods came, and the winds blew, and beat upon that house; and it fell not: for it was founded upon a rock.
And every one that heareth these sayings of mine, and doeth them not, shall be likened unto a foolish man, which built his house upon the sand:
And the rain descended, and the floods came, and the winds blew, and beat upon that house; and it fell: and great was the fall of it.

Jesus said it; I didn't. A wise man builds upon a rock, and the rock we are dealing with is Jesus Christ. What are you building your life on? God said: if you build your life on Christ, you won't be disappointed. He is, after all, The Rock, God's perfect work. You cannot lay a better foundation.

I Corinthians 3:9- 11
For we are labourers together with God: ye are God's husbandry, *ye are* **God's building.**
According to the grace of God which is given unto me, as a wise masterbuilder, I have laid the foundation, and another buildeth thereon. But let every man take heed how he buildeth thereupon.
For other foundation can no man lay than that is laid, which is Jesus Christ.

Paul writes of a foundation that he laid and upon which each man is to build with the exhortation of taking care how he builds thereupon. But there can be no doubt of the foundation itself, which is Jesus Christ.

I Corinthians 10:1- 4
Moreover, brethren, I would not that ye should be ignorant, how that all our fathers were under the cloud, and all passed through the sea;
And were all baptized unto Moses in the cloud and in the sea;
And did all eat the same spiritual meat;
And did all drink the same spiritual drink: for they drank of that spiritual Rock that followed them: and that Rock was Christ.

The red thread in the book of Deuteronomy is Jesus Christ, The Rock, God's perfect work and the Rock of our salvation. God sets before us the blessing of Jesus Christ. Will we choose to build on that Rock or will we lay another foundation? The choices are clear and so also is the recompense of that choice.

The Red Thread of Deuteronomy

A Great Stone of Witness

Have you ever awakened to realize that you were separated from God? Mankind has been living in sin ever since Adam. Sin is a state of separation from God. That's what sin is, that which separates you from God. Adam left man in a perpetual state of sin; we simply compound the issue by our own actions. Let me ask you, have you ever desired sanctuary, a place where you were safe from sin? Sin has the ultimate consequence of death. Whenever you are separated from God, there can only be one final outcome. Sanctuary offers a place of refuge and protection, a place in which you can worship God. In the book of Joshua, you find a stone of witness placed by the sanctuary, a great stone which heard all the words the Lord had spoken. This stone stood as a witness unto all the people that God would fulfill His Word. Jesus Christ would prove to be this great stone as the red thread passing through the book of Joshua.

Joshua 24:15
And if it seem evil unto you to serve the LORD, choose you this day whom ye will serve; whether the gods which your fathers served that *were* on the other side of the flood, or the gods of the Amorites, in whose land ye dwell: but as for me and my house, we will serve the LORD.

Joshua told the people they couldn't serve the Lord the way they had been, serving the Lord God along with other gods. They needed to decide who they were going to trust. Would it be the God who is the life giver, or would they forsake the Lord and serve strange gods, which would do them harm and consume them?

Joshua 24:21
And the people said unto Joshua, Nay; but we will serve the LORD.

Joshua 24:25- 28
So Joshua made a covenant with the people that day, and set them a statute and an ordinance in Shechem.
And Joshua wrote these words in the book of the law of God, and took a great stone, and set it up there under an oak, that *was* by the sanctuary of the LORD.

And Joshua said unto all the people, Behold, this stone shall be a witness unto us; for it hath heard all the words of the LORD which he spake unto us: it shall be therefore a witness unto you, lest ye deny your God.
So Joshua let the people depart, every man unto his inheritance.

There stood a day when all the people believed. It was a rare day in the history of the children of Israel, but one which I enjoy reading about. The book of Joshua sadly opens with the statement, "Moses, My servant is dead." But God doesn't leave it there, He says, "Now arise and go over this Jordan." God said that He would give them everything He had said unto Moses. The people seemed to fight Moses every step of the way as they wandered in the wilderness those forty years. Now there is a new page being turned, and all those who disbelieved, those of the generation who spent their days on the wilderness side of Jordan, are gone.

The people have the promised land stretching out before them, and all that separates them from their prize is the Jordan.

Joshua 3:5
And Joshua said unto the people, Sanctify yourselves: for tomorrow the LORD will do wonders among you.

Joshua told the people what they were to do. Even though the Jordan was at flood stage, this posed no problem for God. You see, God had practice when He parted the Red Sea for the children of Israel who left Egypt. It proved to be no more difficult here either; again God parted the waters, and the children of Israel passed over on dry ground. It was here that God had them take twelve stones from the river's bed, where the feet of the priest stood for a memorial unto the children of Israel.

Joshua 4:6-8
That this may be a sign among you, *that* when your children ask *their fathers* in time to come, saying, What *mean* ye by these stones?
Then ye shall answer them, That the waters of Jordan were cut off before the ark of the covenant of the LORD; when it passed over Jordan, the waters of Jordan were cut off: and these stones shall be for a memorial unto the children of Israel for ever.
And the children of Israel did so as Joshua commanded, and took up twelve stones out of the midst of Jordan, as the LORD spake unto Joshua, according to the number of the tribes of the children of Israel, and carried them over with them unto the place where they

lodged, and laid them down there.

You may not find these stones any longer in their place, but God had Joshua put twelve others in a place where you will still find them today.

Joshua 4:9
And Joshua set up twelve stones in the midst of Jordan, in the place where the feet of the priests which bare the ark of the covenant stood: and they are there unto this day.

When your children shall ask their fathers in time to come, "What do these stones mean?", what will you tell them? Will it be concerning myths and fables or of God's wonders and power made manifest for all to see? Abraham was circumcised because he believed God, and it was a token of the covenant between them. God had Joshua circumcise the children of Israel after crossing Jordan, for this generation again would prove to be men who would believe God and recognize the token of the covenant they had between themselves and God.

Joshua 5:4- 7
And this *is* the cause why Joshua did circumcise: All the people that came out of Egypt, *that were* males, *even* all the men of war, died in the wilderness by the way, after they came out of Egypt.
Now all the people that came out were circumcised: but all the people *that were* born in the wilderness by the way as they came forth out of Egypt, *them* they had not circumcised.
For the children of Israel walked forty years in the wilderness, till all the people *that were* men of war, which came out of Egypt, were consumed, because they obeyed not the voice of the LORD:
unto whom the LORD sware that he would not show them the land, which the LORD sware unto their fathers that he would give us, a land that floweth with milk and honey.
And their children, *whom* he raised up in their stead, them Joshua circumcised: for they were uncircumcised, because they had not circumcised them by the way.

When you get a group of people together who believe, it is amazing what you will see happen. It is no wonder Joshua said, "Sanctify yourselves today for tomorrow God will do wonders among you." God is always in the business of doing wonderful things for His people, but He needs for them to believe Him when He speaks. What a joy it is to see a nation in league with

God, watching God at work. The children of Israel passed over Jordan and camped in the plains of Jericho. God had the captain of his host, an angel whose name is Michael to be precise, show up to help with the defeat of Jericho. God had declared the whole city to be accursed.

Joshua 6:17- 19
And the city shall be accursed, *even* it, and all that *are* therein, to the LORD: only Rahab the harlot shall live, she and all that *are* with her in the house, because she hid the messengers that we sent.

And ye, in any wise keep *yourselves* from the accursed thing, lest ye make *yourselves* accursed, when ye take of the accursed thing, and make the camp of Israel a curse, and trouble it.

But all the silver, and gold, and vessels of brass and iron, *are* consecrated unto the LORD: they shall come into the treasury of the LORD.

Now, things went smoothly with one exception. It happened when the city was taken that Achan, who was soon to be ache'n (sorry, I couldn't resist), became accursed by taking of the accursed thing. The entire city and its contents were accursed, because they carried with them evil and harm. Everything gives off something, and you wouldn't want anything this city had to offer. This caused the children of Israel to fall before the men of Ai and their hearts melted and became as water.

Joshua 7:12, 13
Therefore the children of Israel could not stand before their enemies, *but* turned *their* backs before their enemies, because they were accursed: neither will I be with you any more, except ye destroy the accursed from among you.

Up, sanctify the people, and say, Sanctify yourselves against tomorrow: for thus saith the LORD God of Israel, *There is* an accursed thing in the midst of thee, O Israel: thou canst not stand before thine enemies, until ye take away the accursed thing from among you.

One man can have a profound affect upon the whole group. It may be a positive effect or, in this case, a negative effect. Joshua went from family to family asking who had done such a thing to the nation of their brethren by taking of the accursed thing, thus causing Israel to be accursed. When he came to the family of Judah, in the family of Zabdi, Achan stepped forward and confessed and told all that he had done.

Joshua 7:25, 26

And Joshua said, Why hast thou troubled us? the LORD shall trouble thee this day. And all Israel stoned him with stones, and burned them with fire, after they had stoned them with stones.

And they raised over him a great heap of stones unto this day. So the LORD turned from the fierceness of his anger. Wherefore the name of that place was called, The valley of Achor, unto this day.

This happens to be the first stoning recorded in the Word. There was a time when I thought that getting stoned meant being high on drugs. Sometimes the meanings of words change, but the truth of the Word is that Achan died, and they heaped up a great pile of stones on top of him. Today we still place a headstone over someone when they die as a memorial and a witness to the dead body buried below. Joshua and Israel took the city of Ai and burnt it and hanged the king of Ai on a tree until eventide. As the sun went down, they took the carcass down and raised a great heap of stones thereon at the gate of the city. This, too, was a witness to all who passed by of the desolation of the city of Ai, but perhaps a sign also of the stone of witness yet to come.

Joshua 8:30- 32

Then Joshua built an altar unto the LORD God of Israel in mount Ebal,

As Moses the servant of the LORD commanded the children of Israel, as it is written in the book of the law of Moses, an altar of whole stones, over which no man hath lift up *any* iron: and they offered thereon burnt offerings unto the LORD, and sacrificed peace offerings.

And he wrote there upon the stones a copy of the law of Moses, which he wrote in the presence of the children of Israel.

When Joshua built an altar, he used whole stones. He did not shape or fashion them after his own imagination or liking. He simply used what God provided. God has provided something for us in Christ that is fashioned in God's likeness, and it is by God's design. If you are looking for peace with God, if you are looking for a sanctuary from sin, then look no farther than to the stone of witness that God has set up, which is the Lord Jesus Christ. We must now go to the book of Isaiah as we consider the red thread here in the book of Joshua.

Isaiah 8:11- 14

For the LORD spake thus to me with a strong hand, and

instructed me that I should not walk in the way of this people, saying,
　　Say ye not, A confederacy, to all *them to* whom this people shall say, A confederacy; neither fear ye their fear, nor be afraid.
　　Sanctify the LORD of hosts himself; and *let* him *be* your fear, and *let* him *be* your dread.
　　And he shall be for a sanctuary; but for a stone of stumbling and for a rock of offence to both the houses of Israel, for a gin and for a snare to the inhabitants of Jerusalem.

Even though Israel believed God in the days of Joshua, it was not always so. As time passed, Israel again stopped believing and moved away from God and the stone that he had set as a witness to the truth of their salvation. The great stone set by the sanctuary turned into a stumbling block. By the time Jesus Christ came to Israel, he had only this to say.

　　Luke 20:17, 18
　　And he beheld them, and said, What is this then that is written, The stone which the builders rejected, the same is become the head of the corner?
　　Whosoever shall fall upon that stone shall be broken; but on whomsoever it shall fall, it will grind him to powder.

This is the stone that God set to be the headstone, the corner stone of Christianity. Israel did believe concerning this stone for awhile in the time of Joshua, and it was a sight to behold. Israel as a whole later rejected this stone, and for them it became a stone of stumbling, a stone rejected. When the children of Israel moved away from believing the Word, they became religious in their own right. Even the law of Moses in its adherence ended up just another religion of the world. The law of Moses became a ritual to them, their separation from God widened, and their believing was lost.

　　Romans 9:31- 33
　　But Israel, which followed after the law of righteousness, hath not attained to the law of righteousness.
　　Wherefore? Because *they sought it* not by faith [believing], but as it were by the works of the law. For they stumbled at that stumblingstone;
　　As it is written, Behold, I lay in Sion a stumblingstone and rock of offence: and whosoever believeth on him shall not be ashamed.

If you believe in Jesus Christ, you will not be disappointed. Don't let

Jesus Christ be a stumbling stone or a rock of offence to you. Do what Israel did in the days of Joshua and believe God. Sanctify the Lord God in your hearts, and be ready always to give an answer to every man that asketh you a reason of the hope that is in you.

I Peter 2:1- 8
Wherefore laying aside all malice, and all guile, and hypocrisies, and envies, and all evil speakings,

As newborn babes, desire the sincere milk of the word, that ye may grow thereby:

If so be ye have tasted that the Lord *is* **gracious.**

To whom coming, *as unto* **a living stone, disallowed indeed of men, but chosen of God,** *and* **precious,**

Ye also, as lively stones, are built up a spiritual house, an holy priesthood, to offer up spiritual sacrifices, acceptable to God by Jesus Christ.

Wherefore also it is contained in the scripture, Behold, I lay in Sion a chief corner stone, elect, precious: and he that believeth on him shall not be confounded.

Unto you therefore which believe *he is* **precious: but unto them which be disobedient, the stone which the builders disallowed, the same is made the head of the corner,**

And a stone of stumbling, and a rock of offence, *even to them* **which stumble at the word, being disobedient: whereunto also they were appointed.**

We, also, as living stones are built up to be a spiritual house where our offerings and sacrifices are acceptable to God by Jesus Christ. We have the sanctuary we desired. In Christ we are made whole. We are wonderfully saved from sin. There is only one way back to God, and that way is through Jesus Christ. We now worship God in spirit and in truth in the sanctuary of the body of Christ.

If you want to be made whole – if you no longer want to be separated from God – then look to the stone which God has placed for salvation, that stone upon which we build, the only name under heaven given among men whereby we must be saved.

Acts 4:8- 12
Then Peter, filled with the Holy Ghost, said unto them, Ye rulers of the people, and elders of Israel,

If we this day be examined of the good deed done to the impotent

man, by what means he is made whole;
> Be it known unto you all, and to all the people of Israel, that by the name of Jesus Christ of Nazareth, whom ye crucified, whom God raised from the dead, *even* by him doth this man
> stand here before you whole.
> This is the stone which was set at nought of you builders, which is become the head of the corner.
> Neither is there salvation in any other: for there is none other name under heaven given among men, whereby we must be saved.

This is the stone that bore witness to all that God had said. This is the stone that became the head of the corner. This is Jesus Christ, in whom there is salvation. In no other name given under heaven will you find salvation. This is the great stone Joshua set up by the sanctuary as the red thread; a stone of witness, what could be more enduring?

> **Genesis 31:44- 46**
> Now therefore come thou, let us make a covenant, I and thou; and let it be for a witness between me and thee.
> And Jacob took a stone, and set it up *for* a pillar.
> And Jacob said unto his brethren, Gather stones; and they took stones, and made an heap: and they did eat there upon the heap.

What about you and I? Can we climb on the heap and eat together, sharing in the believing we have in Christ Jesus our Lord?

The Red Thread of Judges

Our Saviour and Judge

A judge is one who upholds the law, but he is also one who should be able to get to the bottom of a matter. A judge raised up by God passes judgment according to the Word and counsel of God. We may think of a judge as one who sits behind the bench wielding the gavel of blind justice, but the judges we will be looking at were far from bench sitters. After the mess that Adam left, we needed a judge who would not be so quick to condemn, but who would come to deliver us. As we look for the red thread in the book of Judges, we should define the word "deliverer," which is used in the text. The word "deliverer" could just as well be translated as the word "saviour." One who delivers here in Judges is one who saves. We are dealing with peoples' lives here; one who delivers peoples' lives is one who saves lives. This plays an important role in our study, because Jesus Christ is our saviour. Jesus Christ is the ultimate judge and deliverer for all mankind. The very name of Jesus means saviour. In the book of Judges, Jesus Christ is the red thread as God's perfect saviour and judge.

A man without the spirit of God has a hard time judging anything. He cannot discern between his right hand and his left hand. This perhaps explains some of the reason why the children of Israel seemed to wander so easily away from God from one generation to the next.

Judges 2:1, 2
And an angel of the LORD came up from Gilgal to Bochim, and said, I made you to go up out of Egypt, and have brought you unto the land which I sware unto your fathers; and I said, I will never break my covenant with you.

And ye shall make no league with the inhabitants of this land; ye shall throw down their altars: but ye have not obeyed my voice: why have ye done this?

No one is without a reason for his actions. Everyone has an excuse, and most excuses seem to get recycled from one generation to the next. Suppose when the children of Israel were asked by God, "why have you done this?", they replied with some timeless excuses. They may have used one of the following frequently used examples: *Well, everyone else is doing it*; *She made me do it*; *It doesn't hurt anybody*; *It seemed like a good idea at the time*. Or perhaps they said: *It's progress*; or, *Things change, so get with the times*. Then there is my favorite, an all-time classic example: *I don't know*. This seems to be an all too common theme, when asked, "why have you done this?" To respond with "I don't know" shows a lack of understanding. I can't imagine that they would not obey God's voice, if they knew what was going on spiritually. But you cannot know nor perceive spirit without spirit.

Judges 2:10- 12
And also all that generation were gathered unto their fathers: and there arose another generation after them, which knew not the LORD [Without spirit it is impossible to know or perceive God who is spirit], **nor yet the works which he had done for Israel.**
And the children of Israel did evil in the sight of the LORD, and served Baalim:
And they forsook the LORD God of their fathers, which brought them out of the land of Egypt, and followed other gods, of the gods of the people that *were* **round about them, and bowed themselves unto them, and provoked the LORD to anger.**

Judges 2:16- 18
Nevertheless the LORD raised up judges, which delivered them out of the hand of those that spoiled them.
And yet they would not hearken unto their judges, but they went a whoring after other gods, and bowed themselves unto them: they turned quickly out of the way which their fathers walked in, obeying the commandments of the LORD; *but* **they did not so.**
And when the LORD raised them up judges, then the LORD was with the judge, and delivered them out of the hand of their enemies all the days of the judge: for it repented the LORD because of their groanings by reason of them that oppressed them and vexed them.

The only way any judge is able to succeed is if the Lord is with him. This holds true when dealing with Jesus Christ as well. When looking at the life and ministry of Jesus Christ, it is clear that God made him responsible for judging all men. God has always desired for men to know Him. God's judge has not come looking to condemn you, but with the desire to deliver you from them who oppress and vex you. God's desire can clearly be seen, and His desire is not to come to man with a judgment of condemnation but with a judgment of salvation. It all depends on your acceptance or rejection of God's perfect judge and saviour, Jesus Christ.

John 5:22, 23
For the Father judgeth no man, but hath committed all judgment unto the Son:
That all *men* should honour the Son, even as they honour the Father. He that honoureth not the Son honoureth not the Father which hath sent him.

Jesus was very clear as to how he was able to accomplish such a task of judging all men. His judgment was not made unilaterally. Any time Jesus judged anyone, God was with him giving counsel. You should have God with you and accept His counsel in every situation.

John 8:15, 16
Ye judge after the flesh; I judge no man [after the flesh].
And yet if I judge, my judgment is true: for I am not alone, but I and the Father that sent me.

The acceptance or rejection of this saviour will prove to be a most dramatic judgment upon each individual come the last day. It is your response to the Word that will determine the judgment handed down in your case.

John 12:47- 50
And if any man hear my words, and believe not, I judge him not: for I came not to judge the world, but to save the world.
He that rejecteth me, and receiveth not my words, hath one that judgeth him: the word that I have spoken, the same shall judge him in the last day.
For I have not spoken of myself; but the Father which sent me, he gave me a commandment, what I should say, and what I should speak.
And I know that his commandment is life everlasting: whatsoever I speak therefore, even as the Father said unto me, so I speak.

Jesus Christ came as the saviour of the world. He is the fulfillment of all deliverance and judgment that God desires for you and I. It is the very name of Jesus Christ in which we can see our deliverance.

Matthew 1:18- 21
Now the birth of Jesus Christ was on this wise: When as his

mother Mary was espoused to Joseph, before they came together, she was found with child of the Holy Ghost.

Then Joseph her husband, being a just *man*, **and not willing to make her a public example, was minded to put her away privily.**

But while he thought on these things, behold, the angel of the Lord appeared unto him in a dream, saying, Joseph, thou son of David, fear not to take unto thee Mary thy wife: for that which is conceived in her is of the Holy Ghost.

And she shall bring forth a son, and thou shalt call his name JESUS: for he shall save his people from their sins.

The fulfillment of which all the prophets have spoken may be seen in only one. That one, declared to be God's son even by God Himself, is Jesus Christ. In the book of Judges, God raised up judges to deliver the children of Israel out of the hand of those who spoiled them. All together there are twelve judges recorded by name in the book of Judges. The red thread is woven through the spirit of Othniel, the left hand of Ehud, and the ox goad of Shamgar. The red thread wraps around the song of Deborah and Barak and the sword of Gideon and flows through the water of the jawbone of the ass that revived Samson.

Judges 3:9, 10
And when the children of Israel cried unto the LORD, the LORD raised up a deliverer to the children of Israel, who delivered them, *even* **Othniel the son of Kenaz, Caleb's younger brother.**

And the spirit of the LORD came upon him, and he judged Israel,

The first thing any man needs is the spirit of God. The five senses limit a man's perception to that which he can see, hear, smell, taste, and touch. The spirit allows a man to judge things from a whole different perspective. Jesus also had the spirit placed upon him when he was baptized of John in the Jordan. It is the spirit which gives a man the ability that he is otherwise missing.

Acts 10:38
How God anointed Jesus of Nazareth with the Holy Ghost [holy spirit] **and with power: who went about doing good, and healing all that were oppressed of the devil; for God was with him.**

Jesus Christ sees all who are oppressed and vexed of the Devil and delivers them. You may not have picked Jesus as the most likely candidate to deliver the world. Some today even look at it as a left-handed gift. A left-handed gift would be perceived as something distasteful and not of the hand of blessing. Biblically the right hand would be considered the hand of blessing. But God knew what He was doing even when He chose Ehud, a left-handed man, to deliver a present unto Eglon. And God knew what He was doing in choosing Jesus.

Judges 3:15
But when the children of Israel cried unto the LORD, the LORD raised them up a deliverer, Ehud the son of Gera, a Benjamite, a man left handed: and by him the children of Israel sent a present unto Eglon the king of Moab.

A man left-handed, how could this be? You wouldn't pick a left-handed man to present a gift.

Matthew 13:53- 57
And it came to pass, *that* when Jesus had finished these parables, he departed thence.
And when he was come into his own country, he taught them in their synagogue, insomuch that they were astonished, and said, Whence hath this *man* this wisdom, and *these* mighty works?
Is not this the carpenter's son? is not his mother called Mary? and his brethren, James, and Joses, and Simon, and Judas?
And his sisters, are they not all with us? Whence then hath this *man* all these things?
And they were offended in him. But Jesus said unto them, A prophet is not without honour, save in his own country, and in his own house.

Jesus came to deliver a gift. Some may be leery, and others may not believe, but he is the best man to judge and deliver us all from the oppression of the enemy. Some thought him to be the carpenter's son. The people around him thought they knew his situation and his family. Therefore, they were offended by him and said, *how could this man have all these things?*

Judges 3:31
And after him was Shamgar the son of Anath, which slew of the

Philistines six hundred men with an ox goad: and he also delivered Israel.

An ox goad. What is the significance of an ox goad? A goad is a sharp pointed stick used to keep the ox going; and in the right direction, not a soothing thing by which to be prodded.

Ecclesiastes 12:11, 13, 14
The words of the wise *are* as goads, and as nails fastened *by* the masters of assemblies, *which* are given from one shepherd.
Let us hear the conclusion of the whole matter: Fear God, and keep his commandments: for this *is* the whole *duty* of man.
For God shall bring every work into judgment, with every secret thing, whether *it be* good, or whether *it be* evil.

Jesus' words were pointed at times, and some who heard him were offended, but he always cut to the heart of the matter. He didn't mess around when it came to the job God had given him to do. His judgment was right when he was dealing with good or with evil.

Judges 5: 1, 2
Then sang Deborah and Barak the son of Abinoam on that day, saying,
Praise ye the LORD for the avenging of Israel, when the people willingly offered themselves.

The Lord is able to avenge His people when they willingly offer themselves. God is always waiting for us to willingly come to Him and offer ourselves to His judgment.

Judges 5:9, 10, 12
My heart *is* toward the governors of Israel, that offered themselves willingly among the people. Bless ye the LORD.
Speak, ye that ride on white asses, ye that sit in judgment, and walk by the way.
Awake, awake, Deborah: awake, awake, utter a song: arise, Barak, and lead thy captivity captive, thou son of Abinoam.

These governors of Israel wanted God's involvement in their lives. They wanted to know what God thought. The judges rode on asses. When it says that they were on white asses, it tells you the judgments they were carrying were pure and right judgments. They also had the last word on the matter. God should always be afforded the final word on any matter.

Ephesians 4:7, 8
But unto every one of us is given grace according to the measure of the gift of Christ.
Wherefore he saith, When he ascended up on high, he led captivity captive, and gave gifts unto men.

Jesus Christ led captivity captive and gave gifts unto men; let us also awake and utter a song. Now we have something to fight with. I know we were hiding out, afraid of our own shadow just like Gideon was. But Christ is our Judge and saviour, and this is where the sword of the Lord and of Gideon comes in.

Judges 6:11, 12
And there came an angel of the LORD, and sat under an oak which *was* in Ophrah, that *pertained* unto Joash the Abiezrite: and his son Gideon threshed wheat by the winepress, to hide *it* from the Midianites.
And the angel of the LORD appeared unto him, and said unto him, The LORD *is* with thee, thou mighty man of valour.

Gideon didn't feel much like a mighty man of valour when the angel first showed up and talked with him. He wasn't at all convinced until he took up the sword of the Lord and began to do that which God judged him worthy of. God wasn't looking for an army, all He wanted were those who were not fearful and who would believe His Word.

Judges 7:20
And the three companies blew the trumpets, and brake the pitchers, and held the lamps in their left hands, and the trumpets in their right hands to blow *withal*: and they cried, The sword of the LORD, and of Gideon.

We have access to the sword of the Lord as well, a sword far superior to any blade of steel. It is able to cut to the heart of the matter, a sword that will make you a mighty man of valor also.

Ephesians 6:16, 17
Above all, taking the shield of faith, wherewith ye shall be able to

quench all the fiery darts of the wicked.
And take the helmet of salvation, and the sword of the Spirit, which is the word of God:

Hebrews 4:12
For the word of God *is* quick, and powerful, and sharper than any twoedged sword, piercing even to the dividing asunder of soul and spirit, and of the joints and marrow, and *is* a discerner of the thoughts and intents of the heart.

From birth, Samson was a Nazarite unto God, and the Lord blessed him. When it began that the spirit moved him, he went forth with the judgments of God to victory.

Judges 15:16, 18, 19
And Samson said, With the jawbone of an ass, heaps upon heaps, with the jaw of an ass have I slain a thousand men.
And he was sore athirst, and called on the LORD, and said, Thou hast given this great deliverance into the hand of thy servant: and now shall I die for thirst, and fall into the hand of the uncircumcised?
But God clave an hollow place that *was* in the jaw, and there came water thereout; and when he had drunk, his spirit came again, and he revived:

Jesus Christ came to judge, but he also came to save; and with his judgments he wrought salvation for you and I. It was a great deliverance when he revived us with the spirit which God returned to us in the new birth. We can now receive the gift of God and drink of the living water that Jesus offered to the woman at the well.

John 4:10
Jesus answered and said unto her [the woman at the well], **If thou knewest the gift of God, and who it is that saith to thee, Give me to drink; thou wouldest have asked of him, and he would have given thee living water.**

God made the water to flow for Samson. He can and He will make the living water flow into you. The judge has spoken, the judgment has been passed, and deliverance can be found in the new birth.

John 3:3- 7
Jesus answered and said unto him, Verily, verily, I say unto thee, Except a man be born again, he cannot see the kingdom of God.
Nicodemus saith unto him, How can a man be born when he is old? can he enter the second time into his mother's womb, and be born?
Jesus answered, Verily, verily, I say unto thee, Except a man be born of water and *of* **the Spirit, he cannot enter into the kingdom of God.**
That which is born of the flesh is flesh; and that which is born of the Spirit is spirit.
Marvel not that I said unto thee, Ye must be born again.

Jesus Christ as the red thread is the perfect saviour and Judge, for he brought into fruition all that the Judges of old could not and provided for us the new birth. He delivered us from the oppression and vexation of the Devil, returning to us the spirit that was lost through the amazing judgment of God.

The Red Thread of Judges

The Kinsman Redeemer

The book of Ruth opens on the heels of the book of Judges, when every man was doing that which was right in his own eyes. The Word declares that there was a famine in the land in those days. A famine may mean that there is a lack of bread to eat, but even more important to realize is that a physical famine is only an indicator of the greater famine, that of the Word of God. People bring themselves into desperate times; but even out of a desperate situation, God brought forth a kinsman redeemer. Jesus Christ is the red thread as the kinsman redeemer in the book of Ruth. I know the question on everyone's mind in times like these. Can we find grace to help in the time of need?

Judges 21: 24, 25
And the children of Israel departed thence at that time, every man to his tribe and to his family, and they went out from thence every man to his inheritance.

In those days *there was* no king in Israel: every man did *that which was* right in his own eyes.

The problem wasn't that they didn't have a king. The problem was they were doing that which seemed right in their own eyes and not that which was right in God's eyes. As we come now to the book of Ruth, we begin to understand why there was a famine in the land.

Ruth 1: 1
Now it came to pass in the days when the judges ruled, that there was a famine in the land. And a certain man of Bethlehemjudah went to sojourn in the country of Moab, he, and his wife, and his two sons.

Amos speaks also of a famine far greater than that of the want of bread alone. A physical famine may be an indicator of a much more deeply rooted problem.

Amos 8: 11
Behold, the days come, saith the Lord GOD, that I will send a famine in the land, not a famine of bread, nor a thirst for water, but of hearing the words of the LORD:

In Hosea chapter four verse six, God says, "My People are destroyed for lack of knowledge," and this knowledge is the knowledge of God and His Word. When men are separated from God and His Word, they are in need of a redeemer. For who can fend off the destruction that is sure to follow?

Ruth 1: 3- 6
And Elimelech Naomi's husband died; and she was left, and her two sons.
And they took them wives of the women of Moab; the name of the one *was* Orpah, and the name of the other Ruth: and they dwelled there about ten years.
And Mahlon and Chilion died also both of them; and the woman was left of her two sons and her husband.
Then she arose with her daughters in law, that she might return from the country of Moab: for she had heard in the country of Moab how that the Lord had visited his people in giving them bread.

Naomi then gave her daughters-in-law a choice. She encouraged them to stay and try to remarry, because she was most assuredly going to return to her God and country.

Ruth 1: 14- 16
And they lifted up their voice, and wept again: and Orpah kissed her mother in law; but Ruth clave unto her.
And she said, Behold, thy sister in law is gone back unto her people, and unto her gods: return thou after thy sister in law.
And Ruth said, Entreat me not to leave thee, *or* to return from following after thee: for whither thou goest, I will go; and where thou lodgest, I will lodge: thy people *shall be* my people, and thy God my God:

Orpah chose to stay with her people and her gods, but Ruth chose to go with Naomi and to make Naomi's people, her people and Naomi's God, her God. So they returned wondering if they would find grace to help in their time of need.

Ruth 2: 1, 2
And Naomi had a kinsman of her husband's, a mighty man of wealth, of the family of Elimelech; and his name *was* Boaz.
And Ruth the Moabitess said unto Naomi, Let me now go to the

field, and glean ears of corn after *him* in whose sight I shall find grace. And she said unto her, Go, my daughter.

Naomi knew of a kinsman who might have the means to help. So they went knowing the situation they were faced with and trusting they would find the grace that was needed.

Ruth 2: 10- 12
Then she fell on her face, and bowed herself to the ground, and said unto him, Why have I found grace in thine eyes, that thou shouldest take knowledge of me, seeing I *am* a stranger?
And Boaz answered and said unto her, It hath fully been showed me, all that thou hast done unto thy mother in law since the death of thine husband: and *how* thou hast left thy father and thy mother, and the land of thy nativity, and art come unto a people which thou knewest not heretofore.
The LORD recompense thy work, and a full reward be given thee of the LORD God of Israel, under whose wings thou art come to trust.

And so Ruth and Naomi found the grace that they needed in their kinsman, Boaz. He redeemed their lives from destruction and married Ruth, who would conceive and bear Obed, who was the father of Jesse, who happened to be the father of David.

Ruth 4: 14, 15
And the women said unto Naomi, Blessed *be* the LORD, which hath not left thee this day without a kinsman, that his name may be famous in Israel.
And he shall be unto thee a restorer of *thy* life, and a nourisher of thine old age:

Even greater than the kinsman redeemer found in Boaz is the red thread found in the book of Ruth, and this is the kinsman redeemer found in Jesus Christ. In the days preceding the birth of Jesus Christ, Zacharias, the father of John the Baptist, prophesied this.

Luke 1: 68- 75
Blessed *be* the Lord God of Israel; for he hath visited and redeemed his people,
And hath raised up an horn of salvation for us in the house of his

servant David;
>
> As he spake by the mouth of his holy prophets, which have been since the world began:
>
> That we should be saved from our enemies, and from the hand of all that hate us;
>
> To perform the mercy *promised* to our fathers, and to remember his holy covenant;
>
> The oath which he sware to our father Abraham,
>
> That he would grant unto us, that we being delivered out of the hand of our enemies might serve him without fear,
>
> In holiness and righteousness before him, all the days of our life.

It was time for God to redeem His people, but most did not understand that He had designs on much more than a physical plot of land. So when Jesus died, no one saw what he was purchasing with his blood. Even Jesus' disciples on the road to Emmaus were seemingly unaware of what was going on.

> Luke 24: 20- 27
>
> And how the chief priests and our rulers delivered him to be condemned to death, and have crucified him.
>
> But we trusted that it had been he which should have redeemed Israel: and beside all this, to day is the third day since these things were done.
>
> Yea, and certain women also of our company made us astonished, which were early at the sepulchre; And when they found not his body, they came, saying, that they had also seen a vision of angels, which said that he was alive.
>
> And certain of them which were with us went to the sepulchre, and found *it* even so as the women had said: but him they saw not.
>
> Then he said unto them, O fools, and slow of heart to believe all that the prophets have spoken:
>
> Ought not Christ to have suffered these things, and to enter into his glory?
>
> And beginning at Moses and all the prophets, he expounded unto them in all the scriptures the things concerning himself.

What a day, what a moment in time to have Jesus expound the scriptures concerning himself. I call it the red thread, but however you choose to look at it, it is quite a bit of knowledge to possess. In Titus chapter two, verse fourteen, we find it recorded that Jesus Christ gave himself for us that he might redeem us from all iniquity and purify unto himself a peculiar or special people, zealous of good works. Once you know the kinsman redeemer you have in Jesus Christ, don't be afraid to find the grace God has placed there for you, so that you can become one of the redeemed of the Lord, who is not ashamed to say so.

I Peter 1: 18- 23
Forasmuch as ye know that ye were not redeemed with corruptible things, *as* **silver and gold, from your vain conversation** *received* **by tradition from your fathers;**
But with the precious blood of Christ, as of a lamb without blemish and without spot:
Who verily was foreordained before the foundation of the world, but was manifest in these last times for you,
Who by him do believe in God, that raised him up from the dead, and gave him glory; that your faith [believing] **and hope might be in God.**
Seeing ye have purified your souls in obeying the truth through the spirit unto unfeigned love of the brethren, *see that ye* **love one another with a pure heart fervently:**
Being born again, not of corruptible seed, but of incorruptible, by the word of God, which liveth and abideth for ever.

As the red thread Jesus Christ is the kinsman redeemer in the book of Ruth. Today there is grace available to each of us who would like the redemption, which is in Jesus Christ our Lord.

Ephesians 1: 2- 9
Grace *be* **to you, and peace, from God our Father, and** *from* **the Lord Jesus Christ.**
Blessed *be* **the God and Father of our Lord Jesus Christ, who hath blessed us with all spiritual blessings in heavenly** *places* **in Christ:**
According as he hath chosen us in him [Christ] **before the foundation of the world, that we should be holy and without blame before him in love:**
Having predestinated [foreknown] **us unto the adoption** [sonship] **of children by Jesus Christ to himself, according to the good pleasure of his will,**
To the praise of the glory of his grace, wherein he hath made us accepted in the beloved.
In whom we have redemption through his blood, the forgiveness

of sins, according to the riches of his grace;
 Wherein he hath abounded toward us in all wisdom and prudence;
 Having made known unto us the mystery of his will,

Don't get caught up in the famine that is in the world today. Do not be ignorant of the mystery of God's will concerning the riches of His grace and the redemption of our kinsman redeemer.

The Lord's Anointed

When dealing with the red thread, I Samuel points to the Lord's Anointed. As the plight of man takes a downward spiral, there are few stars that shine as bright as Samuel, who was lent to the Lord by his mother. Samuel learned of the Lord early on in his life, even when the Word and the Lord were a scarcity around him. He grew, and the Lord was with him and let none of his words fall to the ground. Everyone knew that Samuel was established, a prophet of the Lord. And Samuel judged Israel all the days of his life. When Hannah brought Samuel to the house of the Lord in Shiloh to leave the child with Eli, she had this to say:

I Samuel 1:28
Therefore also I have lent him to the LORD; as long as he liveth he shall be lent to the LORD. And he worshiped the LORD there.

To be lent to the Lord, to spend your life with the Lord and in service to the Lord... is this a downer, a sub-par way to live? Your answer to this question will be very telling when it comes to understanding and appreciating the Lord's anointed.

I Samuel 2:1, 9, 10
And Hannah prayed, and said, My heart rejoiceth in the LORD, mine horn [strength and position] is exalted in the LORD: my mouth is enlarged over mine enemies; because I rejoice in thy salvation.
He will keep the feet of his saints, and the wicked shall be silent in darkness; for by strength shall no man prevail.
The adversaries of the LORD shall be broken to pieces; out of heaven shall he thunder upon them: the LORD shall judge the ends of the earth; and he shall give strength unto his king, and exalt the horn of His Anointed.

That which Hannah spoke of was not found in Saul, who would become king over Israel. The people wanted a king other than God to judge them, so they could be like all of the other nations. The people of Israel could only see an earthly kingdom, while God was looking to bring back the heavenly one. God would anoint His king with holy spirit and power. However, He needed the right person, who would accept it and use it for the purpose which God intended. Israel started something here that would never play out to their benefit, but God never took His eyes off the captain of our salvation, which is a good thing for all of us. Israel steadily went downhill from here, but God forged ahead, working with the few that were willing to work with Him.

I Samuel 12:16- 25

Now therefore stand and see this great thing, which the LORD will do before your eyes.

Is it not wheat harvest to day? I will call unto the LORD, and he shall send thunder and rain; that ye may perceive and see that your wickedness *is* great, which ye have done in the sight of the LORD, in asking you a king.

So Samuel called unto the LORD; and the LORD sent thunder and rain that day: and all the people greatly feared the LORD and Samuel.

And all the people said unto Samuel, Pray for thy servants unto the LORD thy God, that we die not: for we have added unto all our sins *this* evil, to ask us a king.

And Samuel said unto the people, Fear not: ye have done all this wickedness: yet turn not aside from following the LORD, but serve the LORD with all your heart;

And turn ye not aside: for *then should ye go* after vain *things*, which cannot profit nor deliver; for they *are* vain.

For the LORD will not forsake his people for his great name's sake: because it hath pleased the LORD to make you his people.

Moreover as for me, God forbid that I should sin against the LORD in ceasing to pray for you: but I will teach you the good and the right way:

Only fear the LORD, and serve him in truth with all your heart; for consider how great *things* he hath done for you.

But if ye shall still do wickedly, ye shall be consumed, both ye and your king.

Hannah prophesied concerning the Lord's anointed and how God would exalt the horn of His anointed and give strength unto His king. God wasn't about to forsake His people, but they forsook Him.

I Samuel 13:13, 14

And Samuel said to Saul, Thou hast done foolishly: thou hast not kept the commandment of the LORD thy God, which he commanded thee: for now would the LORD have established thy kingdom upon

Israel for ever.

But now thy kingdom shall not continue: the LORD hath sought him a man after his own heart, and the LORD hath commanded him *to be* captain over his people, because thou hast not kept *that* which the LORD commanded thee.

God was looking for a man after His own heart, and David, who according to God was exactly that, did not prove to be the captain of our salvation. This was yet to be fulfilled by the Lord's Anointed, Jesus Christ. This Jesus Christ would be the Lord's Anointed, spoken of by Hannah in the book of I Samuel.

Luke 1:68, 69
Blessed *be* the Lord God of Israel; for he hath visited and redeemed his people, And hath raised up an horn of salvation for us in the house of his servant David.

God would anoint this Jesus to be Christ the Lord. God would raise up for us a horn of salvation in the house of David. Unto us was born a saviour, which is Christ Jesus the Lord.

Luke 2:11
For unto you is born this day in the city of David a Saviour, which is Christ the Lord.

Jesus was the Anointed of the Lord. When it came time for him to begin his work here upon earth, God exalted the horn of His Anointed with the spirit and the authority to use it.

Luke 4:14 and 18-21
And Jesus returned in the power of the Spirit into Galilee: and there went out a fame of him through all the region round about.
{And as Jesus taught he said;}
The Spirit of the Lord *is* upon me, because he hath anointed me to preach the gospel to the poor; he hath sent me to heal the brokenhearted, to preach deliverance to the captives, and recovering of sight to the blind, to set at liberty them that are bruised, To preach the acceptable year of the Lord.
And he closed the book, and he gave *it* again to the minister, and sat down. And the eyes of all them that were in the synagogue were fastened on him.

And he began to say unto them, This day is this scripture fulfilled in your ears.

There is no other who could carry the name of Christ, for it is only in Jesus Christ that man can find salvation and be made whole. Jesus was anointed with the spirit, so he could do the job that was given him. He was anointed, so he could fulfill the scripture that was recorded concerning him.

Acts 4:8- 12
Then Peter, filled with the Holy Ghost [holy spirit]**, said unto them, Ye rulers of the people, and elders of Israel, If we this day be examined of the good deed done to the impotent man, by what means he is made whole;**
Be it known unto you all, and to all the people of Israel, that by the name of Jesus Christ of Nazareth, whom ye crucified, whom God raised from the dead, *even* **by him doth this man stand here before you whole.**
This is the stone which was set at nought of you builders, which is become the head of the corner.
Neither is there salvation in any other: for there is none other name under heaven given among men, whereby we must be saved.

There is no salvation in any other. Jesus Christ did what no other could do, and although he had to suffer, he led many sons to glory.

Acts 4:27, 28
For of a truth against thy holy child Jesus, whom thou hast anointed, both Herod, and Pontius Pilate, with the Gentiles, and the people of Israel, were gathered together,
For to do whatsoever thy hand and thy counsel determined before to be done.

God had a plan, and Jesus Christ was anointed to do the job. He did not fail as the Lord's Anointed. Jesus was a holy child, and when it came time, the prophecy was fulfilled. God did anoint him, and he did all that was determined before to be done.

Hebrews 2:9- 13
But we see Jesus, who was made a little lower than the angels for the suffering of death, crowned with glory and honour; that he by the grace of God should taste death for every man.

> For it became him, for whom *are* all things, and by whom *are* all things, in bringing many sons unto glory, to make the captain of their salvation perfect through sufferings.
>
> For both he that sanctifieth and they who are sanctified *are* all of one: for which cause he is not ashamed to call them brethren, Saying, I will declare thy name unto my brethren, in the midst of the church will I sing praise unto thee.
>
> And again, I will put my trust in him. And again, Behold I and the children which God hath given me.

We are God's children when we believe on the Lord Jesus Christ. He is the captain of our salvation. We are his brethren, and by him we also receive an anointing. We have the spirit to use in our lives, and we are to live our lives with God. This is the reason why Jesus Christ suffered the things he did, so that we could be established in Christ with the anointing that God has given us.

> **II Corinthians 1:18- 22**
>
> But *as* God *is* true, our word toward you was not yea and nay [wishy washy].
>
> For the Son of God, Jesus Christ, who was preached among you by us, *even* by me and Silvanus and Timotheus, was not yea and nay, but in him was yea [in the affirmative].
>
> For all the promises of God in him *are* yea, and in him Amen, unto the glory of God by us.
>
> Now he which stablisheth us with you in Christ, and hath anointed us, *is* God;
>
> Who hath also sealed us, and given the earnest of the spirit in our hearts.

God's word to us is a sure thing. We are established in Christ by the anointing of God who gave unto us the spirit. We have the spirit of God for a purpose, and that purpose is to use it. How good is it to live your life with God and to be in service to Him with the anointing He has given us? The proof is in doing it, but there is an answer for us in the Word as well.

> **I Timothy 6:6 and 11- 15**
>
> But godliness with contentment is great gain.
>
> But thou, O man of God, flee these things; and follow after righteousness, godliness, faith [believing], love, patience, meekness.
>
> Fight the good fight of faith [believing], lay hold on eternal life,

whereunto thou art also called, and hast professed a good profession before many witnesses.

I give thee charge in the sight of God, who quickeneth all things, and *before* **Christ Jesus, who before Pontius Pilate witnessed a good confession;**

That thou keep *this* **commandment without spot, unrebukeable, until the appearing of our Lord Jesus Christ:**

Which in his times he shall show, *who is* **the blessed and only Potentate, the King of kings, and Lord of lords.**

Hannah said that God would give strength unto His king and exalt the horn of His anointed. I say, He most certainly has. And when Jesus Christ comes back as king of kings and lord of lords, every man will know the Lord's Anointed.

My Son

In the book of II Samuel, the red thread moves through the life of David, however not with regard to his strengths or his frailties, but with regard to his desire. In II Samuel, the red thread is woven through the life and genealogy of King David, yet it would still be years before it would come into fruition in the person of Jesus Christ. David was concerned at this time with building a house for God. A house involves more than just a structure in which to live. David had built his own house, he had wives and children and a place for his name to grow and dwell. He was also concerned that God was without a place for His name to be established and grow into a wonderful family. David's desire was that the house of God would be established, and there would be a family bearing God's name. This then is where we find the red thread in the book of II Samuel.

II Samuel 7:1-5
And it came to pass, when the king sat in his house, and the LORD had given him rest round about from all his enemies;
That the king said unto Nathan the prophet, See now, I dwell in an house of cedar, but the ark of God dwelleth within curtains.
And Nathan said to the king, Go, do all that *is* in thine heart; for the LORD *is* with thee.
And it came to pass that night, that the word of the LORD came unto Nathan, saying,
Go and tell my servant David, Thus saith the LORD, Shalt thou build me an house for me to dwell in?

Nathan spoke presumptuously and God asked, "Shalt thou build me a house for me to dwell in?" David had a nice house with wives and children, but for God there was only an ark residing in a tent getting shuffled about from one place to the next. David's heart was in the right place, albeit God said, "I took you from the sheepcote and made you ruler over my people, Israel," *and now you think you can build me a house?* God said, *need I remind you that it was I who told you that I would make you a house?*

II Samuel 7:11-16
And as since the time that I commanded judges *to be* over my people Israel, and have caused thee to rest from all thine enemies. Also the LORD telleth thee that he will make thee an house.

And when thy days be fulfilled, and thou shalt sleep with thy fathers, I will set up thy seed after thee, which shall proceed out of thy bowels, and I will establish his kingdom.

He shall build an house for my name, and I will stablish the throne of his kingdom for ever.

I will be his father, and he shall be my son. If he commit iniquity, I will chasten him with the rod of men, and with the stripes of the children of men:

But my mercy shall not depart away from him, as I took *it* from Saul, whom I put away before thee.

And thine house and thy kingdom shall be established for ever before thee: thy throne shall be established for ever.

God did fulfill His promise to David's seed in Solomon, David's son. God did set up David's seed after him, which proceeded out of David's bowels. God also established Solomon's kingdom, and God even allowed Solomon to build a temple where He placed His name.

II Chronicles 7:11, 12, 15-21

Thus Solomon finished the house of the LORD, and the king's house: and all that came into Solomon's heart to make in the house of the LORD, and in his own house, he prosperously effected.

And the LORD appeared to Solomon by night, and said unto him, I have heard thy prayer, and have chosen this place to myself for an house of sacrifice.

Now mine eyes shall be open, and mine ears attent unto the prayer *that is made* in this place.

For now have I chosen and sanctified this house, that my name may be there for ever: and mine eyes and mine heart shall be there perpetually.

And as for thee, if thou wilt walk before me, as David thy father walked, and do according to all that I have commanded thee, and shalt observe my statutes and my judgments;

Then will I stablish the throne of thy kingdom, according as I have covenanted with David thy father, saying, There shall not fail thee a man *to be* ruler in Israel.

But if ye turn away, and forsake my statutes and my commandments, which I have set before you, and shall go and serve other gods, and worship them;

Then will I pluck them up by the roots out of my land which I have given them; and this house, which I have sanctified for my name, will I cast out of my sight, and will make it *to be* a proverb and a byword among all nations.

And this house, which is high, shall be an astonishment to every one that passeth by it; so that he shall say, Why hath the LORD done thus unto this land, and unto this house?

Houses of cedar and temples of gold are built for men. God's house, which He will build for His name, will be built by His son. David's lineage will have something to do with the coming of God's son, although God's house and His kingdom will be established forever by Jesus Christ. God's son would pass through the house of David, for his mother was of the lineage of king David. It would be God's son that would build a house for God's name, thereby establishing David's house and kingdom forever. The only abiding kingdom is a spiritual one, and the throne of His kingdom will be established forever. God's son would bring many sons into the household of God. David himself will one day be brought into the household of God because of the resurrection and the promise of God.

Matthew 3:16, 17
And Jesus, when he was baptized, went up straightway out of the water: and, lo, the heavens were opened unto him, and he saw the Spirit of God descending like a dove, and lighting upon him:
And lo a voice from heaven, saying, This is my beloved Son, in whom I am well pleased.

God always knew that it would be His son that would build a house for His name and that it would be His kingdom that would be established forever.

Matthew 4:17
From that time Jesus began to preach, and to say, Repent: for the kingdom of heaven is at hand.

The kingdom of heaven, or you could say the kingdom from heaven, is a spiritual kingdom not a kingdom of or from this world.

John 18:36
Jesus answered, My kingdom is not of this world: if my kingdom were of this world, then would my servants fight, that I should not be delivered to the Jews: but now is my kingdom not from hence.

Jesus said "my kingdom is not of this world," therefore it could be established forever. It is according to the sure mercies of David that God would bring His son into the world to save us. God has made promises to Israel that are yet to be fulfilled even today. Yet one thing is certain, we have received already the sure mercies of David through Jesus Christ our Lord.

Isaiah 55:3
Incline your ear, and come unto me: hear, and your soul shall live; and I will make an everlasting covenant with you, *even* **the sure mercies of David.**

Acts 2:22-36, 38, 39
Ye men of Israel, hear these words; Jesus of Nazareth, a man approved of God among you by miracles and wonders and signs, which God did by him in the midst of you, as ye yourselves also know:
Him, being delivered by the determinate counsel and foreknowledge of God, ye have taken, and by wicked hands have crucified and slain:
Whom God hath raised up, having loosed the pains of death: because it was not possible that he should be holden of it.
For David speaketh concerning him, I foresaw the Lord always before my face, for he is on my right hand, that I should not be moved:
Therefore did my heart rejoice, and my tongue was glad; moreover also my flesh shall rest in hope:
Because thou wilt not leave my soul in hell [David knew he would be getting up in the resurrection], **neither wilt thou suffer thine Holy One to see corruption.**
Thou hast made known to me the ways of life; thou shalt make me full of joy with thy countenance.
Men *and* **brethren, let me freely speak unto you of the patriarch David, that he is both dead and buried, and his sepulchre is with us unto this day.** [The resurrection for David is yet in the future, but you and I have salvation available in the present.]
Therefore being a prophet, and knowing that God had sworn with an oath to him, that of the fruit of his loins, according to the flesh, he would raise up Christ to sit on his throne;
He seeing this before spake of the resurrection of Christ, that his soul was not left in hell, neither his flesh did see corruption.
This Jesus hath God raised up, whereof we all are witnesses.
Therefore being by the right hand of God exalted [that would be

Jesus Christ], **and having received of the Father the promise of the Holy Ghost** [this was the apostles on the day of Pentecost], **he hath shed forth this, which ye now see and hear.**

For David is not ascended into the heavens: but he saith himself, The Lord said unto my Lord, Sit thou on my right hand, Until I make thy foes thy footstool.

Therefore let all the house of Israel know assuredly, that God hath made that same Jesus, whom ye have crucified, both Lord and Christ.

Then Peter said unto them, Repent, and be baptized every one of you in the name of Jesus Christ for the remission of sins, and ye shall receive the gift of the Holy Ghost [holy spirit].

For the promise is unto you, and to your children, and to all that are afar off, *even* **as many as the Lord our God shall call.**

Salvation is here, and the day for God's kingdom has come. The gift of the holy spirit is given; the promise is to you and as many as the Lord our God shall call.

Acts 13:32-39, 47, 48
And we declare unto you glad tidings, how that the promise which was made unto the fathers,

God hath fulfilled the same unto us their children, in that he hath raised up Jesus again; as it is also written in the second psalm, Thou art my Son, this day have I begotten thee.

And as concerning that he raised him up from the dead, *now* **no more to return to corruption, he said on this wise, I will give you the sure mercies of David.**

Wherefore he saith also in another *psalm***, Thou shalt not suffer thine Holy One to see corruption.**

For David, after he had served his own generation by the will of God, fell on sleep, and was laid unto his fathers, and saw corruption: But he, whom God raised again, saw no [not] corruption.

Be it known unto you therefore, men *and* **brethren, that through this man is preached unto you the forgiveness of sins:**

And by him all that believe are justified from all things, from which ye could not be justified by the law of Moses.

For so hath the Lord commanded us, *saying***, I have set thee to be a light of the Gentiles, that thou shouldest be for salvation unto the ends of the earth.**

And when the Gentiles heard this, they were glad, and glorified

the word of the Lord: and as many as were ordained to eternal life believed.

    My son shall build a house for my name. God has foreknowledge: He knew of His son even in the days of David the king. God's house is built for the spirit, for it is a spiritual house bearing God's name. You and I have been given the gift of holy spirit through God's son, Jesus Christ. It is he who has brought us into the household of God. We are a habitation of God through the spirit, not a building made with cedar or gold, but a holy temple in the Lord.

    Ephesians 2:18-22
    For through him we both have access by one spirit unto the Father.
    Now therefore ye are no more strangers and foreigners, but fellowcitizens with the saints, and of the household of God;
    And are built upon the foundation of the apostles and prophets, Jesus Christ himself being the chief corner *stone*;
    In whom all the building fitly framed together groweth unto an holy temple in the Lord:
    In whom ye also are builded together for an habitation of God through the spirit.

    It is God's son that has made it all possible. God's son was born of a woman according to the flesh out of the house of David. David saw some things, because God revealed it unto him concerning the fruit of his loins. David foresaw the Lord, which is God's son, and kept him always before his face. David kept him in sight, or you could say he kept him in mind, so that he should not be moved. When David died, he rested in hope, because he knew God's son would come. He knew that God would not leave his soul in the grave, because he believed that God's holy one would not see total decay, for God had made known unto him the way of life. Furthermore, he was full of joy knowing also that he was going to be seeing his Lord in the land of the living. The place for God to dwell is not in a house of cedar or in any structure that man could make. Through Jesus Christ, God prepared a body, a place for him to dwell. For it is in the body of Christ that we bear God's name, having received the gift of holy spirit which He has given us.

    Hebrews 10:5, 9, 10
    Wherefore when he [Jesus] cometh into the world, he saith,

Sacrifice and offering thou wouldest not, but a body hast thou prepared me:

Then said he, Lo, I come to do thy will, O God. He taketh away the first, that he may establish the second.

By the which will we are sanctified through the offering of the body of Jesus Christ once *for all.*

Ephesians 2:15, 16
Having abolished in his [Jesus Christ's] flesh the enmity, *even* **the law of commandments** *contained* **in ordinances; for to make in himself of twain one new man,** *so* **making peace;**

And that he might reconcile both unto God in one body by the cross, having slain the enmity thereby:

Ephesians 1:22, 23
And hath put all *things* **under his [Jesus Christ's] feet, and gave him** *to be* **the head over all** *things* **to the church, which is his body, the fulness of him that filleth all in all.**

I Corinthians 12:27
Now ye are the body of Christ, and members in particular.

This is where we belong, and this is how God built a house for His name through His son, our Lord and saviour Jesus Christ. My son shall build a house for my name, and I will establish the throne of his kingdom forever. So in the book of II Samuel, the red thread is found in the desire of king David and the son of God, Jesus Christ.

Psalm 132:1-5
LORD, remember David, *and* **all his afflictions:**
How he sware unto the LORD, *and* **vowed unto the mighty** *God* **of Jacob;**
Surely I will not come into the tabernacle of my house, nor go up into my bed;
I will not give sleep to mine eyes, *or* **slumber to mine eyelids,**
Until I find out a place for the LORD, an habitation for the mighty *God* **of Jacob.**

The Red Thread of II Samuel

The Red Thread of I Kings

A Man

God was looking for a man, one who would love Him, one who would walk before Him in truth with all his heart and with all his soul. God needed a man with integrity of heart, an upright man who would fulfill His will. God knew of such a man and spoke to David of him even before this man was born. This is the red thread in the book of I Kings, for God had a man in mind, a man who would be all of this, a man who would sit on the throne of Israel, and that man is Jesus Christ. The book of I Kings begins at the end of King David's reign. The kings of Israel hold the book's primary focus, although the kings of Judah are noted. The books of I Kings and II Kings have been identified as one book in the Hebrew Canon, just as the books of I Samuel and II Samuel and I Chronicles and II Chronicles. These three books were later divided by the translators of the Septuagint. It is clear that at the end of these books, the man that God had spoken of had not yet come to rule, yet God knew that the red thread would not unravel with the transgressions of Israel.

I Kings 2:1- 4
Now the days of David drew nigh that he should die; and he charged Solomon his son, saying,
I go the way of all the earth: be thou strong therefore, and show thyself a man;
And keep the charge of the LORD thy God, to walk in his ways, to keep his statutes, and his commandments, and his judgments, and his testimonies, as it is written in the law of Moses, that thou mayest prosper in all that thou doest, and whithersoever thou turnest thyself:
That the LORD may continue his word which he spoke concerning me, saying, If thy children take heed to their way, to walk before me in truth with all their heart and with all their soul, there shall not fail thee (said He) a man on the throne of Israel.

David told Solomon to "show thyself a man." You hear the term "be a man" being used today, but what does it mean to be a man? Is there a standard that we can fashion ourselves after? Solomon was told to be a man, but you can bet David wasn't talking about just any man. There was a man about whom God had told David; it was this man that David set as the standard. When David told Solomon to show thyself a man, he wanted Solomon to set the type for the man who is yet to be. Even sitting here today

I still say, "I wish I were the man I know to be," and that man is Christ in me. Israel needed to turn to the Lord and walk before Him in truth with all their hearts and with all their souls. Israel was fast becoming like all of the other nations of the world in following other gods and rejecting God as the one to lead them. Israel sought a man to sit on the throne, although they failed to see the man that God saw. God had a man in sight, and it is this man that happens to be the red thread in the book of I Kings, a man named Jesus Christ.

I Kings 8:25
Therefore now, LORD God of Israel, keep with thy servant David my father that thou promisedst him, saying, There shall not fail thee a man in my sight to sit on the throne of Israel;

God said, "There shall not fail thee a man in my sight," as He saw beyond the demise of Israel. God saw all the way through to Jesus Christ.

I Kings 9:1- 9
And it came to pass, when Solomon had finished the building of the house of the LORD, and the king's house, and all Solomon's desire which he was pleased to do,
That the LORD appeared to Solomon the second time, as he had appeared unto him at Gibeon.
And the LORD said unto him, I have heard thy prayer and thy supplication, that thou hast made before me: I have hallowed this house, which thou hast built, to put my name there for ever; and mine eyes and mine heart shall be there perpetually.
And if thou wilt walk before me, as David thy father walked, in integrity of heart, and in uprightness, to do according to all that I have commanded thee, *and* wilt keep my statutes and my judgments:
Then I will establish the throne of thy kingdom upon Israel for ever, as I promised to David thy father, saying, There shall not fail thee a man upon the throne of Israel.
***But* if ye shall at all turn from following me, ye or your children, and will not keep my commandments *and* my statutes which I have set before you, but go and serve other gods, and worship them:**
Then will I cut off Israel out of the land which I have given them; and this house, which I have hallowed for my name, will I cast out of my sight; and Israel shall be a proverb and a byword among all people:
And at this house, *which* is high, every one that passeth by it

shall be astonished, and shall hiss; and they shall say, Why hath the LORD done thus unto this land, and to this house?

And they shall answer, Because they forsook the LORD their God, who brought forth their fathers out of the land of Egypt, and have taken hold upon other gods, and have worshipped them, and served them...

God's promise to David was sure because of the man God had in mind. Jesus Christ would be the fulfillment of the promise to David. As for the continuance of the kingdom of Israel, well they failed to walk before God and keep His commandments even through the life and times of Solomon. Solomon himself ended his life on a very sour note. I Kings shows how quickly the nation of Israel became a byword, and it has remains so even today.

I Kings 11:1- 9

But king Solomon loved many strange women, together with the daughter of Pharaoh, women of the Moabites, Ammonites, Edomites, Zidonians, *and* Hittites;

Of the nations *concerning* which the LORD said unto the children of Israel, Ye shall not go in to them, neither shall they come in unto you: *for* surely they will turn away your heart after their gods: Solomon clave unto these in love.

And he had seven hundred wives, princesses, and three hundred concubines: and his wives turned away his heart.

For it came to pass, when Solomon was old, *that* his wives turned away his heart after other gods: and his heart was not perfect with the LORD his God, as *was* the heart of David his father.

For Solomon went after Ashtoreth the goddess of the Zidonians, and after Milcom the abomination of the Ammonites.

And Solomon did evil in the sight of the LORD, and went not fully after the LORD, as *did* David his father.

Then did Solomon build an high place for Chemosh, the abomination of Moab, in the hill that *is* before Jerusalem, and for Molech, the abomination of the children of Ammon.

And likewise did he for all his strange wives, which burnt incense and sacrificed unto their gods.

And the LORD was angry with Solomon, because his heart was turned from the LORD God of Israel, which had appeared unto him twice.

God wasn't looking for another god, for He is the Lord God, the one and only. God needed a man that He could put on the throne of Israel. A man that would be equal to the task. A man who could sit next to God. A man who would be faithful to lead God's people and intercede on their behalf. The throne is a seat of position and rank, and the man that God had in mind would neither deny nor abuse his rank or position.

I Timothy 2:5
For *there is* one God, and one mediator between God and men, the man Christ Jesus;

There is one God and one mediator between God and men, the man Christ Jesus. Jesus Christ is not a god or a god man. Jesus Christ is the son of God and a man of God. However, he never was, nor is he now, God.

Hebrews 10:12
But this man, after he had offered one sacrifice for sins for ever, sat down on the right hand of God;

Jesus Christ is the man of Hebrews 10:12. The name Jesus Christ is used to show how Jesus humbled himself yet is now exalted. The name of Christ Jesus denotes the now exalted one who was once humbled and suffered for us. Christ Jesus sat down on the right hand of God when it was all done. Christ Jesus is the man God put on the throne beside Himself.

Hebrews 8:1, 2
Now of the things which we have spoken *this is* the sum: We have such an high priest, who is set on the right hand of the throne of the Majesty in the heavens;
A minister of the sanctuary, and of the true tabernacle, which the Lord pitched, and not man.

God built this tabernacle, not Solomon. Jesus Christ is the man that ministers in the sanctuary doing the work which no other man could do. God seated him at His own right hand, for he is well deserving of the honor.

Hebrews 12:2
Looking unto Jesus the author and finisher of *our* faith; who for the joy that was set before him endured the cross, despising the shame, and is set down at the right hand of the throne of God.

Jesus not only started but finished that which we needed to believe. God was working with him. Even his death and resurrection were part of God's plan and will. We all needed a man like Jesus Christ, and God knew there would only ever be one Jesus.

Acts 2:22
Ye men of Israel, hear these words; Jesus of Nazareth, a man approved of God among you by miracles and wonders and signs, which God did by him in the midst of you, as ye yourselves also know...

Jesus, a man approved of God. God was at work in Jesus. This is true, but He is also at work within you. The work that was wrought in Christ is now perfected in you when you believe on the Lord Jesus Christ. It is a work of grace finished in glory, for it is now and will always be Christ in you, the hope of glory. Jesus was not who he was for himself alone. He showed us who we are and who we can become in him. Jesus Christ led the way for all the sons of God.

John 1:30, 32- 34
This is he of whom I said, After me cometh a man which is preferred before me: for he was before me.
And John bare record, saying, I saw the Spirit descending from heaven like a dove, and it abode upon him.
And I knew him not: but he that sent me to baptize with water, the same said unto me, Upon whom thou shalt see the Spirit descending, and remaining on him, the same is he which baptizeth with the Holy Ghost [holy spirit] **.**
And I saw, and bare record that this is the Son of God.

John said, "after me cometh a man," a man marked out by God. He will be a man who will baptize with holy spirit making it available to all those who will believe on him; for he is the son of God.

John 5:18
Therefore the Jews sought the more to kill him, because he not only had broken the sabbath, but said also that God was his Father, making himself equal with God.

Jesus dared to believe what God had said about him. Jesus made himself equal with God, because God was at work with him. Jesus did not seek to do his own will but the will of God, his father.

John 5:30
I can of mine own self do nothing: as I hear, I judge: and my judgment is just; because I seek not mine own will, but the will of the Father which hath sent me.

Jesus made God's will his will by keeping the word of God. It was Jesus who put God's words in his mind and thereby took on the form or shape of God.

John 5:37- 39
And the Father himself, which hath sent me, hath borne witness of me. Ye have neither heard his voice at any time, nor seen his shape.

And ye have not his word abiding in you: for whom he hath sent, him ye believe not.

Search the scriptures; for in them ye think ye have eternal life: and they are they which testify of me.

John 8:28- 32
Then said Jesus unto them, When ye have lifted up the Son of man, then shall ye know that I am *he*, and *that* I do nothing of myself; but as my Father hath taught me, I speak these things.

And he that sent me is with me: the Father hath not left me alone; for I do always those things that please him.

As he spoke these words, many believed on him.

Then said Jesus to those Jews which believed on him, If ye continue in my word, *then* are ye my disciples indeed;

And ye shall know the truth, and the truth shall make you free.

Jesus kept God's word in his mind. He allowed God to be at work within him both to will and to do of his good pleasure. God will work with you to do of His good pleasure according to your willingness. It is a matter of will; God will not overstep your freedom of will. Therefore, let God's good pleasure be your good pleasure. We can do those things that please Him as well, if we keep His word in our minds and allow God to be at work within us.

Philippians 2:5- 11
Let this mind be in you, which was also in Christ Jesus:

Who, being in the form of God, thought it not robbery to be equal with God:

But made himself of no reputation, and took upon him the form of a servant, and was made in the likeness of men:

And being found in fashion as a man, he humbled himself, and became obedient unto death, even the death of the cross.

Wherefore God also hath highly exalted him, and given him a name which is above every name:

That at the name of Jesus every knee should bow, of *things* in heaven, and *things* in earth, and *things* under the earth;

And *that* every tongue should confess that Jesus Christ *is* Lord, to the glory of God the Father.

Let God's Word be in your mind just as Christ Jesus kept God's Word in mind. This is the man that God would have you fashion yourself after. This is the man that He showed David. This is the kind of man that Solomon was encouraged to be. This is the man who, being in the form of God, did not think it was robbery to be equal with God. It is not wrong to want to be like our heavenly Father. The form of words that we hold in our minds determines our shape. God's form is also defined by His word. You will never know God's form without knowing God's Word because that is how He makes Himself known. Shape yourself according to God's Word and allow God to fulfill His will in your life.

Philippians 2:13
For it is God which worketh in you both to will and to do of *his* good pleasure.

This is the man, the red thread in the book of I Kings. This Jesus Christ is a man, not a god nor a god man. When God encourages you to show thyself a man, this is the one He has in mind. It is this man that has made salvation available to all who will believe on his name. Don't become a byword, but rather a wonderful believer in Christ.

The Red Thread of I Kings

The Resurrection

In the book of II Kings, the red thread passes through the lives and ministries of two men and can be found in the last miracle of each. The last miracle of Elijah speaks not only of death but also of an ascension. The last miracle of Elisha speaks after his death by a resurrection, showing the reviving effect it would have upon another. Elisha was not resurrected in this final miracle, because Christ is the resurrection and the life. The final miracle of Elisha foretold of the effect that the resurrection would have on others. It is not the attributes and characteristics exemplified in Christ that make up the red thread, because those things show up in others also. Elisha was a man of God, and Elijah was a man of God. Both men had attributes and characteristics that were shared with Jesus Christ. The study of the red thread contains those things that are peculiar to Christ, things that could only be fulfilled in him. That is why in the miracles of Elijah and Elisha, death is tied with an ascension and a resurrection shows the effect that the resurrection will have upon another. Christ is the resurrection, and without him there would be no resurrection for any other. Therefore, Christ is the link that ties the two miracles of II Kings together. For Christ is the resurrection and the title of this study.

II Kings 2:1
And it came to pass, when the LORD would take up Elijah into heaven by a whirlwind, that Elijah went with Elisha from Gilgal.

The last miracle in Elijah's ministry was this: God was going to take Elijah up into heaven by a whirlwind. This shows an ascension, and the means by which he was taken up. A whirlwind has its significance in that it places Elijah in God's hands. He was borne by the hands of the Spirit, putting him in the presence of the omniscient one.

II Kings 2:9-12
And it came to pass, when they were gone over, that Elijah said unto Elisha, Ask what I shall do for thee, before I be taken away from thee. And Elisha said, I pray thee, let a double portion of thy spirit be upon me.
And he said, Thou hast asked a hard thing: *nevertheless*, if thou see me *when I am* taken from thee, it shall be so unto thee; but if not, it shall not be *so*.

And it came to pass, as they still went on, and talked, that, behold, *there appeared* a chariot of fire, and horses of fire, and parted them both asunder; and Elijah went up by a whirlwind into heaven.

And Elisha saw *it*, and he cried, My father, my father, the chariot of Israel, and the horsemen thereof. And he saw him no more: and he took hold of his own clothes, and rent them in two pieces.

The chariot of fire and the horses of fire show the strength and marshaled forces of God. They also made a delivery to Elisha of a double portion of the spirit that was on Elijah; for he saw when Elijah was taken up by the whirlwind. This expression, "My father, my father, the chariot of Israel, and the horsemen thereof" links this miracle with the last miracle of Elisha's ministry being used only in connection with those two events.

II Kings 13:14
Now Elisha was fallen sick of his sickness whereof he died. And Joash the king of Israel came down unto him, and wept over his face, and said, O my father, my father, the chariot of Israel, and the horsemen thereof.

II Kings 13:20, 21
And Elisha died, and they buried him. And the bands of the Moabites invaded the land at the coming in of the year.

And it came to pass, as they were burying a man, that, behold, they spied a band *of men*; and they cast the man into the sepulchre of Elisha: and when the man was let down, and touched the bones of Elisha, he [the man] revived, and stood up on his feet.

Even in death the power of God is able to reach you. Elisha was dead and buried yet the last miracle of Elisha's ministry shows the reviving effect of the resurrection. Jesus Christ is the resurrection and life available to all. If you touch him in death, you are with him in the resurrection. If you die, there is a resurrection, which is to get you up again. Elisha and Elijah died, but in the resurrection, they will live again.

John 11:23- 26
Jesus saith unto her, Thy brother shall rise again.
Martha saith unto him, I know that he shall rise again in the resurrection at the last day.
Jesus said unto her, I am the resurrection, and the life: he that believeth in me, though he were dead, yet shall he live:

And whosoever liveth and believeth in me shall never die. Believest thou this?

Jesus put the resurrection in the present tense when he said, "I am the resurrection;" and we can enjoy the reviving effect here and now, if we care to.

Romans 6:3-11

Know ye not, that so many of us as were baptized into Jesus Christ were baptized into his death?

Therefore we are buried with him by baptism into death: that like as Christ was raised up from the dead by the glory of the Father, even so we also should walk in newness of life.

For if we have been planted together in the likeness of his death, we shall be also *in the likeness* of *his* resurrection:

Knowing this, that our old man is crucified with *him*, that the body of sin might be destroyed, that henceforth we should not serve sin.

For he that is dead is freed from sin.

Now if we be dead with Christ, we believe that we shall also live with him:

Knowing that Christ being raised from the dead dieth no more; death hath no more dominion over him.

For in that he died, he died unto sin once: but in that he liveth, he liveth unto God.

Likewise reckon ye also yourselves to be dead indeed unto sin, but alive unto God through Jesus Christ our Lord.

In touching Jesus in his death, we also can enjoy a walk in newness of life because of the resurrection. Even if we happen to fall asleep before Christ returns, there is yet a rising up with the return of Christ that will not leave us dead and buried, but alive with Christ in glory.

I Corinthians 15:20-23

But now is Christ risen from the dead, *and* become the firstfruits of them that slept.

For since by man [Adam] *came* death, by man [Jesus] *came* also the resurrection of the dead.

For as in Adam all die, even so in Christ shall all be made alive.

But every man in his own order: Christ the firstfruits; afterward they that are Christ's at his coming.

I Thessalonians 4:16, 17
For the Lord himself shall descend from heaven with a shout, with the voice of the archangel, and with the trump of God: and the dead in Christ shall rise first:

Then we which are alive *and* **remain shall be caught up together with them in the clouds, to meet the Lord in the air: and so shall we ever be with the Lord.**

With the first coming of Christ, there was an ascension where he himself became the first fruits. Then in his second coming, there will be a resurrection, but not before those of us who are alive and remain and those who are dead in Christ shall rise and be caught up together. We shall meet the Lord in the air, and forever be with the Lord. There is a course and order as to when everyone lives again, but be assured, there will be a resurrection of the dead. Some will be rising again to life everlasting and some will be rising again to meet with a second death, but all will live to recognize the Lord of Glory.

John 20:1, 2
The first *day* **of the week cometh Mary Magdalene early, when it was yet dark, unto the sepulchre, and seeth the stone taken away from the sepulchre.**

Then she runneth, and cometh to Simon Peter, and to the other disciple, whom Jesus loved, and saith unto them, They have taken away the Lord out of the sepulchre, and we know not where they have laid him.

Mary knew Jesus was dead, and when she saw the stone had been taken away, she thought there was mischief afoot. When they came back to the sepulcher, they saw an odd sight, but Jesus was already gone.

John 20:9- 13
For as yet they knew [understood] not the scripture, that he must rise again from the dead.
Then the disciples went away again unto their own home.
But Mary stood without at the sepulchre weeping: and as she wept, she stooped down, *and looked* **into the sepulchre,**
And seeth two angels in white sitting, the one at the head, and the other at the feet, where the body of Jesus had lain.
And they say unto her, Woman, why weepest thou? She saith unto them, Because they have taken away my Lord, and I know not

where they have laid him.

For as yet they didn't understand the scripture revealing to them that he must rise up from the dead. Jesus was to be the resurrection, and if Christ didn't rise from among the dead, how could there be a resurrection for anyone? There couldn't be, that's right.

I Corinthians 15:12-14
Now if Christ be preached that he rose from the dead, how say some among you that there is no resurrection of the dead?
But if there be no resurrection of the dead, then is Christ not risen:
And if Christ be not risen, then *is* our preaching vain, and your faith [believing] ***is* also vain.**

But Jesus did get up, and Mary Magdalene was the first to see him after he was risen from the dead. She didn't recognize him at first, but then again, she wasn't looking for the resurrection, only for a dead body.

John 20:17
Jesus saith unto her, Touch me not; for I am not yet ascended to my Father: but go to my brethren, and say unto them, I ascend unto my Father, and your Father; and *to* my God, and your God.

Jesus ascended to the Father after he was raised from the dead to present himself as a wave offering of the first fruits. Jesus was the first fruits from the dead, and his rising and ascension set in motion all that was to follow. Jesus Christ's death and ascension resulted in a resurrection and will have a reviving effect upon everyone that ever lives. Some will be revived only to die again, but others who believe on Jesus Christ shall live. There was a promise made, and God said he is coming back.

Acts 1:9-11
And when he had spoken these things, while they beheld, he was taken up; and a cloud received him out of their sight.
And while they looked stedfastly toward heaven as he went up, behold, two men stood by them in white apparel;
Which also said, Ye men of Galilee, why stand ye gazing up into heaven? this same Jesus, which is taken up from you into heaven, shall so come in like manner as ye have seen him go into heaven.

The Red Thread of II Kings

The red thread in the book of II Kings has to do with death, an ascension, and a resurrection. Jesus Christ said, "I am the resurrection and the life. He that believeth in me, though he were dead, yet shall he live: And whosoever liveth and believeth in me shall never die. Believest thou this?" Well, do you believe? There is life to those who believe in the resurrection.

The Way

The children of Israel had a unique opportunity extended to them; God wanted to be like a father to them. He wanted to give them the birthright of a firstborn son. He wanted to build them a house and to have all those who were willing to bear His name live there. The children of Israel were God's chosen people, but it's still up to God to keep track of every person and what they have done. The chronicling of names recorded in the opening chapters of the book of I Chronicles shows the care and concern which God has for each individual life and indicates that God won't forget when it comes to the resurrection. A chronicle is a record or register. We are working in the book of I Chronicles, but we are also going to be dealing with a genealogy. A genealogy is given for the purpose of pedigree. The children of Israel had an opportunity to be a part of God's household and to have the birthright of a firstborn, but their place was not secured by pedigree alone. There is a way for a person to enter God's family and house, and this is where the red thread passes through the book of I Chronicles. Jesus said, when it comes to having a place in my father's house, I am the way.

I Chronicles 17:9-14
Also I will ordain a place for my people Israel, and will plant them, and they shall dwell in their place, and shall be moved no more; neither shall the children of wickedness waste them any more, as at the beginning,
And since the time that I commanded judges *to be* over my people Israel. Moreover I will subdue all thine enemies. Furthermore I tell thee that the LORD will build thee an house.
And it shall come to pass, when thy days be expired that thou must go *to be* with thy fathers, that I will raise up thy seed after thee, which shall be of thy sons; and I will establish his kingdom.
He shall build me an house, and I will stablish his throne for ever.
I will be his father, and he shall be my son: and I will not take my mercy away from him, as I took *it* from *him* that was before thee:
But I will settle him in mine house and in my kingdom for ever: and his throne shall be established for evermore.

There is one whom God would settle in His house and in His kingdom forever. It is he who will build a house for God in which God's people, Israel, will dwell. This one would come out of the genealogy of Israel, but not necessarily after the birthright given to the firstborn.

I Chronicles 5:1, 2
Now the sons of Reuben the firstborn of Israel, (for he *was* the firstborn; but, forasmuch as he defiled his father's bed, his birthright was given unto the sons of Joseph the son of Israel: and the genealogy is not to be reckoned after the birthright.

For Judah prevailed above his brethren, and of him *came* the chief ruler; but the birthright *was* Joseph's:)

The genealogy of Christ would come through Judah, but the birthright was given to Joseph. You will find many twists and turns when following the linage of Israel through the years, but God is keeping track of each life.

Revelation 20:11-15
And I saw a great white throne, and him that sat on it, from whose face the earth and the heaven fled away; and there was found no place for them.

And I saw the dead, small and great, stand before God; and the books were opened: and another book was opened, which is *the book* of life: and the dead were judged out of those things which were written in the books, according to their works.

And the sea gave up the dead which were in it; and death and hell delivered up the dead which were in them: and they were judged every man according to their works.

And death and hell were cast into the lake of fire. This is the second death.

And whosoever was not found written in the book of life was cast into the lake of fire.

It is up to God to keep the record straight. This is a good thing, for God is good with details; He even has the hairs on your head numbered.

Luke 12:7
But even the very hairs of your head are all numbered. Fear not therefore: ye are of more value than many sparrows.

David realized how much God cared for His people, and he praised Him for it.

I Chronicles 16:8-17, 33-36
Give thanks unto the LORD, call upon his name, make known his deeds among the people.
Sing unto him, sing psalms unto him, talk ye of all his wondrous works.
Glory ye in his holy name: let the heart of them rejoice that seek the LORD.
Seek the LORD and his strength, seek his face continually.
Remember his marvellous works that he hath done, his wonders, and the judgments of his mouth;
O ye seed of Israel his servant, ye children of Jacob, his chosen ones.
He *is* the LORD our God; his judgments *are* in all the earth.
Be ye mindful always of his covenant; the word *which* he commanded to a thousand generations;
Even of the covenant which he made with Abraham, and of his oath unto Isaac;
And hath confirmed the same to Jacob for a law, *and* to Israel *for* an everlasting covenant, Saying, Unto thee will I give the land of Canaan, the lot of your inheritance;
Then shall the trees of the wood sing out at the presence of the LORD, because he cometh to judge the earth.
O give thanks unto the LORD; for *he is* good; for his mercy *endureth* for ever.
And say ye, Save us, O God of our salvation, and gather us together, and deliver us from the heathen, that we may give thanks to thy holy name, *and* glory in thy praise.
Blessed *be* the LORD God of Israel for ever and ever. And all the people said, Amen, and praised the LORD.

David was the youngest son of his father, who was a descendent of Judah, but it was he who rose to be ruler over God's people. It was also from his linage that Christ came.

I Chronicles 11:1-3, 9
Then all Israel gathered themselves to David unto Hebron, saying, Behold, we *are* thy bone and thy flesh.
And moreover in time past, even when Saul was king, thou *wast* he that leddest out and broughtest in Israel: and the LORD thy God said unto thee, Thou shalt feed my people Israel, and thou shalt be ruler

over my people Israel.

 Therefore came all the elders of Israel to the king to Hebron; and David made a covenant with them in Hebron before the LORD; and they anointed David king over Israel, according to the word of the LORD by Samuel.

 So David waxed greater and greater: for the LORD of hosts *was* with him.

David was a wonderful man, but Satan stood up against Israel and had David number them. He still tries doing this today. David had Joab go out and number all of Israel, but how could any man number God's people? Only God could do justice in numbering His people. This is why Joab didn't want to do it, and this is why God said it would be a cause of trespass to Israel.

I Chronicles 21:1-4

 And Satan stood up against Israel, and provoked David to number Israel.

 And David said to Joab and to the rulers of the people, Go, number Israel from Beersheba even to Dan; and bring the number of them to me, that I may know *it*.

 And Joab answered, The LORD make his people an hundred times so many more as they *be*: but, my lord the king, *are* they not all my lord's servants? why then doth my lord require this thing? why will he be a cause of trespass to Israel?

 Nevertheless the king's word prevailed against Joab. Wherefore Joab departed, and went throughout all Israel, and came to Jerusalem.

 And Joab gave the sum of the number of the people unto David.

It is only God who could possibly number Israel, for only God knows who believes in Him and in His son. Jesus spoke to the children of Israel concerning his father's house and how it was that he was going to prepare a place for them.

John 14:1-6

 Let not your heart be troubled: ye believe in God, believe also in me.

 In my Father's house are many mansions: if *it were* not *so*, I would have told you. I go to prepare a place for you.

 And if I go and prepare a place for you, I will come again, and receive you unto myself; that where I am, *there* ye may be also.

And whither I go ye know, and the way ye know.

Thomas saith unto him, Lord, we know not whither thou goest; and how can we know the way?

Jesus saith unto him, I am the way, the truth, and the life: no man cometh unto the Father, but by me.

Jesus said, "I am the way." Jesus was talking to Israel, to those God had numbered and written in the book of life which will be opened in the resurrection of the last day. The question still stands, who of the genealogy of the linage of Israel believes in the resurrection?

Matthew 22:23-33

The same day came to him the Sadducees, which say that there is no resurrection, and asked him,

Saying, Master, Moses said, If a man die, having no children, his brother shall marry his wife, and raise up seed unto his brother.

Now there were with us seven brethren: and the first, when he had married a wife, deceased, and, having no issue [no offspring], left his wife unto his brother:

Likewise the second also, and the third, unto the seventh.

And last of all the woman died also.

Therefore in the resurrection whose wife shall she be of the seven? for they all had her.

Jesus answered and said unto them, Ye do err, not knowing the scriptures, nor the power of God.

For in the resurrection they neither marry, nor are given in marriage, but are as the angels of God in heaven.

But as touching the resurrection of the dead, have ye not read that which was spoken unto you by God, saying,

I am the God of Abraham, and the God of Isaac, and the God of Jacob? God is not the God of the dead, but of the living.

And when the multitude heard *this*, they were astonished at his doctrine.

When it comes to Israel, how many err not knowing the scripture or the power of God when it comes to the resurrection and Jesus Christ who is the way and the truth and the life? How many won't know the way home when Christ returns? How many live in darkness not knowing the Father or the son? God has prepared a place for Israel; and in the resurrection, they will find that in our father's house are many mansions. If it were not so, he would not have said so. As the red thread Jesus said, *"I am the way"* to my *father's house*. His absence merely indicates that he has gone to prepare a place for you in His Father's House.

The Red Thread of II Chronicles

A Light

Darkness was falling over the nation of Israel. As a people, Israel kept moving further and further away from God and His Word. After the death of David, his son Solomon reigned in Jerusalem over all of Israel for forty years. As a nation, Israel became split into two nations. After the death of Solomon, his son Rehoboam reigned over the house of Judah and of Benjamin only. He remained in Jerusalem, and these two tribes became known as the nation of Judah. II Chronicles focuses primarily on this nation of Judah and the kings which followed Rehoboam until they were carried away to Babylon and ceased to be. The books of I and II Kings focus more on the nation of Israel and its kings. The books of I and II Kings follow Jeroboam, the son of Nebat, and the ten tribes which went to the north under his reign, and the kings which came after him, known now as the nation of Israel. So Israel was also carried away out of their own land to Assyria and ceased to be even before the nation of Judah fell prey to the same fate. They groped about in darkness, fading into obscurity, and this is where you see the red thread passing through the book of II Chronicles. The children of Israel would have ceased to exist had it not been for the promise of God. Only God could fulfill a promise to give a light in the face of such a dismal setting, and Jesus Christ is that light.

II Chronicles 21:7
Howbeit the LORD would not destroy the house of David, because of the covenant that he had made with David, and as he promised to give a light to him and to his sons for ever.

God promised to give a light to David and to his sons forever. These years were a real roller coaster ride for the children of Israel, yet the Lord would not destroy Judah for His servant David's sake.

II Kings 8:16-19
And in the fifth year of Joram the son of Ahab king of Israel, Jehoshaphat *being* then king of Judah, Jehoram the son of Jehoshaphat king of Judah began to reign.
Thirty and two years old was he when he began to reign; and he reigned eight years in Jerusalem.
And he walked in the way of the kings of Israel, as did the house of Ahab: for the daughter of Ahab was his wife: and he did evil in the

sight of the LORD.
Yet the LORD would not destroy Judah for David his servant's sake, as he promised him to give him alway a light, *and* to his children.

When one group couldn't get into enough trouble on their own, they married into it. Things never really got any better. Sure, there were periods of brief reprieve, but it was all downhill from here.

II Chronicles 12:1, 13, 14
And it came to pass, when Rehoboam had established the kingdom, and had strengthened himself, he forsook the law of the LORD, and all Israel with him.
So king Rehoboam strengthened himself in Jerusalem, and reigned: for Rehoboam *was* one and forty years old when he began to reign, and he reigned seventeen years in Jerusalem, the
city which the LORD had chosen out of all the tribes of Israel, to put his name there. And his mother's name was Naamah an Ammonitess.
And he did evil, because he prepared not his heart to seek the LORD.

Rehoboam set a standard that would be hard to break, but there were a few that came after him that tried to beat back the darkness at least for a little while.

II Chronicles 14:1, 2, 7
So Abijah slept with his fathers, and they buried him in the city of David: and Asa his son reigned in his stead. In his days the land was quiet ten years.
And Asa did *that which was* good and right in the eyes of the LORD his God: Therefore he said unto Judah, Let us build these cities, and make about *them* walls, and towers, gates, and bars, *while* the land *is* yet before us; because we have sought the LORD our God, we have sought *him*, and he hath given us rest on every side. So they built and prospered.

Through it all God never threw in the towel. God wants us to live in peace and have rest on every side. If we seek Him, He will always be found.

II Chronicles 15:1-4
And the Spirit of God came upon Azariah the son of Oded:

And he went out to meet Asa, and said unto him, Hear ye me, Asa, and all Judah and Benjamin; The LORD *is* with you, while ye be with him; and if ye seek him, he will be found of you; but if ye forsake him, he will forsake you.

Now for a long season Israel *hath been* without the true God, and without a teaching priest, and without law.

But when they in their trouble did turn unto the LORD God of Israel, and sought him, he was found of them.

It is hard to know God without a teacher. When you take the knowledge of God out of a nation, how can the people not forsake Him? When people get in trouble, it's interesting how they seem to find their way back to God.

II Chronicles 15:8-15

And when Asa heard these words, and the prophecy of Oded the prophet, he took courage, and put away the abominable idols out of all the land of Judah and Benjamin, and out of the cities which he had taken from mount Ephraim, and renewed the altar of the LORD, that *was* before the porch of the LORD.

And he gathered all Judah and Benjamin, and the strangers with them out of Ephraim and Manasseh, and out of Simeon: for they fell to him out of Israel in abundance, when they saw that the LORD his God *was* with him.

So they gathered themselves together at Jerusalem in the third month, in the fifteenth year of the reign of Asa.

And they offered unto the LORD the same time, of the spoil *which* they had brought, seven hundred oxen and seven thousand sheep.

And they entered into a covenant to seek the LORD God of their fathers with all their heart and with all their soul;

That whosoever would not seek the LORD God of Israel should be put to death, whether small or great, whether man or woman.

And they sware unto the LORD with a loud voice, and with shouting, and with trumpets, and with cornets.

And all Judah rejoiced at the oath: for they had sworn with all their heart, and sought him with their whole desire; and he was found of them: and the LORD gave them rest round about.

God's ready whenever we are. Whenever we get around to seeking Him out and we believe His Word, God will see and come running to show Himself strong on our behalf.

II Chronicles 16:9
For the eyes of the LORD run to and fro throughout the whole earth, to show himself strong in the behalf of *them* whose heart *is* perfect toward him.

Asa did well for a while in following the Lord, and so did his son Jehoshaphat, who reigned after him.

II Chronicles 17:3- 6
And the LORD was with Jehoshaphat, because he walked in the first ways of his father David, and sought not unto Baalim;
But sought to the *LORD* God of his father, and walked in his commandments, and not after the doings of Israel.
Therefore the LORD stablished the kingdom in his hand; and all Judah brought to Jehoshaphat presents; and he had riches and honour in abundance.
And his heart was lifted up in the ways of the LORD: moreover he took away the high places and groves out of Judah.

Jehoshaphat lifted up his heart in the ways of the Lord. He became really excited about learning about God and doing His will. Therefore, he benefited because of it, and the people also were blessed under his reign. Yet Jehoshaphat joined affinity with Ahab, in that he had his son marry the daughter of Ahab. This proved to be an unwise move, for even though Jehoshaphat walked in the ways of his father David, the people had not yet prepared their hearts unto God, and Jehoshaphat's son was swept up in the ways of the kings of Israel.

II Chronicles 20:30, 32, 33 and 21:5- 7
So the realm of Jehoshaphat was quiet: for his God gave him rest round about.
And he walked in the way of Asa his father, and departed not from it, doing *that which was* right in the sight of the LORD.
Howbeit the high places were not taken away: for as yet the people had not prepared their hearts unto the God of their fathers.
Jehoram [Jehoshaphat's son] *was* thirty and two years old when he began to reign, and he reigned eight years in Jerusalem.
And he walked in the way of the kings of Israel, like as did the house of Ahab: for he had the daughter of Ahab to wife: and he wrought *that which was* evil in the eyes of the LORD.

Howbeit the LORD would not destroy the house of David, because of the covenant that he had made with David, and as he promised to give a light to him and to his sons for ever.

There was another king that stood in the breach before Israel and Judah were taken away captive, and that was Hezekiah. He had a dramatic effect on his day, but for the most part, the people would not hear nor return to the Lord.

II Chronicles 30:6- 10
So the posts went with the letters from the king and his princes throughout all Israel and Judah, and according to the commandment of the king, saying, Ye children of Israel, turn again
unto the LORD God of Abraham, Isaac, and Israel, and he will return to the remnant of you, that are escaped out of the hand of the kings of Assyria.
And be not ye like your fathers, and like your brethren, which trespassed against the LORD God of their fathers, *who* therefore gave them up to desolation, as ye see.
Now be ye not stiffnecked, as your fathers *were*, *but* yield yourselves unto the LORD, and enter into his sanctuary, which he hath sanctified for ever: and serve the LORD your God, that the fierceness of his wrath may turn away from you.
For if ye turn again unto the LORD, your brethren and your children *shall find* compassion before them that lead them captive, so that they shall come again into this land: for the LORD your God *is* gracious and merciful, and will not turn away *his* face from you, if ye return unto him.
So the posts passed from city to city through the country of Ephraim and Manasseh even unto Zebulun: but they laughed them to scorn, and mocked them.

Darkness was engulfing them. There seemed to be no hope for Israel. I cannot help feeling disheartened reading this, yet I know that God promised a light. God said He would leave a light on for them, even though they were heading into a long and arduous dark period for the next four hundred years.

II Chronicles 33:1- 6, 9- 11
Manasseh *was* twelve years old when he began to reign, and he reigned fifty and five years in Jerusalem:

But did *that which was* evil in the sight of the LORD, like unto the abominations of the heathen, whom the LORD had cast out before the children of Israel.

For he built again the high places which Hezekiah his father had broken down, and he reared up altars for Baalim, and made groves, and worshiped all the host of heaven, and served them.

Also he built altars in the house of the LORD, whereof the LORD had said, In Jerusalem shall my name be for ever.

And he built altars for all the host of heaven in the two courts of the house of the LORD.

And he caused his children to pass through the fire in the valley of the son of Hinnom: also he observed times, and used enchantments, and used witchcraft, and dealt with a familiar spirit, and with wizards: he wrought much evil in the sight of the LORD, to provoke him to anger.

So Manasseh made Judah and the inhabitants of Jerusalem to err, *and* to do worse than the heathen, whom the LORD had destroyed before the children of Israel.

And the LORD spake to Manasseh, and to his people: but they would not hearken.

Wherefore the LORD brought upon them the captains of the host of the king of Assyria, which took Manasseh among the thorns, and bound him with fetters, and carried him to Babylon.

Now when Jesus Christ came, what God had promised proved to be true. Darkness was overcome by the light, and Jesus Christ is that light.

John 9:5
As long as I am in the world, I am the light of the world.

Jesus said, "As long as I am in the world, I am the light of the world." As long as Jesus was in the world, he was the light that God had promised.

John 8:12
Then spake Jesus again unto them, saying, I am the light of the world: he that followeth me shall not walk in darkness, but shall have the light of life.

This is the red thread in the book of II Chronicles. Jesus Christ is the light of the world. Follow him and you shall not walk in darkness, but you shall have the light of life.

> **Ephesians 5:6-14**
> **Let no man deceive you with vain words: for because of these things cometh the wrath of God upon the children of disobedience.**
> **Be not ye therefore partakers with them.**
> **For ye were sometimes darkness, but now *are ye* light in the Lord: walk as children of light:**
> **(For the fruit of the Spirit [light] *is* in all goodness and righteousness and truth;)**
> **Proving what is acceptable unto the Lord.**
> **And have no fellowship with the unfruitful works of darkness, but rather reprove *them*.**
> **For it is a shame even to speak of those things which are done of them in secret.**
> **But all things that are reproved are made manifest by the light: for whatsoever doth make manifest is light.**
> **Wherefore he saith, Awake thou that sleepest, and arise from the dead, and Christ shall give thee light.**

God promised to give us a light, and now we can be the children of light when we accept the work that Jesus Christ accomplished for us. Wherefore he said, "Awake thou that sleepest and arise from the dead and Christ shall give thee light." As the red thread in the book of II Chronicles, Jesus Christ is the light that God promised. Light always dispels darkness, and there is no greater light than that which is found in the face of Jesus Christ.

The Red Thread of II Chronicles

A Nail

In their captivity, Israel was given grace for a little space. Now, in the first year of Cyrus, King of Persia, God stirred it within him to make a proclamation throughout all his kingdom. Cyrus was going to allow God's people to go back to Jerusalem and build the house of the Lord God of Israel. All those that desired to go were allowed to go, and he gave them provisions and all that they needed for the task. This is how Ezra ended up back in Jerusalem, rebuilding the wall of the city and the temple. It is no wonder then that this is where we find the red thread in the Book of Ezra: as a nail in God's holy place.

Ezra 9:8
And now for a little space grace hath been *showed* from the LORD our God, to leave us a remnant to escape, and to give us a nail in his holy place, that our God may lighten our eyes, and give us a little reviving in our bondage.

This nail was surely driven in and secured in His holy place upon, which Israel could hang all their hope. Ezra desired the light that God had promised. Some of the reviving he knew was yet to come, but he didn't know how much was available for him in his day and time. Ezra understood that they were in over their heads in their trespasses against their God.

Ezra 9:5- 7
And at the evening sacrifice I arose up from my heaviness; and having rent my garment and my mantle, I fell upon my knees, and spread out my hands unto the LORD my God,
And said, O my God, I am ashamed and blush to lift up my face to thee, my God: for our iniquities are increased over *our* head, and our trespass is grown up unto the heavens.
Since the days of our fathers *have* we *been* in a great trespass unto this day; and for our iniquities have we, our kings, *and* our priests, been delivered into the hand of the kings of the lands, to the sword, to captivity, and to a spoil, and to confusion of face, as *it is* this day.

A remnant held to the hope of Christ's coming, and to those God continued to reveal His Word. God continued to reveal the red thread and added to the knowledge of who and what this red thread would be.

Isaiah 22:20- 25
And it shall come to pass in that day, that I will call my servant Eliakim [the name Eliakim means, *he whom God sets up*] the son of Hilkiah:

And I will clothe him with thy robe, and strengthen him with thy girdle, and I will commit thy government into his hand: and he shall be a father to the inhabitants of Jerusalem, and to the house of Judah.

And the key of the house of David will I lay upon his shoulder; so he shall open, and none shall shut; and he shall shut, and none shall open.

And I will fasten him *as* a nail in a sure place; and he shall be for a glorious throne to his father's house.

And they shall hang upon him all the glory of his father's house, the offspring and the issue, all vessels of small quantity, from the vessels of cups, even to all the vessels of flagons.

In that day, saith the LORD of hosts, shall the nail that is fastened in the sure place be removed, and be cut down, and fall; and the burden that *was* upon it shall be cut off: for the LORD hath spoken *it*.

The key of the house of David will be given to the one who God sets up or appoints. It is he who will be a nail in a sure place, and all they from the least to the greatest shall hang all the glory of his father's house upon him. Isaiah declares, *in that day shall the nail be cut down, and the burden that was hanging upon it shall be cut off*. God speaks of the day when Christ shall come, not only of the first coming but also of the second. We see Christ with his second coming having the key of the house of David. It is Christ's first coming where we find the nail that was fastened in a sure place being cut off along with the burden that was hanging upon it.

Revelation 1:10, 11, 17, 18
I was in the Spirit on the Lord's day, and heard behind me a great voice, as of a trumpet,

Saying, I am Alpha and Omega, the first and the last: and, What thou seest, write in a book, and send *it* unto the seven churches which are in Asia; unto Ephesus, and unto Smyrna, and unto Pergamos, and unto Thyatira, and unto Sardis, and unto Philadelphia, and unto Laodicea.

And when I saw him, I fell at his feet as dead. And he laid his right hand upon me, saying unto me, Fear not; I am the first and the last:

I *am* he that liveth, and was dead; and, behold, I am alive for evermore, Amen; and have the keys of hell [gravedom] and of death.

This is the Lord's day, the time of the Lord's second coming, where we find Christ alive after having been dead and now having the keys of the grave and of death.

Revelation 3:7- 9
And to the angel of the church in Philadelphia write; These things saith he that is holy, he that is true, he that hath the key of David, he that openeth, and no man shutteth; and shutteth, and no man openeth;
I know thy works: behold, I have set before thee an open door, and no man can shut it: for thou hast a little strength, and hast kept my word, and hast not denied my name.
Behold, I will make them of the synagogue of Satan, which say they are Jews, and are not, but do lie; behold, I will make them to come and worship before thy feet, and to know that I have loved thee.

He that has the key of David is Christ. So he shall open the door to the house and none shall shut it, and he shall shut the door and none shall open, for it is he that holds the key. As the nail, Christ would not only carry the glory, but also the burden of death and sin. The burdens of the world were on his shoulders, but they were also cut off in that day. What day? The day of his death, when he hung upon the tree accomplishing that which God had promised.

Colossians 2:13- 15
And you, being dead in your sins and the uncircumcision of your flesh, hath he quickened [made alive] together with him, having forgiven you all trespasses;
Blotting out the handwriting of ordinances that was against us, which was contrary to us, and took it out of the way, nailing it to his cross;
And having spoiled principalities and powers, he made a show of them openly, triumphing over them in it.

All the burdens which were hanging on that nail were cut off when Christ took it out of the way, triumphing over them not only in death, but much more in that he got up from the dead.

I Peter 3:18
For Christ also hath once suffered for sins, the just for the unjust, that he might bring us to God, being put to death in the flesh, but quickened [made alive] **by the Spirit:**

Christ died for us that he might bring us to God. This was the work which he accomplished for us; he reconnected us with God.

Hebrews 10:10
By the which will [God's will] **we are sanctified through the offering of the body of Jesus Christ once *for all*.**

Christ had to die once, but for us death is not the way to God. For us the way to God is through Christ. Death doesn't bring a man any closer to God. Only Christ can bring a man closer to God.

II Corinthians 5:21
For he [God] **hath made him** [Christ] *to be* **sin for us, who knew no sin; that we might be made the righteousness of God in him.**

Christ bore the burden that we could not bear. He was the nail upon which all hope was hung, but when that nail was cut off, we were able to be made the righteousness of God in Christ.

I Peter 2:24
Who his own self bare our sins in his own body on the tree, that we, being dead to sins, should live unto righteousness: by whose stripes ye were healed.

We were dead, but now we are alive in Christ and have been healed by his stripes. God said that a remnant would escape. This was true in the day of Ezra as well as in the day of Christ. For Israel, there always is a remnant who will believe. Christ has done so much for us, but it seems that with Israel it is always a remnant, a few who have the will to believe.

Isaiah 10:20- 27
And it shall come to pass in that day, *that* the remnant of Israel, and such as are escaped of the house of Jacob, shall no more again stay [focus] **upon him that smote them; but shall stay upon the LORD, the**

Holy One of Israel, in truth.

The remnant shall return, *even* **the remnant of Jacob, unto the mighty God.**

For though thy people Israel be as the sand of the sea, *yet* **a remnant of them shall return: the consumption** [the finished work] **decreed shall overflow with righteousness.**

For the Lord GOD of hosts shall make a consumption [a finished work], **even determined, in the midst of all the land.**

Therefore thus saith the Lord GOD of hosts, O my people that dwellest in Zion, be not afraid of the Assyrian: he shall smite thee with a rod, and shall lift up his staff against thee, after the manner of Egypt.

For yet a very little while, and the indignation shall cease, and mine anger in their destruction.

And the LORD of hosts shall stir up a scourge for him according to the slaughter of Midian at the rock of Oreb: and *as* **his rod** *was* **upon the sea, so shall he lift it up after the manner of Egypt.**

And it shall come to pass in that day, *that* **his burden shall be taken away from off thy shoulder, and his yoke from off thy neck, and the yoke shall be destroyed because of the anointing** [the choosing] .

God chose one to finish the work, to carry the burden, to be the nail upon which all hope was hung. Christ is that nail and the red thread in the book of Ezra. God did not forget; thus out of the house of Judah came the nail, as God upheld His promise to David.

Zechariah 10:3, 4
For the LORD of hosts hath visited his flock the house of Judah, and hath made them as his goodly horse in the battle.

Out of him came forth the corner, out of him the nail, out of him the battle bow, out of him every oppressor [governor or ruler] **together.**

Romans 11:5
Even so then [as it was then] **at this present time also there is a remnant according to the election of grace.**

Even today in this age of grace, there is a remnant of Israel that will believe on Jesus Christ and hang all their hope on the nail.

The Red Thread of Ezra

The Door

In the book of Nehemiah, the walls and the gates of the city of Jerusalem are rebuilt. Israel had long since forgotten the salvation of the Lord, and the city lay in ruin. Nehemiah said that God put it in his heart to rise up and build the wall and hang the gates. The wall represents God's salvation, and in one of the gates, there is a door which allows all to enter into the salvation which God has prepared. Some would say that God has forgotten our walls; therefore, we must build our own salvation. But God has not forgotten. The book of Nehemiah sets the red thread as the door of the sheep gate, through which all that enter shall be saved and shall go in and out and find good pasture.

Nehemiah 2:11- 18
So I came to Jerusalem, and was there three days.
And I arose in the night, I and some few men with me; neither told I *any* **man what my God had put in my heart to do at Jerusalem: neither** *was there any* **beast with me, save the beast that I rode upon.**
And I went out by night by the gate of the valley, even before the dragon [wailing] **well,** [named this for all the wailing and complaining done around it] **and to the dung port, and viewed the walls of Jerusalem, which were broken down, and the gates thereof were consumed with fire.**
Then I went on to the gate of the fountain, and to the king's pool: but *there was* **no place for the beast** *that was* **under me to pass.**
Then went I up in the night by the brook, and viewed the wall, and turned back, and entered by the gate of the valley, and *so* **returned.**
And the rulers knew not whither I went, or what I did; neither had I as yet told *it* **to the Jews, nor to the priests, nor to the nobles, nor to the rulers, nor to the rest that did the work.**
Then said I unto them, Ye see the distress that we *are* **in, how Jerusalem** *lieth* **waste, and the gates thereof are burned with fire: come, and let us build up the wall of Jerusalem, that we be no more a reproach.**

Man needs to know the walls of God's salvation in order to feel safe and protected from the thief that lurks outside. Man also needs to know the door leading into the salvation of the Lord.

Nehemiah 3:1
Then Eliashib the high priest rose up with his brethren the priests, and they builded the sheep gate; they sanctified it, and set up the doors of it; even unto the tower of Meah they sanctified it, unto the tower of Hananeel.

When Eliashib, the high priest, and his brethren built the sheep gate, they put a door in the gate. From reading the verse the way it's written, it would appear to be doors as plural. Upon closer scrutiny you will notice the Hebrew word used here describes a door hanging on hinges. The high priest sanctified this one door which set it apart from all others. Why is there only one? For there is only one Jesus Christ, who is the door into the safety of God's salvation.

John 10:1- 9
Verily, verily, I say unto you, He that entereth not by the door into the sheepfold, but climbeth up some other way, the same is a thief and a robber.
But he that entereth in by the door is the shepherd of the sheep.
To him the porter openeth; and the sheep hear his voice: and he calleth his own sheep by name, and leadeth them out.
And when he putteth forth his own sheep, he goeth before them, and the sheep follow him: for they know his voice.
And a stranger will they not follow, but will flee from him: for they know not the voice of strangers.
This parable spake Jesus unto them: but they understood not what things they were which he spake unto them.
Then said Jesus unto them again, Verily, verily, I say unto you, I am the door of the sheep.
All that ever came before me are thieves and robbers: but the sheep did not hear them.
I am the door: by me if any man enter in, he shall be saved, and shall go in and out, and find pasture.

It's very telling what door a man will enter for safety. Those who know the name of the Lord will choose him for their strong tower.

Proverbs 18:10, 11
The name of the LORD *is* a strong tower: the righteous runneth into it, and is safe.

The rich man's wealth *is* **his strong city, and as an high wall in his own conceit.**

A man's own conceit is found in his imagination, for conceit is a lofty or vain conception of ones own person. For the man who enters that door, there is no safety, but instead a fearful awaiting of sudden destruction. The man who does not know Jesus Christ will never have control over his own life; and therefore, he will never know the protection of the walls of the Lord's salvation.

Proverbs 25:28
He that *hath* **no rule over his own spirit** [life] *is like* **a city** *that is* **broken down,** *and* **without walls.**

Without the Lord's salvation, a man can have no rule over his own life; and therefore, he can have no control over what comes in and what goes out. Only in Christ Jesus do we have victory over such a thief who would enter at will to steal from you and try to kill you and even attempt to destroy you. Only God can give a man control over his life, again and this happens when the man enters by the door, Jesus Christ.

Isaiah 25:7 - 26:1
And he will destroy in this mountain the face of the covering cast over all people, and the veil that is spread over all nations.
He will swallow up death in victory; and the Lord GOD will wipe away tears from off all faces; and the rebuke of his people shall he take away from off all the earth: for the LORD hath spoken *it.*
And it shall be said in that day, Lo, this *is* **our God; we have waited for him, and he will save us: this** *is* **the LORD; we have waited for him, we will be glad and rejoice in his salvation.**
For in this mountain shall the hand of the LORD rest, and Moab shall be trodden down under him, even as straw is trodden down for the dunghill.
And he shall spread forth his hands in the midst of them, as he that swimmeth spreadeth forth *his hands* **to swim: and he shall bring down their pride together with the spoils of their hands.**
And the fortress of the high fort of thy walls shall he bring down, lay low, *and* **bring to the ground,** *even* **to the dust.**
In that day shall this song be sung in the land of Judah; We have a strong city; salvation will *God* **appoint** *for* **walls and bulwarks.**

It can be said that salvation shall be the bulwark against that day because a bulwark is anything that defends or protects. Isaiah said, "in that day," what kind of a day would that be? A day of salvation, a day in which we can rejoice in his salvation.

Isaiah 49:8, 9
Thus saith the LORD, In an acceptable time have I heard thee, and in a day of salvation have I helped thee: and I will preserve thee, and give thee for a covenant of the people, to establish the earth, to cause to inherit the desolate heritages;
That thou mayest say to the prisoners, Go forth; to them that *are* **in darkness, Show yourselves. They shall feed in the ways, and their pastures** *shall be* **in all high places.**

This day of salvation has come upon us at this present time, for it is an acceptable time. God has heard all that have called on Him. God has helped us, for we of our own selves were helpless. The prisoners can now go free. We have been reconciled to God by Jesus Christ.

II Corinthians 6:1, 2
We then, *as* **workers together** *with him*, **beseech** *you* **also that ye receive not the grace of God in vain.**
(For he saith, I have heard thee in a time accepted, and in the day of salvation have I succoured thee: behold, now *is* **the accepted time; behold, now** *is* **the day of salvation.)**

Behold, now is the day of salvation. Behold, now is the accepted time. Wait a minute. What about Jacob? What about the children? Has the Lord forgotten Zion? What about all who went before of God's people?

Isaiah 49:14- 18
But Zion said, The LORD hath forsaken me, and my Lord hath forgotten me.
Can a woman forget her sucking child, that she should not have compassion on the son of her womb? yea, they may forget, yet will I not forget thee.
Behold, I have graven thee upon the palms of *my* **hands; thy walls** *are* **continually before me.**
Thy children shall make haste; thy destroyers and they that made thee waste shall go forth of thee.
Lift up thine eyes round about, and behold: all these gather

themselves together, *and* come to thee. *As* I live, saith the LORD, thou shalt surely clothe thee with them all, as with an ornament, and bind them *on thee*, as a bride *doeth.*

God didn't forget Zion. God said that thy walls, thy salvation, are continually before me. God has made the day of salvation to extend even unto thy children. All these that went before shall gather together, and the bride of Israel shall be clothed with salvation.

Isaiah 49:23- 26
... and thou shalt know that I *am* the LORD: for they shall not be ashamed that wait for me.

Shall the prey be taken from the mighty, or the lawful captive delivered?

But thus saith the LORD, Even the captives of the mighty shall be taken away, and the prey of the terrible shall be delivered: for I will contend with him that contendeth with thee, and I will save thy children.

And I will feed them that oppress thee with their own flesh; and they shall be drunken with their own blood, as with sweet wine: and all flesh shall know that I the LORD *am* thy Saviour and thy Redeemer, the mighty One of Jacob.

Shall the prey be taken from the mighty or the lawful captive delivered? The answer is most unequivocally 'yes' in Christ. The door has opened to all of God's people, and that door to salvation is Jesus Christ. We may be strangers to Israel, but we now have and enjoy the victory in Christ, and even though the sons of strangers shall build up the walls of thy salvation for a while, God has not forgotten Zion.

Isaiah 60:10- 14
And the sons of strangers shall build up thy walls, and their kings shall minister unto thee: for in my wrath I smote thee, but in my favour have I had mercy on thee.

Therefore thy gates shall be open continually; they shall not be shut day nor night; that *men* may bring unto thee the forces of the Gentiles, and *that* their kings *may be* brought.

For the nation and kingdom that will not serve thee shall perish; yea, *those* nations shall be utterly wasted.

The glory of Lebanon shall come unto thee, the fir tree, the pine tree, and the box together, to beautify the place of my sanctuary; and I

will make the place of my feet glorious.
    The sons also of them that afflicted thee shall come bending unto thee; and all they that despised thee shall bow themselves down at the soles of thy feet; and they shall call thee, The city of the LORD, The Zion of the Holy One of Israel.

    If God has promised, will it not come to pass? No one is ever ashamed if he waits on the Lord. God spoke in the days of Nehemiah, just as He had before in the days of Isaiah, and the promise still holds true today concerning Israel.

Isaiah 60:18- 22
    Violence shall no more be heard in thy land, wasting nor destruction within thy borders; but thou shalt call thy walls Salvation, and thy gates Praise.
    The sun shall be no more thy light by day; neither for brightness shall the moon give light unto thee: but the LORD shall be unto thee an everlasting light, and thy God thy glory.
    Thy sun shall no more go down; neither shall thy moon withdraw itself: for the LORD shall be thine everlasting light, and the days of thy mourning shall be ended.
    Thy people also *shall be* all righteous: they shall inherit the land for ever, the branch of my planting, the work of my hands, that I may be glorified.
    A little one shall become a thousand, and a small one a strong nation: I the LORD will hasten it in his [Jesus Christ's] **time.**

    Jesus Christ is the door to salvation, and anyone desiring to enter that sheepfold must come through the door which has been sanctified for that use. If anyone is to enter that strong city, he cannot climb up some other way. The porter is the keeper of the gate, and he knows those who are his. The door is open, and it's not the voice of a stranger that you hear calling, "I am the door." Jesus said, "I am come that they might have life and that they might have it more abundantly." Jesus Christ is the door as the red thread in the book of Nehemiah. Nehemiah closes with this thought recorded in the last verse.

Nehemiah 13:31
... Remember me, O my God, for Good.

I Am

In the days of Esther, the world lay in darkness, having no prophet for some four hundred years between Malachi and John the Baptist. The children of Israel were without a prophet, and Jesus Christ remained hidden in God. God, for the most part, remained hidden from His people. In the book of Esther, God's name is not openly mentioned, in contrast to the venerable king Ahasuerus, who is mentioned one hundred and ninety two times. Many in the Gentile nations, whether it be today or in Esther's day, think they have a better plan than God has. Therefore, for all practical purposes, God is removed from the community. God's rule and God's law is cast aside, and they become a liberal society filled with modern thinkers and new ideas. God is not given a place in such an enlightened and progressive social experiment. The king's name is always mentioned more than God's name, and it is forbidden that God's name should be spoken in connection with the king. All who govern think that theirs is a better plan, but one thing holds true where you find good, you find God, and where you find evil, you find God's adversary. It makes it hard when you have to search to find the good upon which to focus. It's hard when even the rudimentary aspects of God have been forsaken and are no longer taught, no longer being passed down from father to son and from mother to daughter. Praise God for the brave soul who happens across some of these truly worthwhile things and chooses to hang on to them.

Without God's name even being mentioned in the book of Esther, you begin to wonder where the red thread could possibly be. As for the mystery of locating God and the red thread in Esther, they can be found in the book's five acrostics. God's name appears five times, written four times as Jehovah or our English word Lord and once as Ehyeh, which in English translates into the words "I am," also found in Exodus chapter three.

Exodus 3:13 and 14
And Moses said unto God, Behold, *when* I come unto the children of Israel, and shall say unto them, The God of your fathers hath sent me unto you; and they shall say to me, What *is* his name? what shall I say unto them?

And God said unto Moses, I AM THAT I AM: and he said, Thus shalt thou say unto the children of Israel, I AM hath sent me unto you.

Sometimes when people get far enough away from God, He has to go back to the beginning. He has to get down to the basics of letting us know that He is and that you can believe that He will be what He will be.

Hebrews 11:6
But without faith [believing] ***it is*** **impossible to please *him*: for he that cometh to God must believe that he is, and *that* he is a rewarder of them that diligently seek him.**

Jesus Christ can be found in the "I am" of God's name. Jesus has always been hidden in God, even from the foundation of the world until the time he was made known by his presence in the flesh. And now being risen, he sitteth on the right hand of God. Jesus said, *You believe in God believe also in me for "I am."*

John 5:39 and 43
Search the scriptures; for in them ye think ye have eternal life: and they are they which testify of me.
I am come in my Father's name, and ye receive me not: if another shall come in his own name, him ye will receive.

Jesus said, "I am come in my father's name," because that is where he has always been. But they wouldn't receive his name or his Father's.

John 6:35
And Jesus said unto them, I am the bread of life: he that cometh to me shall never hunger; and he that believeth on me shall never thirst.

Again he said, "I am the bread of life," showing that he will be what he will be, but will we believe?

John 8:12 and 24
Then spake Jesus again unto them, saying, I am the light of the world: he that followeth me shall not walk in darkness, but shall have the light of life.
I said therefore unto you, that ye shall die in your sins: for if ye believe not that I am *he*, ye shall die in your sins.

When dealing with the italicized words found in the King James version of the Bible, it is needful to realize that they were added by the translators. The use of italics lets us know that there is no corresponding Greek word in the text. If we remove one of these italicized words we are not hurting the text knowing it is what the translators had added to the translation. Where it reads, "for if ye believe not that I am *he*," we can remove the word "he," which is in italics. The emphasis is on the words "I am." Jesus said, "for if you believe not that I am, ye shall die in your sins."

John 8:25 and 28- 30
Then said they unto him, Who art thou? And Jesus saith unto them, Even *the same* that I said unto you from the beginning.
Then said Jesus unto them, When ye have lifted up the Son of man, then shall ye know that I am *he*, and *that* I do nothing of myself; but as my Father hath taught me, I speak these things.
And he that sent me is with me: the Father hath not left me alone; for I do always those things that please him.
As he spake these words, many believed on him.

Everybody wanted to know who Jesus was, but he first had to get them to believe *that* he was. Only then could they accept *who* he was.

John 10: 9-11
I am the door: by me if any man enter in, he shall be saved, and shall go in and out, and find pasture.
The thief cometh not, but for to steal, and to kill, and to destroy: I am come that they might have life, and that they might have *it* more abundantly.
I am the good shepherd: the good shepherd giveth his life for the sheep.

"I am the door." "I am the good shepherd." "I am the light." "I am the bread of life." "I am come that they might have life." But who is he really?

John 10:36
Say ye of him, whom the Father hath sanctified, and sent into the world, Thou blasphemest; because I said, I am the Son of God?

The son of God. This is the "I am," and this is Jesus Christ.

John 11:25 and 26
Jesus said unto her, I am the resurrection, and the life: he that

believeth in me, though he were dead, yet shall he live:
 And whosoever liveth and believeth in me shall never die. Believest thou this?

John 13:13 and 19
 Ye call me Master and Lord: and ye say well; for *so* <u>I am</u>.
 Now I tell you before it come, that, when it is come to pass, ye may believe that <u>I am</u> *he*.

John 14:6
 Jesus saith unto him, <u>I am</u> the way, the truth, and the life: no man cometh unto the Father, but by me.

John 14:10
 Believest thou not that <u>I am</u> in the Father, and the Father in me? the words that I speak unto you I speak not of myself: but the Father that dwelleth in me, he doeth the works.

Jesus Christ is the "I am" of the book of Esther just as much as God is. "I am" shows that Jesus Christ is, and it also shows who he is and what he is. Jesus came, so that we could get to God. He came, so that we could live and know that he was in God and God was in him. God has worked it all out, so that we can all be together in him. This is the purpose for Jesus Christ's existence.

John 14:19 and 20
 Yet a little while, and the world seeth me no more; but ye see me: because I live, ye shall live also.
 At that day ye shall know that I *am* in my Father, and ye in me, and I in you.

This sets the direction which God is headed, but back in the book of Esther, you see that God was hidden. The course in which the people were headed allowed no room for God and His purposes, yet God cannot be denied His will. An acrostic is a figure of speech where certain corresponding letters in a grouping of words spell out another word that was purposefully hidden there. God uses acrostics in the book of Esther to show us a hidden message. When it comes to the English translation from the Hebrew language, the translators would have to be aware of these markings and concerned enough to translate it over to the English rendering of the words. In some versions these markings are identified, but the translation itself may not allow us to see what God has done.

In the first occurrence of this figure of speech found in the book of Esther, the king wanted to parade queen Vashti around to show everyone how good looking she was. The queen refused to come to the party, and the king's advisors could see the rippling effects this would have throughout the kingdom. So a law was passed that all wives shall give to their husbands honor, both small and great.

Esther 1:20
And when the king's decree which he shall make shall be published throughout all his empire, (for it is great,) all the wives shall give to their husbands honour, both to great and small.

It is in these words, "all the wives shall give to their husbands honor," we find the acrostic in the Hebrew words. When it comes to the English words, it is difficult to identify by the King James version what it should look like. Another way of translating this into English has been offered, so as to be able to see the figure of speech present here. It reads: "**D**ue **R**espect **O**ur **L**adies shall give to their husbands, both great and small." The word **LORD** is spelled backwards by the first letters of the words Due Respect Our Ladies and is perhaps the closest we'll get to seeing the acrostic of the name Jehovah, which is in the Hebrew language. Here we find God's marking and what it is that He thinks of the king's decree. Having His name spelled out backwards shows how they got it all backwards, because you can't force a woman to honor a man. God's name is in here at this point, because the door opened for Esther to move into the estate of Vashti as queen.

The second occurrence shows up in chapter five, and this time the letters for the word Lord are spelled out forward, not backwards as in the previous occurrence. It shows God at work taking the initiative with Esther, now the queen.

Esther 5:3 and 4
Then said the king unto her, What wilt thou, queen Esther? and what *is* thy request? it shall be even given thee to the half of the kingdom.
And Esther answered, If *it seem* good unto the king, let the king

and Haman come this day unto the banquet that I have prepared for him.

"Let the king and Haman come this day unto the banquet." These are the words in question in the King James version. We could use these other words to represent the figure here: "**L**et **O**ur **R**oyal **D**inner be graced by the king and Haman." This allows us to see the acrostic, which is present in this verse. The third occurrence is also found in chapter five, but here again the lettering is reversed, for it always avails me nothing to go against God.

Esther 5:13
Yet all this availeth me nothing, so long as I see Mordecai the Jew sitting at the king's gate.

Haman wanted to do away with all Jews, and it plagued him to see Mordecai sitting in a place of influence and power. Therefore, he could never be happy with God's invitation and what He had prepared for him. Haman was at odds with God and moving in the opposite direction. That is why God had it backwards for him. "All this availeth me nothing" is where the name of the Lord is placed. Yet all this is goo**D** fo**R** n**O** avai**L**, so long as Haman could see Mordecai the Jew sitting at the king's gate. Haman couldn't even see the good when it came to his door for he was too engrossed in the darkness of his day. There is one more time where the word "Lord" is used, and that is in chapter seven, verse seven.

Esther 7:6 and 7
And Esther said, The adversary and enemy *is* this wicked Haman. Then Haman was afraid before the king and the queen.
And the king arising from the banquet of wine in his wrath *went* into the palace garden: and Haman stood up to make request for his life to Esther the queen; for he saw that there was evil determined against him by the king.

We can try to do it our way. We may even think our way is better than God's way, but God will prevail. We may leave God completely out of the picture, but He doesn't go away. We might as well believe that He is and that He is a rewarder of them that diligently seek Him. Haman stood up to make request for his life to Esther the queen, for he saw that there was evi**L** t**O** fea**R** determine**D** against him by the king. The Lord's name is once again headed in the right direction. As for Haman, he was hanged on the gallows that he had built for Mordecai. Then was the king's wrath pacified. Having now shared these four accounts with you, we must turn our attention to the seventh chapter and the fifth verse, where we find the last acrostic and the red thread of Esther.

Esther 7:4 and 5
For we are sold, I and my people, to be destroyed, to be slain, and to perish. But if we had been sold for bondmen and bondwomen, I had held my tongue, although the enemy could not countervail the king's damage.

Then the king Ahasuerus answered and said unto Esther the queen, Who is he, and where is he, that durst presume in his heart to do so?

"Who is he and where is he." This is Ehyeh, the "I am." How prophetic. God said, *I am and I am hidden*; and so also is Christ the "I am," for he was hidden in God as well. In Hebrew, the final letters of the phrase spelled out the name "Ehjhe," pronounced *E- he- yhe*, both backwards and forwards. God has Christ covered both coming and going, just as He has all of us covered in Christ when we dare to believe that "I am." This has been the red thread in the book of Esther, where we have uncovered the acrostic and set it straight concerning the "I am" in the name Ehyeh.

The Red Thread of Esther

The Daysman

Even a man like Job felt the separation brought on by the sin of Adam. We find Job caught up in unbelief, which is either due to wrong teaching or to ignorance. The result in a man's life is the same, albeit the calamity does not divulge the difference. Job's vigilance and good intentions became misdirected and turned against him when he began to worry and obsess over the potential for evil, which he saw in his children's actions. Job was under the impression, even as some are today, that from God's hand comes the evil and the good. If mankind had never been separated from God, it could never have been said "the Lord giveth and the Lord taketh away;" it would only be said "the Lord giveth and the Lord giveth good." You may also be a man like Job, full of good intentions, trying to live upright, and overall just be a "good Joe," a God-fearing man. But do you see the need for a Daysman? Job came to know the need for a Daysman, a mediator, an intercessor, someone who could plead his cause and reconcile him to God. You also need to know your Daysman; for no matter how perfect you are, without Jesus Christ you are bound for disaster. Your fear of God holds little hope of being replaced by love and a growing appreciation of your heavenly Father. The enmity which exists between the carnal mind and God can only be done away with in Christ. As the red thread in the book of Job, Jesus Christ is the Daysman, for the day of his mediation and intercession were yet to come.

Job 1:1- 3
There was a man in the land of Uz, whose name *was* Job; and that man was perfect and upright, and one that feared God, and eschewed evil.
And there were born unto him seven sons and three daughters.
His substance also was seven thousand sheep, and three thousand camels, and five hundred yoke of oxen, and five hundred she asses, and a very great household; so that this man was the greatest of all the men of the east.

Job was a man truly blessed by God. It was God who said of this man Job that he was perfect and upright. To be perfect here means Job was without offence; in other words, he believed that God is and that God is a rewarder of those who diligently seek Him. Now, it says Job feared God, and we already know the fear of God is only the beginning of knowledge; for once you truly get to know God, how could you possibly fear Him any longer? Job's fear now begins to unfold, letting us see the destructive nature of fear.

Job 1:4 and 5
And his sons went and feasted *in their* houses, every one his day; and sent and called for their three sisters to eat and to drink with them.

And it was so, when the days of *their* feasting were gone about, that Job sent and sanctified them, and rose up early in the morning, and offered burnt offerings *according* to the number of them all: for Job said, It may be that my sons have sinned, and cursed God in their hearts. Thus did Job continually.

Job's incessant worrying was nothing more than advanced interest paid on the fear that he harbored about the possible sin of his children. As we will see, this only sealed the destruction that fear brings to a man's life. Because when and where you have fear, you cannot be believing God. Fear prevents you from having a continuing assurance of God's promise to you. This believing and assurance can only be found in a true knowledge of God and the will of His word.

Job 1:12-16
And the LORD said unto Satan, Behold, all that he hath *is* in thy power; only upon himself put not forth thine hand. So Satan went forth from the presence of the LORD.

And there was a day when his sons and his daughters *were* eating and drinking wine in their eldest brother's house:

And there came a messenger unto Job, and said, The oxen were plowing, and the asses feeding beside them:

And the Sabeans fell *upon them*, and took them away; yea, they have slain the servants with the edge of the sword; and I only am escaped alone to tell thee.

While he *was* yet speaking, there came also another, and said, The fire of God is fallen from heaven, and hath burned up the sheep, and the servants, and consumed them; and I only am escaped alone to tell thee.

Job's own fear opened the door for Satan to enter and bring the calamity that so devastated Job's whole world. But who did Satan make it appear had done the deed? He just played into the false notion Job already had preconceived. The Word says, "The fire of God is fallen from heaven and consumed them." Up to this point, whenever a man wanted to offer sacrifice to God, he would lay it out. If God accepted the sacrifice, God would set fire to it, and the sacrifice would be consumed. If Job thought that the good and the evil both came at God's hand, what would he think?

Job 1:20 and 21
Then Job arose, and rent his mantle, and shaved his head, and fell down upon the ground, and worshiped,
And said, Naked came I out of my mother's womb, and naked shall I return thither: the LORD gave, and the LORD hath taken away; blessed be the name of the LORD.

Most people would curse God at this point and throw away any hope they might have of ever knowing any different. At this point, Job was willing to take the good and the bad at the Lord's hand, but what Job did not know was Satan is never satisfied; and it was not God's hand which brought the evil upon him.

Job 2:6- 9
And the LORD said unto Satan, Behold, he *is* in thine hand; but save his life.
So went Satan forth from the presence of the LORD, and smote Job with sore boils from the sole of his foot unto his crown.
And he took him a potsherd to scrape himself withal; and he sat down among the ashes.
Then said his wife unto him, Dost thou still retain thine integrity? curse God, and die.

If Satan can keep us in the dark concerning who he is and who God is, then he has an open door to ride a man's fears to his death. He doesn't care who he uses to accomplish the task. Job's wife was being used to close the door and seal the fate of her own husband. If possible, Satan will use those who are closest to us to keep us from God. Job didn't allow his wife to level the last blow, but he was still unaware of who he was dealing with.

Job 2:10
But he said unto her, Thou speakest as one of the foolish women speaketh. What? shall we receive good at the hand of God, and shall we

not receive evil? In all this did not Job sin with his lips.

Job made a very revealing confession by his own lips, although at this point, he was still ignorant of its ramifications.

Job 3:25 and 26
For the thing which I greatly feared is come upon me, and that which I was afraid of is come unto me.
I was not in safety, neither had I rest, neither was I quiet; yet trouble came.

Some would try to tell you that a little fear is a good thing, but fear is never a good thing. Fear brings results just as believing brings results. Job said, "I was not in safety." He didn't feel safe. Well, why not? He feared, that's why. He couldn't rest. Why not? He was afraid. He thought worry was a part of a parent's responsibility, but what you fear will get you. Job didn't know why trouble came, but not knowing brings little comfort to calamity.

Job 6:1, 2 and 24
But Job answered and said,
Oh that my grief were thoroughly weighed, and my calamity laid in the balances together!
Teach me, and I will hold my tongue: and cause me to understand wherein I have erred.

The weight of Job's calamity caused him to wonder if he erred, and so it starts when he said "teach me," for we must be ready to be taught before the cycle of unbelief can be broken.

Job 9:1 and 2
Then Job answered and said,
I know *it is* so of a truth: but how should man be just with God?

The word "how" should be in all capital letters, because you can tell a man all day long just what he should do, but that doesn't help him unless you can tell him HOW. Job was wondering how he could possibly come before God to contend a matter. How could a man be just as if he had never sinned, so that he could stand before God and be held innocent?

Job 9:28-33

I am afraid of all my sorrows, I know that thou wilt not hold me innocent.

If I be wicked, why then labour I in vain?

If I wash myself with snow water, and make my hands never so clean;

Yet shalt thou plunge me in the ditch, and mine own clothes shall abhor me.

For *he is* not a man, as I *am, that* I should answer him, *and* we should come together in judgment.

Neither is there any Daysman betwixt us, *that* might lay his hand upon us both.

"I am afraid of all my sorrows." What Job is saying here is that he is afraid he is failing the test of not handling his sorrows properly. Many today believe God tests them through sickness and disease. If this then proves Job's wickedness, it wouldn't matter what he has done before to be so perfect and good, because all that labor is now proven to be in vain. All of his past accomplishments now mean nothing. From Job's vantage point, he was in quite a predicament. Job wanted a Daysman, someone to mediate the matter, someone to intercede between him and God. But who could that possibly be?

I Timothy 2:5

For *there is* one God, and one mediator between God and men, the man Christ Jesus;

Today we know our Daysman, for there is only one mediator between God and men, the man Christ Jesus. This is the red thread in the book of Job, because Jesus Christ is the only mediator between God and man. Job, on the other hand, couldn't know Christ like you and I know him, for he hadn't come yet in Job's day. Whenever a man is not clear on a matter, he will suffer from confusion. Job recognized the need for a mediator, but he still needed to clear up a few matters which continued to plague him.

Job 10:15

If I be wicked, woe unto me; and *if* I be righteous, *yet* will I not lift up my head. *I am* full of confusion; therefore see thou mine affliction;

Job didn't think he was wicked. At the same time, he said: *if I be righteous and this has happened to me, who am I to say anything since it is God who I am dealing with?*

Job 12:9 and 10
Who knoweth not in all these that the hand of the LORD hath wrought this?
In whose hand *is* the soul of every living thing, and the breath of all mankind.

Well, in whose hand is the soul life of all mankind? We have already learned that in the beginning of man's existence God gave the responsibility of every living thing to Adam. Soul life was in his hands, the breath of all mankind, but Adam transferred that which God had conferred unto him over to God's arch enemy, Satan. Apparently Job was not aware of this, but one thing he knew, he wanted someone to intercede on his behalf.

Job 16:21
O that one might plead for a man with God, as a man *pleadeth* for his neighbour!

Where is the intercessor? Who is the one that can undo what Adam brought upon all mankind? How can a man regain his strength and godliness? Does God have a plan for our redemption?

Romans 5:6-11
For when we were yet without strength [because we had no spirit], **in due time Christ died for the ungodly** [those who were without God's nature].
For scarcely for a righteous man will one die: yet peradventure for a good man some would even dare to die.
But God commendeth his love toward us, in that, while we were yet sinners, Christ died for us.
Much more then, being now justified by his blood, we shall be saved from wrath through him.
For if, when we were enemies, we were reconciled to God by the death of his Son, much more, being reconciled, we shall be saved by his life.
And not only *so*, but we also joy in God through our Lord Jesus Christ, by whom we have now received the atonement.

Romans 8:31- 34
What shall we then say to these things? If God *be* for us, who *can be* against us?
He that spared not his own Son, but delivered him up for us all, how shall he not with him also freely give us all things?
Who shall lay any thing to the charge of God's elect? *It is* God that justifieth. [the words "It is" are in italics, you may take them out without harming the scripture. This is a question not a statement.]
Who *is* he that condemneth? *It is* Christ that died, yea rather, that is risen again, who is even at the right hand of God, who also maketh intercession for us.

In these verses you have a rhetorical question, where the answer is so obvious that it should not have to be stated. Christ is the one to make intercession. Christ brought the atonement. Christ's soul life was given for ours. Jesus Christ pleaded our cause to God, giving us the victory. What about Job? Well, Job saw something too. He could not enjoy the same privilege as you and I do today, because it was not available yet. However, he had the hope that God gave to every man of his day.

Job 19:23- 26
Oh that my words were now written! oh that they were printed in a book!
That they were graven with an iron pen and lead in the rock for ever!
For I know *that* my redeemer liveth, and *that* he shall stand at the latter *day* upon the earth:
And *though* after my skin *worms* destroy this *body*, yet in my flesh shall I see God:

Job knew he had a redeemer. He just didn't know his redeemer like you and I can know him. Job thought for a while that God brought the evil and the good, just as some today believe that God kills. Because of Job's desire to know, God showed him some things about his adversary. Job overcame his fear by desiring to know. Ignorance can be overcome by instruction, and wrong teaching may be corrected with right teaching.

Job 31:35
Oh that one would hear me! behold, my desire *is, that* the

Almighty would answer me, and *that* mine adversary had written a book.

Job told us his desire, but what is your desire? Is your desire to know God up close and personal? If so, we must become well acquainted with the Daysman, our mediator Jesus Christ.

Job 42:3
Who *is* he that hideth counsel without knowledge? therefore have I uttered that I understood not; things too wonderful for me, which I knew not.

Who is he that hides counsel? The question is here in this scripture. There should be no question mark after the word "knowledge," because it is in the middle of the next thought. Job said: *without knowledge I have spoken of things which I did not understand.* Now, Job says: *I know it is Satan who keeps us in the dark. Therefore, without knowledge I tried to understand things that were beyond me, and I presumed some things about you, God, which were not true.* Here at the close of the book of Job, he speaks this which is recorded next.

Job 42:5
I have heard of thee by the hearing of the ear: but now mine eye seeth thee.

Job's unbelief was overcome in the end, and he ended up closer to God. He saw things that he did not see before. We also have an opportunity to see some things previously hidden to all those who came before. Since the day of Pentecost, we enjoy a better covenant built upon better promises. We have someone who took away the enmity that existed between the mind of man and God. We not only can hear about God, but we have the ability to see Him as He really is. This all came to us through the Daysman, Jesus Christ.

Thine Holy One

Bless the Lord, oh my soul and all that is within me, bless His holy name.

In the book of the Psalms, the red thread is identified in the Holy One. As God is holy so also is Thine Holy One. God is the essence of all that is holy. The word "holy" describes the nature and being of God and all that is touched by God. Anything described as holy becomes special, because God's hand is upon it. It is an infinite truth expressed by a finite language. It is a spiritual concept hoped to be grasped by the frail and fallible mind of man. Jesus Christ is God's Holy One, because God's hand is all over his life – from his birth to his death and everywhere in between. God's name is holy, God's son is holy, and God's spirit is holy. The beauty of it is that we can now put on the new man, which after God is created in this true holiness.

Psalms 29:1 and 2
Give unto the LORD, O ye mighty, give unto the LORD glory and strength.
Give unto the LORD the glory due unto his name; worship the LORD in the beauty of holiness.

David could only look ahead to the time that this worship of God in the beauty of holiness would be available. He saw the day, and he thanked God and praised Him for it. The red thread can be clearly seen in the Psalms, but it is here in the sixteenth Psalm that Thine Holy One is so profoundly felt.

Psalms 16:5- 11
The LORD *is* the portion of mine inheritance and of my cup: thou maintainest my lot.
The lines are fallen unto me in pleasant *places*; yea, I have a goodly heritage.
I will bless the LORD, who hath given me counsel: my reins also instruct me in the night seasons.
I have set the LORD always before me: because *he is* at my right hand, I shall not be moved.
Therefore my heart is glad, and my glory rejoiceth: my flesh also

shall rest in hope.
> For thou wilt not leave my soul in hell; neither wilt thou suffer thine Holy One to see corruption.
> Thou wilt show me the path of life: in thy presence *is* fulness of joy; at thy right hand *there are* pleasures for evermore.

We all have our inheritance in the Lord. In Jesus Christ our Lord we are sons, and if sons, then heirs according to the promise. The cup is the new testament in Christ's blood. This is how God is able to maintain our lot in life; we remain in existence only in Jesus Christ. Because of David's circumstance, he could only be in line for a pleasant place which exists in the future.

His right of birth could only be seen far off. Therefore what he saw and what he believed, he held onto even in death.

Hebrews 11:13-16
> These all died in faith [believing], **not having received the promises, but having seen them afar off, and were persuaded of** *them,* **and embraced** *them,* **and confessed that they were strangers and pilgrims on the earth.**
> **For they that say such things declare plainly that they seek a country.**
> **And truly, if they had been mindful of that** *country* **from whence they came out, they might have had opportunity to have returned.**
> **But now they desire a better** *country,* **that is, an heavenly: wherefore God is not ashamed to be called their God: for he hath prepared for them a city.**

David said, "I have set the Lord always before me." He did not turn back in unbelief, because he knew he would not be disappointed in his expectations. The word "hell" in Psalm sixteen is referring to a grave or gravedom, a state of being dead and continuing in the grave. David knew that his soul would not be left in the grave. When Christ came, he would fix the problem of death, and David would live again in the end. Well, Jesus did come, and you and I stand in a day where we can look back upon the life and times of Jesus Christ. God's promise in Christ for us is not only a future expectation but a present tense reality.

Acts 2:22-29
> **Ye men of Israel, hear these words; Jesus of Nazareth, a man**

approved of God among you by miracles and wonders and signs, which God did by him in the midst of you, as ye yourselves also know:

Him, being delivered by the determinate counsel and foreknowledge of God, ye have taken, and by wicked hands have crucified and slain:

Whom God hath raised up, having loosed the pains of death: because it was not possible that he should be holden of it.

For David speaketh concerning him, I foresaw the Lord always before my face, for he is on my right hand, that I should not be moved:

Therefore did my heart rejoice, and my tongue was glad; moreover also my flesh shall rest in hope:

Because thou wilt not leave my soul in hell, neither wilt thou suffer thine Holy One to see corruption.

Thou hast made known to me the ways of life; thou shalt make me full of joy with thy countenance.

Men *and* brethren, let me freely speak unto you of the patriarch David, that he is both dead and buried, and his sepulchre is with us unto this day.

God did not allow His Holy One to see corruption, which is total decay. Jesus Christ died and was in the grave for three nights and three days, but God raised him from the dead before his body saw total decomposition. Jesus Christ is God's Holy One; and therefore, it became impossible for Jesus to be held in death. If you are holy, my friend, you can transcend the finite limits of this world. David was not the Holy One, couldn't be, for he is still dead and buried unto this day.

Acts 2:31- 36

He [David] seeing this before spake of the resurrection of Christ, that his soul was not left in hell, neither his flesh did see corruption.

This Jesus hath God raised up, whereof we all are witnesses.

Therefore being by the right hand of God exalted, and having received of the Father the promise of the Holy Ghost [holy spirit], he hath shed forth this, which ye now see and hear.

For David is not ascended into the heavens: but he saith himself, The Lord said unto my Lord, Sit thou on my right hand, Until I make thy foes thy footstool.

Therefore let all the house of Israel know assuredly, that God

hath made that same Jesus, whom ye have crucified, both Lord and Christ.

The promise of the holy spirit has been fulfilled. It is available at this time to be holy through the spirit.

Acts 2:39
For the promise is unto you, and to your children, and to all that are afar off, *even* **as many as the Lord our God shall call.**

Jesus Christ is seated at the right hand of God, being exalted, and we have received of the Father the promise of the holy spirit. It is holy, and it is spirit. That makes it the greatest thing that God could give, because God himself is holy and God is spirit. The promise is unto you, and the provision has been made for you to be a holy one. As you look to God's Holy One, the choice is yours.

Ephesians 4:23 and 24
And be renewed in the spirit of your mind;
And that ye put on the new man, which after God is created in righteousness and true holiness.

The exhortation is clear: put on the new man, for you are now a holy one. God created the spirit within you in righteousness and true holiness. God's Holy One gave his all, so that you and I could be holy as well. Always steal your mind back to the promise of God and let your life be holy, always touched by God's hand.

I Peter 1:14 -16
As obedient children, not fashioning yourselves according to the former lusts in your ignorance:
But as he which hath called you is holy, so be ye holy in all manner of conversation;
Because it is written, Be ye holy; for I am holy.

There are those who have denied the Holy One, but God has glorified him. Don't you be profane when God's Holy One stands before you. Believe in the power of God and in the resurrection of His Holy One, our Lord and saviour, Jesus Christ.

Acts 3:12-16
And when Peter saw *it*, he answered unto the people, Ye men of Israel, why marvel ye at this? or why look ye so earnestly on us, as though by our own power or holiness we had made this man to walk?

The God of Abraham, and of Isaac, and of Jacob, the God of our fathers, hath glorified his Son Jesus; whom ye delivered up, and denied him in the presence of Pilate, when he was determined to let *him* go.

But ye denied the Holy One and the Just, and desired a murderer to be granted unto you;

And killed the Prince of life, whom God hath raised from the dead; whereof we are witnesses.

And his name through faith [believing] in his name hath made this man strong, whom ye see and know: yea, the faith [believing] which is by him hath given him this perfect soundness in the presence of you all.

As our lives begin to reflect the Holy One, there may be opposition. Don't let that deter you from holding forth and holding fast that which is holy and that which is true. Your perfect soundness is wrought by the spirit within you. Don't you deny the Holy One, but believe in his name.

Acts 4:25-31
Who by the mouth of thy servant David hast said, Why did the heathen rage, and the people imagine vain things?

The kings of the earth stood up, and the rulers were gathered together against the Lord, and against his Christ.

For of a truth against thy holy child Jesus, whom thou hast anointed, both Herod, and Pontius Pilate, with the Gentiles, and the people of Israel, were gathered together,

For to do whatsoever thy hand and thy counsel determined before to be done.

And now, Lord, behold their threatenings: and grant unto thy servants, that with all boldness they may speak thy word,

By stretching forth thine hand to heal; and that signs and wonders may be done by the name of thy holy child Jesus.

And when they had prayed, the place was shaken where they were assembled together; and they were all filled with the Holy Ghost [holy spirit], and they spake the word of God with boldness.

So we can either move on with the greatness of all that we have or we can turn back like the children of Israel and limit the Holy One, not remembering nor accepting God's hand upon our life.

Psalms 78:37- 42
For their heart was not right with him, neither were they stedfast in his covenant.

But he, *being* full of compassion, forgave *their* iniquity, and destroyed *them* not: yea, many a time turned he his anger away, and did not stir up all his wrath.

For he remembered that they *were but* flesh; a wind that passeth away, and cometh not again.

How oft did they provoke him in the wilderness, *and* grieve him in the desert!

Yea, they turned back and tempted God, and limited the Holy One of Israel.

They remembered not his hand, *nor* the day when he delivered them from the enemy.

How does a man limit the Holy One? By not believing. We need our heart to be fixed, trusting in the Lord. God knows our frame and the fleeting nature of the flesh, but He has given the spirit. He has touched our lives and delivered us from the enemy. Don't turn back and limit the Holy One; press on toward the mark for the prize of the high calling of God in Christ Jesus.

Psalms 139:1- 14
O LORD, thou hast searched me, and known *me*.

Thou knowest my downsitting and mine uprising, thou understandest my thought afar off.

Thou compassest my path and my lying down, and art acquainted *with* all my ways.

For *there is* not a word in my tongue, *but*, lo, O LORD, thou knowest it altogether.

Thou hast beset me behind and before, and laid thine hand upon me.

***Such* knowledge *is* too wonderful for me; it is high, I cannot *attain* unto it.**

Whither shall I go from thy spirit? or whither shall I flee from thy presence?

If I ascend up into heaven, thou *art* there: if I make my bed in hell [the grave], behold, thou *art there*.

If I take the wings of the morning, *and* dwell in the uttermost parts of the sea;
Even there shall thy hand lead me, and thy right hand shall hold me.
If I say, Surely the darkness shall cover me; even the night shall be light about me.
Yea, the darkness hideth not from thee; but the night shineth as the day: the darkness and the light *are* both alike *to thee*.
For thou hast possessed [had a hand on] my reins: thou hast covered me in my mother's womb.
I will praise thee; for I am fearfully *and* wonderfully made:

O LORD, you have searched me and you know me. How deeply felt is this Psalm of David's? No matter where you are or what you do, God's hand is on your life. We are fearfully and wonderfully made. God brought His Holy One into the world, so that we could see our potential in him. As the red thread in Psalms, Jesus Christ is Thine Holy One, a heartfelt reminder of the awesome nature and being of our Father and his.
Bless the Lord, oh my soul and all that is within me, bless His holy name.

The Red Thread of Psalms

The Wise Son

The book of Proverbs is all about wisdom. Being a wise son and seeing the wisdom of God is what is hoped to be obtained. Wisdom may not always come with age, but when you have wisdom, you may live a long and full life. Without wisdom, there is little hope for man. Even if he did find a little knowledge, he wouldn't know what to do with it. The red thread flows through the book of Proverbs in wisdom and culminates in the prophecy found in chapter thirty. Jesus Christ is the red thread; and in Proverbs, he is not only the wise son, but also the wisdom of God. Through Jesus Christ, we can know God and see the wisdom of the ages.

Proverbs 30:1- 4
The words of Agur the son of Jakeh, *even* the prophecy: the man spake unto Ithiel, even unto Ithiel and Ucal,
Surely I *am* more brutish than *any* man, and have not the understanding of a man.
I neither learned wisdom, nor have the knowledge of the holy.
Who hath ascended up into heaven, or descended? who hath gathered the wind in his fists? who hath bound the waters in a garment? who hath established all the ends of the earth? what *is* his name, and what *is* his son's name, if thou canst tell?

There is something you learn as a workman of the Word, and that is punctuation has no authority. It was all added to the text by the translators. Sometimes it is better left out when reading the Word, if you ever hope to understand what you are reading. The Word says, "**I neither learned wisdom, nor have the knowledge of the holy**" period. Then it starts with a question, "**Who hath ascended up into heaven, or descended**" question mark. The thought is not broken; it is one full statement. "**I neither learned wisdom nor have the knowledge of the holy who hath ascended up into heaven or descended.**" The brutish man does not have any knowledge of the holy who ascended up into heaven or descended, nor does he see any wisdom in it. What purpose could it possibly have, what good could it do to have the holy ascend up into heaven or to descend? It sounds foolish to me. When reading about the holy, it can either be referring to God, who is holy, or to the holy one, who is God's son, Jesus Christ. The context, not the reader, must define just who or what is holy. There is another place in the Bible where this same type of wording appears concerning who has ascended up into heaven or descended. Let's see if it might be helpful in understanding the prophecy here in Proverbs.

Romans 10:1- 11
Brethren, my heart's desire and prayer to God for Israel is, that they might be saved.
For I bear them record that they have a zeal of God, but not according to knowledge.
For they being ignorant of God's righteousness, and going about to establish their own righteousness, have not submitted themselves unto the righteousness of God.
For Christ *is* **the end of the law for righteousness to every one that believeth.**
For Moses describeth the righteousness which is of the law, That the man which doeth those things shall live by them.
But the righteousness which is of faith [believing] **speaketh on this wise, Say not in thine heart, Who shall ascend into heaven? (that is, to bring Christ down** *from above*:**)**
Or, Who shall descend into the deep? (that is, to bring up Christ again from the dead.)
But what saith it? The word is nigh thee, *even* **in thy mouth, and in thy heart: that is, the word of faith** [believing]**, which we preach;**
That if thou shalt confess with thy mouth the Lord Jesus, and shalt believe in thine heart that God hath raised him from the dead, thou shalt be saved.
For with the heart man believeth unto righteousness; and with the mouth confession is made unto salvation.
For the scripture saith, Whosoever believeth on him shall not be ashamed.

Who shall ascend up into heaven or who shall descend? It's all talking about Jesus Christ here in Romans. We must believe on him and what has been done in order to be saved. So, where is the wisdom in Christ ascending up into heaven or him first having to die and be raised again from the dead? It is found in the wisdom of God and not in the wisdom of this world.

I Corinthians 1:18- 24
For the preaching of the cross is to them that perish foolishness; but unto us which are saved it is the power of God.
For it is written, I will destroy the wisdom of the wise, and will

bring to nothing the understanding of the prudent.
Where *is* the wise? where *is* the scribe? where *is* the disputer of this world? hath not God made foolish the wisdom of this world?
For after that in the wisdom of God the world by wisdom knew not God, it pleased God by the foolishness of preaching to save them that believe.
For the Jews require a sign, and the Greeks seek after wisdom:
But we preach Christ crucified, unto the Jews a stumblingblock, and unto the Greeks foolishness;
But unto them which are called, both Jews and Greeks, Christ the power of God, and the wisdom of God.

Christ is the wisdom of God. Now do you see the wisdom in it? Back in Proverbs the man said, "Surely I *am* more brutish than *any* man." To be more brutish is to be more carnal, not gifted with reason. We must get past the wisdom of this world which says the wisdom of God is foolish. For Christ is the wisdom of God and believing on him and in his resurrection is not foolishness, but it is the power of God. Jesus Christ is God's holy one; God raised him from the dead, and he ascended up on high and is seated at the right hand of God. All that we have is because of God and His son, Jesus Christ. If a man lacks this wisdom, all he has to do is ask for it. God promised that if he asks, it shall be given to him.

James 1:5
If any of you lack wisdom, let him ask of God, that giveth to all *men* liberally, and upbraideth not; and it shall be given him.

God won't withhold wisdom from a man if he asks, and even the most brutish man has the ability to ask. We might be born a carnal man, but we do not have to remain a carnal man bound to the five senses. The man of reason can escape the wisdom of this world. The wisdom of God is found in Jesus Christ, and we have the ability to believe in him. It's not out of my reach or beyond my grasp. It's not over my head or past my comprehension. Things residing in the spiritual realm are beyond the ability of the natural man, but it is not beyond my ability to believe in Jesus Christ. It may take a leap of faith to believe that Jesus Christ is God's son and he did what God needed him to do. One may think it is a hard thing to swallow that God raised him from the dead, but with God all things are possible. Once you admit to the possibility of a greater power, you stand on the precipice of the new birth ready to be loosed from the wisdom of the flesh and to see the great power of God. Jesus had a job to do, and being God's son, he believed the scriptures and did that which needed to be done.

Luke 2:42- 48 and 52
And when he [Jesus] **was twelve years old, they went up to Jerusalem after the custom of the feast.**

And when they had fulfilled the days, as they returned, the child Jesus tarried behind in Jerusalem; and Joseph and his mother knew not *of it.*

But they, supposing him to have been in the company, went a day's journey; and they sought him among *their* **kinsfolk and acquaintance.**

And when they found him not, they turned back again to Jerusalem, seeking him.

And it came to pass, that after three days they found him in the temple, sitting in the midst of the doctors, both hearing them, and asking them questions.

And all that heard him were astonished at his understanding and answers.

And when they saw him, they were amazed: and his mother said unto him, Son, why hast thou thus dealt with us? behold, thy father and I have sought thee sorrowing.

And he said unto them, How is it that ye sought me? wist [know] ye not that I must be about my Father's business?

And Jesus increased in wisdom and stature, and in favour with God and man.

The child said, "I must be about my Father's business," and Jesus increased in wisdom. Did Jesus prove to be a wise son? The answer is yes. Jesus is the wisdom of God, because he was willing to make God's will his will and do what was needed to be done.

Matthew 26:39
And he went a little farther, and fell on his face, and prayed, saying, O my Father, if it be possible, let this cup pass from me: nevertheless not as I will, but as thou *wilt.*

Luke 22:41- 44
And he was withdrawn from them about a stone's cast, and kneeled down, and prayed,

Saying, Father, if thou be willing, remove this cup from me: nevertheless not my will, but thine, be done.

And there appeared an angel unto him from heaven, strengthening him.

And being in an agony he prayed more earnestly: and his sweat was as it were great drops of blood falling down to the ground.

John 18:11
Then said Jesus unto Peter, Put up thy sword into the sheath: the cup which my Father hath given me, shall I not drink it?

Jesus did not want to die. Life was not denied him for long, because God raised him from the dead. What Jesus did, he did for us all. Was there wisdom in God sending Jesus Christ to do the job? Was there a reason for Christ's death? Was there any wisdom and reason in raising Christ Jesus from the dead and having him ascend up on high? Yes, in every way, for he is man's salvation and our redeemer. We could not know God if it were not for His son.

I Corinthians 2:1, 2 and 4, 5
And I, brethren, when I came to you, came not with excellency of speech or of wisdom, declaring unto you the testimony [mystery] of God.

For I determined not to know any thing among you, save Jesus Christ, and him crucified.

And my speech and my preaching *was* not with enticing words of man's wisdom, but in demonstration of the Spirit and of power:

That your faith [believing] should not stand in the wisdom of men, but in the power of God.

It all starts with Christ and him being crucified, but it ends in the power of God. In Romans, it said, "Who shall ascend into heaven? (that is, to bring Christ down)." The parenthetical statement is here to expand the question. It all speaks to the same wisdom, whether this has to do with whose idea it was for Jesus to come or why he is where he is still. Jesus Christ had to come and do the work that he did, and he had to ascend to make it all available. It is all in the wisdom and purpose of God that Jesus came the first time, and he is where he is today, and furthermore, he will return again when the time comes.

Ephesians 1:3- 5, 7- 13
Blessed *be* the God and Father of our Lord Jesus Christ, who hath blessed us with all spiritual blessings in heavenly *places* [the heavenlies] **in Christ:**

According as he hath chosen us in him before the foundation of the world, that we should be holy and without blame before him in love:

Having predestinated [foreknown] us unto the adoption [sonship] of children by Jesus Christ to himself, according to the good pleasure of his will.

In whom we have redemption through his blood, the forgiveness of sins, according to the riches of his grace;

Wherein he hath abounded toward us in all wisdom and prudence [common sense];

Having made known unto us the mystery of his will, according to his good pleasure which he hath purposed in himself:

That in the dispensation [administration] of the fulness of times he might gather together in one all things in Christ, both which are in heaven, and which are on earth; *even* in him:

In whom also we have obtained an inheritance, being predestinated [foreknown] according to the purpose of him who worketh all things after the counsel of his own will:

That we should be to the praise of his glory, who first trusted in Christ.

In whom ye also *trusted*, after that ye heard the word of truth, the gospel of your salvation: in whom also after that ye believed, ye were sealed with that holy spirit of promise.

This is the wisdom of God and His will: to have you as a son. We believe in Christ, and we can trust in him, because God first trusted in him. Some may say, "What will this babbler say?" He seems to be putting forth some strange things, "We will hear you again on this matter."

Acts 17:18, 20- 28, 30- 32

Then certain philosophers of the Epicureans, and of the Stoicks, encountered him. And some said, What will this babbler say? other some, He seemeth to be a setter forth of strange gods: because he preached unto them Jesus, and the resurrection.

For thou bringest certain strange things to our ears: we would know therefore what these things mean.

(For all the Athenians and strangers which were there spent their time in nothing else, but either to tell, or to hear some new thing.)

Then Paul stood in the midst of Mars' hill, and said, *Ye* men of Athens, I perceive that in all things ye are too superstitious.

For as I passed by, and beheld your devotions, I found an altar with this inscription, TO THE UNKNOWN GOD. Whom therefore ye ignorantly worship, him declare I unto you.

God that made the world and all things therein, seeing that he is Lord of heaven and earth, dwelleth not in temples made with hands;

Neither is worshipped with men's hands, as though he needed any thing, seeing he giveth to all life, and breath, and all things;

And hath made of one blood all nations of men for to dwell on all the face of the earth, and hath determined the times before appointed, and the bounds of their habitation;

That they should seek the Lord, if haply they might feel after [grope for] **him, and find him, though he be not far from every one of us:**

For in him we live, and move, and have our being; as certain also of your own poets have said, For we are also his offspring.

And the times of this ignorance God winked at; but now commandeth all men every where to repent:

Because he hath appointed a day, in the which he will judge the world in righteousness by *that* **man whom he hath ordained;** *whereof* **he hath given assurance** [believing] **unto all** *men***, in that he hath raised him from the dead.**

And when they heard of the resurrection of the dead, some mocked: and others said, We will hear thee again of this *matter*.

We may be presented the knowledge of God's Word, but do we see the wisdom in it? Jesus Christ is the wisdom of God. Jesus Christ is the red thread, and in the book of Proverbs, he is the wise son whose name is in question. In Proverbs we were asked, "what *is* his name, and what *is* his son's name, if thou canst tell?" We can know God's name and we can know His son's name if we can but see the wisdom in it.

The Red Thread of Proverbs

The Red Thread of Ecclesiastes

A Just Man

In Ecclesiastes, the Preacher came preaching vanity. In the Gospels, Jesus Christ came preaching things of lasting value. In Ecclesiastes, the Preacher pondered the purpose of man's existence. Jesus Christ came to unveil the purpose of God, revealing to us the mystery of His will. The Preacher was looking for the justification of many things. He wanted to know what would vindicate a man's actions and existence. Jesus Christ is man's justification and the vindication for man's existence. Jesus Christ is the red thread in the book of Ecclesiastes as a just man who could do good, because he did not sin. He justified man and showed him the wisdom of God that is hidden in the mystery of God's will.

Ecclesiastes 1: 1- 11
The words of the Preacher, the son of David, king in Jerusalem.
Vanity of vanities, saith the Preacher, vanity of vanities; all *is* vanity.
What profit hath a man of all his labour which he taketh under the sun?
***One* generation passeth away, and *another* generation cometh: but the earth abideth for ever.**
The sun also ariseth, and the sun goeth down, and hasteth to his place where he arose.
The wind goeth toward the south, and turneth about unto the north; it whirleth about continually, and the wind returneth again according to his circuits.
All the rivers run into the sea; yet the sea *is* not full; unto the place from whence the rivers come, thither they return again.
All things *are* full of labour; man cannot utter *it*: the eye is not satisfied with seeing, nor the ear filled with hearing.
The thing that hath been, it *is that* which shall be; and that which is done *is* that which shall be done: and *there is* no new *thing* under the sun.
Is there *any* thing whereof it may be said, See, this *is* new? it hath been already of old time, which was before us.
***There is* no remembrance of former *things*; neither shall there be *any* remembrance of *things* that are to come with *those* that shall come after.**

Solomon was the Preacher, the son of David, and his kingdom and reign was over the earthly realm of men. He saw the earthly realm to be vain with no lasting substance. All of man's efforts were futile, worthless, and empty of any true purpose and value. He even questioned the reason for man's being here on this earth.

Ecclesiastes 1:12- 15
I the Preacher was [became] king over Israel in Jerusalem.
And I gave my heart to seek and search out by wisdom concerning all *things* **that are done under heaven: this sore travail hath God given to the sons of man to be exercised therewith.**
I have seen all the works that are done under the sun; and, behold, all *is* **vanity and vexation of spirit.**
That which is **crooked cannot be made straight: and that which is wanting cannot be numbered.**

Solomon was a wise man, but he could not see the wisdom of God hidden in the mystery. To live in the realm of the natural man is a sore travail, a painful toil, for there is little profit in the exercise of the flesh. Without the spirit, nothing which is crooked can be straightened out. The travail of the flesh is brought on by man's own iniquity.

Psalms 7:14- 16
Behold, he travaileth [toils] with iniquity, and hath conceived mischief, and brought forth falsehood.
He made a pit, and digged it, and is fallen into the ditch *which* **he made.**
His mischief shall return upon his own head, and his violent dealing shall come down upon his own pate [head].

Man dug the pit and then fell in the ditch which he himself had made. Things had become so twisted that the crooked could not be made straight. It would take something more than what man could work out on his own.

Isaiah 59:7- 10
Their feet run to evil, and they make haste to shed innocent blood: their thoughts *are* **thoughts of iniquity; wasting and destruction** *are* **in their paths.**
The way of peace they know not; and *there is* **no judgment in their goings: they have made them crooked paths: whosoever goeth**

therein shall not know peace.
> Therefore is judgment far from us, neither doth justice overtake us: we wait for light, but behold obscurity; for brightness, *but* we walk in darkness.
> We grope for the wall like the blind, and we grope as if *we had* no eyes: we stumble at noon day as in the night; *we are* in desolate places as dead *men*.

Before Jesus Christ, man lived in desolate places. It is no wonder that Solomon, when looking at all of the works under the sun, remarked all is vanity and vexation of the spirit. He knew man could never make straight that which is crooked, and that which was wanting or lacking in man's existence couldn't be numbered. Therefore it, would take another to come and straighten things out.

Luke 3:4-6
> As it is written in the book of the words of Esaias [Isaiah] the prophet, saying, The voice of one crying in the wilderness, Prepare ye the way of the Lord, make his paths straight.
> Every valley shall be filled, and every mountain and hill shall be brought low; and the crooked shall be made straight, and the rough ways *shall be* made smooth;
> And all flesh shall see the salvation of God.

All flesh shall see the salvation of God, and the crooked shall be made straight. Jesus Christ smoothed it all out for us.

Acts 2:38-40
> Then Peter said unto them, Repent, and be baptized every one of you in the name of Jesus Christ for the remission of sins, and ye shall receive the gift of the Holy Ghost [holy spirit].
> For the promise is unto you, and to your children, and to all that are afar off, *even* as many as the Lord our God shall call.
> And with many other words did he testify and exhort, saying, Save yourselves from this untoward [crooked] generation.

Save yourselves from this crooked generation by baptism in the name of Jesus Christ, and you shall receive the gift of holy spirit.

Philippians 2:15
> That ye may be blameless and harmless, the sons of God,

without rebuke, in the midst of a crooked and perverse nation, among whom ye shine as lights in the world;

We have been given an opportunity to become the sons of God, even though we still live in the midst of a crooked and perverse nation. This godliness we now possess makes our being here profitable for the first time in our lives.

I Timothy 4:7 and 8
But refuse profane and old wives' fables, and exercise thyself *rather* **unto godliness.**
For bodily exercise profiteth little: but godliness is profitable unto all things, having promise of the life that now is, and of that which is to come.

In Ecclesiastes, Solomon saw that man could only exercise in the vanity of the flesh. Man had no godliness to put him in the likeness of God. Solomon saw that there was not a just man upon the earth that doeth good and sinneth not. This is where we really begin to see the red thread in the book of Ecclesiastes.

Ecclesiastes 7:20
For *there is* **not a just man upon earth, that doeth good, and sinneth not.**

At this point, all were under sin. All of man's work was in vain. There weren't any righteous. No, not one.

Romans 3:10-18
As it is written, There is none righteous, no, not one: There is none that understandeth, there is none that seeketh after God.
They are all gone out of the way, they are together become unprofitable; there is none that doeth good, no, not one.
Their throat *is* **an open sepulchre; with their tongues they have used deceit; the poison of asps** *is* **under their lips: Whose mouth** *is* **full of cursing and bitterness: Their feet** *are* **swift to shed blood:**
Destruction and misery *are* **in their ways: And the way of peace have they not known:**
There is no fear of God before their eyes.

Solomon wanted to see the wisdom of God. He wanted to know the righteousness of God and the justification of God. Solomon wanted to see man's justification, but it was hidden in the wisdom of God in a mystery.

Ecclesiastes 7:23- 25
All this have I proved by wisdom: I said, I will be wise; but it *was* far from me.
That which is far off, and exceeding deep, who can find it out?
I applied mine heart to know, and to search, and to seek out wisdom, and the reason *of things*, and to know the wickedness of folly, even of foolishness *and* madness:

Solomon desperately wanted to know what the wisdom of God was concerning this matter. Why are people so given to folly and foolishness and madness? Without the Word and the love of God, all is vanity. Man needs to see the wisdom of God hidden in the mystery. Solomon was willing to look everywhere, but he couldn't see it.

I Corinthians 2:7 and 9- 12
But we speak the wisdom of God in a mystery, *even* the hidden *wisdom*, which God ordained before the world unto our glory:
But as it is written, Eye hath not seen, nor ear heard, neither have entered into the heart of man, the things which God hath prepared for them that love him.
But God hath revealed *them* unto us by his Spirit: for the Spirit searcheth all things, yea, the deep things of God.
For what man knoweth the things of a man, save the spirit of man which is in him? even so the things of God knoweth no man, but the Spirit of God.
Now we have received, not the spirit of the world, but the spirit which is of God; that we might know the things that are freely given to us of God.

This wisdom was hidden. Solomon wanted to see, but he couldn't. It was hidden in God only to be revealed to us who love Him and have His spirit at this time of the new birth. Solomon was a wise man, but he couldn't see the wisdom of God hidden in the mystery. He could not appreciate the love of Christ and thereby comprehend what we can today.

Ephesians 3: 4, 5, 11 and 17- 19
Whereby, when ye read, ye may understand my knowledge in the mystery of Christ

Which in other ages was not made known unto the sons of men, as it is now revealed unto his holy apostles and prophets by the Spirit;

According to the eternal purpose which he purposed in Christ Jesus our Lord:

That Christ may dwell in your hearts by faith [believing]; **that ye, being rooted and grounded in love,**

May be able to comprehend with all saints what *is* **the breadth, and length, and depth, and height;** [of this love]

And to know [by experience] **the love of Christ, which passeth knowledge, that ye might be filled with all the fulness of God.**

There was one thing so desperately missing in Solomon's day, and that was the love of God purposed in the mystery. Solomon sought after it, desiring to know, but not finding it. Yet there was one thing he did find.

Ecclesiastes 7:27 and 28
Behold, this have I found, saith the preacher, *counting* **one by one, to find out the account:**

Which yet my soul seeketh, but I find not: one man among a thousand have I found; but a woman among all those have I not found.

"One man among a thousand..." This is a figure of speech. We would say that he was one in a million. There was one man among a million. Solomon was looking for a just man. Solomon wanted to see a man without sin. He was searching with all the wisdom God gave him. It is here that God places the red thread. When Solomon was looking at the result of his search, he saw this one in a thousand. It would be Jesus Christ, a just man; he would be that one in a million man. Man's justification is wrapped around the love of God. The wisdom of the mystery is wrapped in the love of God. Christ was that just man who brought us to God, suffering for sin, the just for the unjust.

I Peter 3:18
For Christ also hath once suffered for sins, the just for the unjust, that he might bring us to God, being put to death in the flesh, but quickened by the Spirit:

This is what Solomon saw; there would be one in a thousand, a just man doing good and sinning not. This one man opened the door for justification and redemption for all of us.

Romans 3:24- 26
Being justified freely by his grace through the redemption that is in Christ Jesus:

Whom God hath set forth *to be* **a propitiation through faith** [believing] **in his blood, to declare his righteousness for the remission of sins that are past, through the forbearance of God;**

To declare, *I say*, **at this time his righteousness: that he might be just, and the justifier of him which believeth in Jesus.**

It was revealed that there would be a just man, and he would bring the justification of God. When Solomon came to the conclusion of the whole matter, he said, "fear God." However, the fear of God can never bring you into the living room of God's heart. Without the spirit, without the love of God, without the mystery, there is only vanity.

Ecclesiastes 12:13
Let us hear the conclusion of the whole matter: Fear God, and keep his commandments: for this *is* **the whole** *duty* **of man.**

The whole duty of man. Today fear has been replaced by believing, and vanity, with the love of God found in the mystery. In the vanity of the flesh, the natural man can at best only fear God. Fear is the natural man's response to that which he does not know or cannot understand. But we have moved on from fear to the knowledge of the will and purpose of God because of a just man, Jesus Christ. This just man is the red thread in the book of Ecclesiastes.

The Red Thread of Ecclesiastes

The Beloved

In The Song of Solomon, everyone was looking for a beloved. It was said that there was a damsel, a shulamite who was looking for a beloved, a certain shepherd who she longed would come. King Solomon had brought her into his court. He desired to have her as a beloved, one of the many which he chose to love, but she hoped for the shepherd, for she desired him. The damsel also inspired others to look for her beloved as she spake of his love and the good ointment of his name. 'The beloved' is the red thread in The Song of Solomon, which became the song of songs.

The Song of Solomon 1:1- 4
The song of songs, which *is* [became] Solomon's.
Let him kiss me with the kisses of his mouth: for thy love [beloved] ***is* better than wine.**
Because of the savour of thy good ointments thy name *is as* ointment poured forth, therefore do the virgins love thee.
Draw me, we will run after thee: the king hath brought me into his chambers: we will be glad and rejoice in thee, we will remember thy love [beloved] **more than wine: the upright love thee.**

This song of songs became Solomon's song because Solomon embraced the beloved, and he knew that only Jesus Christ could fulfill what was spoken here. Even the love and good name of King Solomon could not provide what Jesus Christ's love and good name could provide. His love is better than wine and his good name as good ointments poured forth. Therefore do the virgins, the pure at heart, love him. Therefore she says, "Draw me and we will run after thee: the upright love thee."

The Song of Solomon 1:7 and 8
Tell me, O thou whom my soul loveth, where thou feedest, where thou makest *thy flock* to rest at noon: for why should I be as one that turneth aside by the flocks of thy companions?
If thou know not, O thou fairest among women, go thy way forth by the footsteps of the flock, and feed thy kids beside the shepherds' tents.

The damsel was concerned about where her beloved was at, where it was that she could find him. Her greatest concern was that she be turned aside by another. Some say that absence makes the heart grow fonder, but far too many find that with the absence of even one as dear as a beloved, they turn aside to find another to love. The shepherd's reply was: if you don't know, follow the footsteps of the flock, track me down, and feed beside the tent. If you are fed by another, you will grow to love another. If you feed on my love, her beloved replies, it won't matter who you are with at the moment. You will still remain my beloved.

The Song of Solomon 1:9- 14
I have compared thee, O my love, to a company of horses in Pharaoh's chariots.
Thy cheeks are comely with rows *of jewels*, **thy neck with chains** *of gold*.
We will make thee borders of gold with studs of silver.
While the king *sitteth* **at his table, my spikenard sendeth forth the smell thereof.**
A bundle of myrrh *is* **my well beloved unto me; he shall lie all night betwixt my breasts.**
My beloved *is* **unto me** *as* **a cluster of camphire in the vineyards of Engedi.**

The damsel goes on to tell of the high esteem with which she holds her beloved, even though she sits at the king's table. She compares him to a company of Pharaoh's horses, which are magnificent creatures to behold. His cheeks are comely, handsome with rows. The rows refer to the lines in the skin of a man's face. A boy wouldn't have these distinct markings yet. The damsel says: we, (herself and the others who love him), will make for him borders on his garments of gold to show his stature and worth in the community. She says, my beloved is the sweetest thing. I will never let him go or trade him for another.

The Song of Solomon 2:3- 8
As the apple tree among the trees of the wood, so *is* **my beloved among the sons. I sat down under his shadow with great delight, and his fruit** *was* **sweet to my taste.**
He brought me to the banqueting house, and his banner over me *was* **love.**
Stay me with flagons, comfort me with apples: for I *am* **sick of love.**
His left hand *is* **under my head, and his right hand doth embrace me.**

I charge you, O ye daughters of Jerusalem, by the roes, and by the hinds of the field, that ye stir not up, nor awake *my* love, till he please.

The voice of my beloved! behold, he cometh leaping upon the mountains, skipping upon the hills.

The apple tree is the lover's tree, the tree of love and comfort. The damsel ate from his love. She sat under his shadow with great delight. She was content with his love, and his fruit was sweet to her. Stay me, sustain me, and comfort me for I am sick of love. I am love sick, or you could say, I am full of love. The damsel is saying, I don't want any other love, you are my beloved among the sons. It doesn't matter how long it takes. I will wait for him. I can hear the voice of my beloved. He's coming, he's coming!

The Song of Solomon 5:8- 16

I charge you, O daughters of Jerusalem, if ye find my beloved, that ye tell him, that I *am* sick of love.

What *is* thy beloved more than *another* beloved, O thou fairest among women? what *is* thy beloved more than *another* beloved, that thou dost so charge us?

My beloved *is* white and ruddy, the chiefest among ten thousand.

His head *is as* the most fine gold, his locks *are* bushy, *and* black as a raven.

His eyes *are* as *the eyes* of doves by the rivers of waters, washed with milk, *and* fitly set.

His cheeks *are* as a bed of spices, *as* sweet flowers: his lips *like* lilies, dropping sweet smelling myrrh.

His hands *are as* gold rings set with the beryl: his belly *is as* bright ivory overlaid *with* sapphires.

His legs *are as* pillars of marble, set upon sockets of fine gold: his countenance *is* as Lebanon, excellent as the cedars.

His mouth *is* most sweet: yea, he *is* altogether lovely. This *is* my beloved, and this *is* my friend, O daughters of Jerusalem.

I charge you, if you find my beloved, you tell him I am full of love for him. You tell him how much I love him. What makes my beloved more beloved than any other beloved? My beloved is white, pure as the driven snow and ruddy, healthy as a red apple. As the song says, he's all my fancy pictures in its fairest dreams and more[1]. He has a name which is above every

---

1 Still Sweeter Every Day. Words by: William C. Martin, *circa* 1899. Music by: C. Austin Miles.

name, and he has a love greater than any other. This is my beloved, and this is my friend, O daughters of Jerusalem. At the time Jesus came, God declared him to be beloved, but Israel had found another. Literally, many others. Yet this song of songs is not wasted, for there are those of us who yet sing of our acceptance in the beloved.

Hosea 2:1- 5, 10

Say ye unto your brethren [the children of Israel], **Ammi** [meaning, My people]**; and to your sisters, Ruhamah** [meaning, mercy].

Plead with your mother [the house of Israel]**, plead: for she *is* not my wife, neither *am* I her husband: let her therefore put away her whoredoms out of her sight, and her adulteries from between her breasts;**

Lest I strip her naked, and set her as in the day that she was born, and make her as a wilderness, and set her like a dry land, and slay her with thirst.

And I will not have mercy upon her children; for they *be* the children of whoredoms.

For their mother hath played the harlot: she that conceived them hath done shamefully: for she said, I will go after my lovers, that give *me* my bread and my water, my wool and my flax, mine oil and my drink.

And now will I discover her lewdness in the sight of her lovers, and none shall deliver her out of mine hand.

Israel had lost sight of her beloved. Even in the days of Hosea, God said she had gone after many other lovers. God did not cast away His people, even though they treated Him so shamefully, choosing to be fed and cared for by someone else.

Hosea 2:14- 17

Therefore, behold, I will allure [draw] **her, and bring her into the wilderness, and speak comfortably unto her.**

And I will give her her vineyards from thence, and the valley of Achor [trouble or trial] **for a door of hope: and she shall sing there, as in the days of her youth, and as in the day when she came up out of the land of Egypt.**

And it shall be at that day, saith the LORD, *that* thou shalt call me Ishi [my husband]**; and shalt call me no more Baali** [my lord]**.**

For I will take away the names of Baalim [many lords] **out of her mouth, and they shall no more be remembered by their name.**

God said He would draw her, Israel, and speak comfortably to her. She would be able to sing again the song of her beloved as in the days of her youth. God's desire was to be united with His people, and Jesus Christ came to bring God and His people together again.

Luke 3:21- 23a
Now when all the people were baptized, it came to pass, that Jesus also being baptized, and praying, the heaven was opened,
And the Holy Ghost descended in a bodily shape like a dove upon him, and a voice came from heaven, which said, Thou art my beloved Son; in thee I am well pleased.
And Jesus himself began to be about thirty years of age.

Truly this was he of whom the song of Solomon was sung. It was God who said of Jesus, "thou art My beloved son." Jesus was the man, the beloved for whom Israel had been waiting. But where was the song of Israel's beloved? It was long forgotten. Jesus spoke against the people of his day by a parable, telling of the beloved.

Luke 20:9- 15
Then began he to speak to the people this parable; A certain man planted a vineyard, and let it forth to husbandmen, and went into a far country for a long time.
And at the season he sent a servant to the husbandmen, that they should give him of the fruit of the vineyard: but the husbandmen beat him, and sent *him* away empty.
And again he sent another servant: and they beat him also, and entreated *him* shamefully, and sent *him* away empty.
And again he sent a third: and they wounded him also, and cast *him* out.
Then said the lord of the vineyard, What shall I do? I will send my beloved son: it may be they will reverence *him* when they see him.
But when the husbandmen saw him, they reasoned among themselves, saying, This is the heir: come, let us kill him, that the inheritance may be ours.
So they cast him out of the vineyard, and killed *him*.

Jesus knew what they were going to do to the beloved. Jesus gave his life for Israel, but Israel had turned aside to others. Is the song of Solomon forsaken; has the red thread failed? No, it will be picked up by others.

Romans 9:25 and 26
As he saith also in Osee [Hosea], I will call them my people, which were not my people; and her [Israel] beloved, which was not beloved.
And it shall come to pass, *that* in the place where it was said unto them, Ye *are* not my people; there shall they be called the children of the living God.

For a time, Israel was not beloved like she once was. How can you be beloved if you kill your beloved and run off with others? Yet both Israel and all the people which were not God's people were given an opportunity to come to the place where they shall be called the children of the living God. They could once again be called beloved because of the beloved, Jesus Christ, and what was accomplished in him.

Ephesians 1:3- 7
Blessed *be* the God and Father of our Lord Jesus Christ, who hath blessed us with all spiritual blessings in heavenly *places* in Christ:
According as he hath chosen us in him before the foundation of the world, that we should be holy and without blame before him in love:
Having predestinated [foreknown] us unto the adoption [sonship] of children by Jesus Christ to himself, according to the good pleasure of his will,
To the praise of the glory of his grace, wherein he hath made us accepted in the beloved.
In whom we have redemption through his blood, the forgiveness of sins, according to the riches of his grace.

God truly has blessed us in Christ. He chose us in Christ even before the foundation of the world. We talk about the red thread as seeing Christ foreknown and foretold all the way through the Old Testament, but we were also foreknown in Christ before the foundation of the world. We are now made to be beloved in the beloved, Jesus Christ. Christ is the red thread and the beloved in whom we now have redemption through his blood, the forgiveness of sins. The Song of Solomon sang of the beloved, which is fulfilled in Christ. His love and good name set him apart from all others who were ever called beloved, and he has made it possible for us to be sons of God, children by Jesus Christ. We can now pick up the song of the beloved being made accepted in the beloved, Jesus Christ.

Philippians 2:5- 9
Let this mind be in you, which was also in Christ Jesus:
Who, being in the form [in the way he thought] **of God, thought it not robbery to be equal with God:**
But made himself of no reputation, and took upon him the form [in the way he thought] **of a servant, and was made in the likeness of men:**
And being found in fashion as a man, he humbled himself, and became obedient unto death, even the death of the cross.
Wherefore God also hath highly exalted him, and given him a name which is above every name.

God has given His beloved a name which is above every name, and we now share in that name of the beloved. We are God's children when we are in Christ, and the sweet smelling savour of his name is ours.

Ephesians 5:1 and 2
Be ye therefore followers of God, as dear children;
And walk in love, as Christ also hath loved us, and hath given himself for us an offering and a sacrifice to God for a sweet smelling savour.

II Corinthians 2:14 and 15
Now thanks *be* **unto God, which always causeth us to triumph in Christ, and maketh manifest the savour of his knowledge by us in every place.**
For we are unto God a sweet savour of Christ, in them that are saved, and in them that perish.

The name of Christ is a sweet savour as an ointment poured forth. Therefore we love him as the beloved of the song of Solomon, as the beloved son in whom God is well pleased. "The beloved" is the red thread in the Song of Solomon.

The Red Thread of The Song of Solomon

God's Namesake

Many things are done in the name of God, but only one came bearing God's name. As we continue our search for the red thread, we come to the book of the Prophet Isaiah. Isaiah is full of references pointing to the red thread. There is, as in every book of the Bible, one reference that stands out and defines the book as a whole. In Isaiah, God points to His name and says, "For My name's sake" will I do it. The King James version translates it as "name's sake," but we would say "namesake." God's namesake is Jesus Christ; and as the red thread in the book of Isaiah, Jesus Christ is God's namesake.

Isaiah 48:9 and 11
For my name's sake will I defer mine anger, and for my praise will I refrain for thee, that I cut thee not off.
For mine own sake, *even* **for mine own sake, will I do** *it***: for how should** *my name* **[this is the same as above, my name's sake] be polluted? and I will not give my glory unto another.**

God will not give His glory to any other than whom? His namesake. He will not allow His namesake to be polluted because of what others have done. He was willing to defer His anger for His own sake, because He wanted to. This was so that God could fulfill all of which He had spoken and written in the stars concerning His namesake, Jesus Christ.

Isaiah 48:12-16
Hearken unto me, O Jacob and Israel, my called; I *am* **he; I** *am* **the first, I also** *am* **the last.**
Mine hand also hath laid the foundation of the earth, and my right hand hath spanned the heavens: *when* **I call unto them, they stand up together.**
All ye, assemble yourselves, and hear; which among them [the stars] **hath declared these** *things***? The LORD hath loved him:**
I, *even* **I, have spoken; yea, I have called him: I have brought him, and he shall make his way prosperous.**
Come ye near unto me, hear ye this; I have not spoken in secret from the beginning; from the time that it was, there *am* **I: and now the Lord GOD, and his spirit, hath sent me.**

God laid the foundation. He spanned the heavens as a great canvas in which He wrote His Word in the stars. In the stars God has declared His love for him. God called him; He brought him and shall make his way prosperous. Of whom are we speaking? God says that He hasn't spoken this in secret, even from the beginning. We should know who it is already.

Isaiah 49:1- 6
Listen, O isles, unto me; and hearken, ye people, from far; The LORD hath called me from the womb; from the bowels of my mother hath he made mention of my name.

And he hath made my mouth like a sharp sword; in the shadow of his hand hath he hid me, and made me a polished shaft; in his quiver hath he hid me;

And said unto me, Thou *art* my servant, O Israel, in whom I will be glorified.

Then I said, I have laboured in vain, I have spent my strength for nought, and in vain: *yet* surely my judgment *is* with the LORD, and my work with my God.

And now, saith the LORD that formed me from the womb *to be* his servant, to bring Jacob again to him, Though Israel be not gathered, yet shall I be glorious in the eyes of the LORD, and my God shall be my strength.

And he said, It is a light thing that thou shouldest be my servant to raise up the tribes of Jacob, and to restore the preserved of Israel: I will also give thee for a light to the Gentiles, that thou mayest be my salvation unto the end of the earth.

God called him before he was born. He made mention of his name even before he was conceived in his mother's womb. He would be God's servant. The one in whom God would be glorified. God is the one who would form him in the womb, so that he could do the job of bringing Jacob and God back together again. Not only would his work restore Israel, but he would also be a light to the Gentiles, bringing salvation unto the ends of the earth.

Isaiah 49:7- 10
Thus saith the LORD, the Redeemer of Israel, *and* his Holy One, to him whom man despiseth, to him whom the nation abhorreth, to a servant of rulers, Kings shall see and arise, princes also shall worship, because of the LORD that is faithful, *and* the Holy One of Israel, and he shall choose thee.

Thus saith the LORD, In an acceptable time have I heard thee, and in a day of salvation have I helped thee: and I will preserve thee, and give thee for a covenant of the people, to establish the earth, to cause to inherit the desolate heritages;

That thou mayest say to the prisoners, Go forth; to them that *are* in darkness, Show yourselves. They shall feed in the ways, and their pastures *shall be* in all high places.

They shall not hunger nor thirst; neither shall the heat nor sun smite them: for he that hath mercy on them shall lead them, even by the springs of water shall he guide them.

Isaiah speaks of God's holy one. The one whom man despises, whom the nation of Israel abhors. Kings will see him and stand up; princes shall bow before him. In an acceptable time, there will be a day of salvation, and he will be for a new covenant to the people. He will make available an inheritance. He will let the prisoners go free. He will feed them in the way. No one will hunger or thirst any longer, for he shall guide them. Who is God's holy one, the one who will do all of this? It is Jesus Christ, the one who will bear God's name.

Isaiah 49:24, 25
Shall the prey be taken from the mighty, or the lawful captive delivered?
But thus saith the LORD, Even the captives of the mighty shall be taken away, and the prey of the terrible shall be delivered: for I will contend with him that contendeth with thee, and I will save thy children.

Shall the prey be taken from the mighty, or the lawful captive delivered? The answer is yes, most unequivocally yes. God will save us in Christ. God's namesake will be true to his name. This has been a lengthy introduction, but God's namesake demands a lengthy response.

Isaiah 62:11, 12
Behold, the LORD hath proclaimed unto the end of the world, Say ye to the daughter of Zion, Behold, thy salvation cometh; behold, his reward *is* with him, and his work before him. And they shall call them, The holy people, The redeemed of the LORD.

Jesus Christ's reward is his name, and the work that is before him is our salvation. When he has lived up to his name and has completed his work, then we shall be able to be called the holy people, the redeemed of the Lord. Jesus Christ was given a name to live up to, and he was given a job to do.

John 4:34
Jesus saith unto them, My meat is to do the will of him that sent me, and to finish his work.

God began His work in Christ right after the fall. God laid the foundation and devised the plan, but Christ had to follow through and do God's will.

John 17:1- 8
These words spake Jesus, and lifted up his eyes to heaven, and said, Father, the hour is come; glorify thy Son, that thy Son also may glorify thee:
As thou hast given him power over all flesh, that he should give eternal life to as many as thou hast given him.
And this is life eternal, that they might know thee the only true God, and Jesus Christ, whom thou hast sent.
I have glorified thee on the earth: I have finished the work which thou gavest me to do.
And now, O Father, glorify thou me with thine own self with the glory which I had with thee before the world was.
I have manifested thy name unto the men which thou gavest me out of the world: thine they were, and thou gavest them me; and they have kept thy word.
Now they have known that all things whatsoever thou hast given me are of thee.
For I have given unto them the words which thou gavest me; and they have received *them*, and have known surely that I came out from thee, and they have believed that thou didst send me.

Jesus finished the work which God had given him to do, and God glorified him with His own glory. This is what God promised back in Isaiah. A namesake is one who carries the name of another. He bears the other's name with the purpose of manifesting the essence of that name to others.

Isaiah 52:6
Therefore my people shall know my name: therefore *they shall know* in that day that I *am* he that doth speak: behold, *it is* I.

Jesus spoke, but it was God's Word. Jesus revealed God's name. If you can know God's name, you can know God.

John 14:23, 24
Jesus answered and said unto him, If a man love me, he will keep my words: and my Father will love him, and we will come unto him, and make our abode with him.

He that loveth me not keepeth not my sayings: and the word which ye hear is not mine, but the Father's which sent me.

God is manifest in the world through His Word. Jesus knew God's Word, and he kept that Word. Jesus made God's will, his will; and he did the work that God had given him to do. God brought him into the world, but he made his way prosperous by keeping the Word. It's the Word, the Word and nothing but the Word. God's Word reveals to us God's name. Jesus knew the Word so he could show us who God is through His name.

Matthew 4:4
But he answered and said, It is written, Man shall not live by bread alone, but by every word that proceedeth out of the mouth of God.

Jesus knew what was written. Jesus lived by every word that came from God. Jesus knew if he was ever going to express the essence of God's name, he had to know God's Word. God reveals who He is and what He is through the communication of words. To know my name, what does that tell you? It tells whatever is in that name. What was the wisdom in Jesus knowing what the Word said about God and His name? If Jesus was going to act sagaciously as God's servant, he had to know all that was in God's name.

Isaiah 52:13
Behold, my servant shall deal prudently, he shall be exalted and extolled, and be very high.

Jesus was God's namesake; and as such, it was needful for him to deal prudently and know what service was required of him. If he dealt wisely with the name that he was given and fulfilled the service which was required of the only begotten son of God, then he would be exalted and extolled and be very high.

Philippians 2:5- 11
Let this mind [thinking] **be in you, which was also in Christ Jesus:**
Who, being in the form of God, thought it not robbery to be equal with God:
But made himself of no reputation, and took upon him the form of a servant, and was made in the likeness of men:
And being found in fashion as a man, he humbled himself, and became obedient unto death, even the death of the cross.
Wherefore God also hath highly exalted him, and given him a name which is above every name:
That at the name of Jesus every knee should bow, of *things* in heaven, and *things* in earth, and *things* under the earth;
And *that* every tongue should confess that Jesus Christ *is* Lord, to the glory of God the Father.

Jesus took on the form of God by thinking the way God would and by representing God's name. Jesus took on the form of a servant by doing what was needful to fulfill God's plan for our redemption. God made sure the name of Jesus Christ received the recognition it deserved. There may be some who do not know the name of Jesus Christ, but that does not change the power that is in the name of Jesus Christ, nor does it change the work that has been accomplished by the one bearing God's name.

John 10:24, 25
Then came the Jews round about him, and said unto him, How long dost thou make us to doubt? If thou be the Christ, tell us plainly.
Jesus answered them, I told you, and ye believed not: the works that I do in my Father's name, they bear witness of me.

Are you in doubt as to who Jesus Christ is? Do you understand the fullness of the name of Christ? If we can come to know what's in the name of Christ Jesus our Lord, we can know God. Jesus Christ gets us to God, and it is all through the name. Come to know the name of Christ by getting to know what the Word of God has to say about him. Read what he himself confessed to be true about who he was and what he came to do. Look at what he did in his Father's name.

John 10:27- 33
My sheep hear my voice, and I know them, and they follow me:
And I give unto them eternal life; and they shall never perish,

neither shall any *man* pluck them out of my hand.

My Father, which gave *them* me, is greater than all; and no *man* is able to pluck *them* out of my Father's hand. I and *my* Father are one.

Then the Jews took up stones again to stone him.

Jesus answered them, Many good works have I showed you from my Father; for which of those works do ye stone me?

The Jews answered him, saying, For a good work we stone thee not; but for blasphemy; and because that thou, being a man, makest thyself God.

Did Jesus ever make himself God? Did God ever make Jesus God? No on both accounts. Jesus was acting in God's name. Jesus Christ was representing his Father, doing his Father's will. Then who is the Lord Jesus Christ, if he is not God? Surely he did things that only God could do, or at least God would have to be with him. Others have said many things about who this Jesus was and is, but what did he himself claim to be?

John 10:36
Say ye of him, whom the Father hath sanctified, and sent into the world, Thou blasphemest; because I said, I am the Son of God?

Jesus knows who he is, and God knows who he is. We, too, can know Jesus Christ as we come to know God's namesake, the son of God. Jesus bears the name of his Father, because he came in his Father's name. Isaiah prophesies of his coming in a wonderful way. Jesus Christ stands as the red thread in the book of Isaiah as God's namesake.

The Red Thread of Isaiah

The Lord Our Righteousness

Righteousness has been defined as the ability to stand in the very presence of God without any sense of sin, fear, guilt, or shortcomings. Righteousness is the state and position of being right. God Himself is the standard. Many have sought their own righteousness, but until Jesus Christ came and made available the righteousness of God, man was always fundamentally wrong. In all of man's attempts to be right, he could not escape what was missing, the most vital part of his nature, the spirit of God. The Lord our righteousness stepped up and delivered this to man. Unrighteousness would have prevailed had it not been for Jesus Christ, the Lord our righteousness. As the red thread in the book of Jeremiah, Jehovah Zidkenu is the Lord our righteousness and Jesus Christ is the fulfillment of that name to us in righteousness.

Jeremiah 23:5, 6
Behold, the days come, saith the LORD, that I will raise unto David a righteous Branch, and a King shall reign and prosper, and shall execute judgment and justice in the earth.

In his days Judah shall be saved, and Israel shall dwell safely: and this *is* his name whereby he shall be called, THE LORD OUR RIGHTEOUSNESS.

"Behold, the days come." This concerns days which had not yet come in the time of Jeremiah. It was yet in the future that God would raise up unto David a righteous branch. This word "branch" is a sprout; this branch would sprout off the root of David. Now, you might recognize this as a figure of speech, because you know that David is not a plant nor would the righteous branch be a vegetable. The branch tells of a wonderful truth. Even though the tree may be cut down and appear to be dead on the surface, there can still be life in the root, and new life can sprout forth. In the days of Jeremiah, Israel was not dwelling in safety. Israel was about to vanish from the land which God had given them. They were far from the righteousness of God; yet looking ahead, God knew that the red thread would hold the promise and the answer which was needed for Judah.

Jeremiah 23:1- 4
Woe be unto the pastors that destroy and scatter the sheep of my pasture! saith the LORD.

Therefore thus saith the LORD God of Israel against the pastors that feed my people; Ye have scattered my flock, and driven them away, and have not visited them: behold, I will visit upon you the evil of your doings, saith the LORD.

And I will gather the remnant of my flock out of all countries whither I have driven them, and will bring them again to their folds; and they shall be fruitful and increase.

And I will set up shepherds over them which shall feed them: and they shall fear no more, nor be dismayed, neither shall they be lacking, saith the LORD.

Those who should have been taking care of God's people were not doing so. The pastors were destroying the people, because they were not feeding them the Word. People become dismayed and are overcome by fear when they do not have the Word of God, when they do not know the difference between right and wrong. There were a few men who had spirit upon them at this time, and they were set to protect and bless the people, not to scatter them. Anyone can pervert and distort the truth and accuracy of the Word, but is this what we want in a man of God?

Jeremiah 23:9- 11
Mine heart within me is broken because of the prophets; all my bones shake; I am like a drunken man, and like a man whom wine hath overcome, because of the LORD, and because of the words of his holiness.

For the land is full of adulterers; for because of swearing the land mourneth; the pleasant places of the wilderness are dried up, and their course is evil, and their force *is* not right.

For both prophet and priest are profane; yea, in my house have I found their wickedness, saith the LORD.

Both the prophet and the priest swear that they are right, but the whole time they are actually wrong. They have moved away from the truth of the Word of God, and their course is evil. Their life force is not right within them. There is something fundamentally wrong with them. They are profane. There is not a right spirit in them.

Jeremiah 23:13, 14
And I have seen folly in the prophets of Samaria; they prophesied in Baal, and caused my people Israel to err.

I have seen also in the prophets of Jerusalem an horrible thing:

they commit adultery, and walk in lies: they strengthen also the hands of evildoers, that none doth return from his wickedness: they are all of them unto me as Sodom, and the inhabitants thereof as Gomorrah.

The prophets of Samaria and Jerusalem pervert the Word. They themselves are perverted. They condone wickedness. Some practice it, but they all have become as Sodom and the inhabitants of Gomorrah. If you are not going to speak out against evil and say it is wrong, then you might as well do evil, because one is the same as the other.

Jeremiah 23:15- 17
Therefore thus saith the LORD of hosts concerning the prophets; Behold, I will feed them with wormwood, and make them drink the water of gall: for from the prophets of Jerusalem is profaneness gone forth into all the land.
Thus saith the LORD of hosts, Hearken not unto the words of the prophets that prophesy unto you: they make you vain: they speak a vision of their own heart, *and* not out of the mouth of the LORD.
They say still unto them that despise me, The LORD hath said, Ye shall have peace; and they say unto every one that walketh after the imagination of his own heart, No evil shall come upon you.

When profaneness is allowed to overtake the land, the people will despise God. The ones who should be speaking for God end up speaking from their own heart. All religions have their priests and prophets and pastors. They all want to establish a form of righteousness for their followers. Yet the question remains, how can there ever be peace and safety for any of us with so many religious differences being embraced? Everyone likes to be right, but without the Lord our righteousness, what chance do any of us really have?

Jeremiah 23:20- 22
The anger of the LORD shall not return, until he have executed, and till he have performed the thoughts of his heart: in the latter days ye shall consider it perfectly.
I have not sent these prophets, yet they ran: I have not spoken to them, yet they prophesied.
But if they had stood in my counsel, and had caused my people to hear my words, then they should have turned them from their evil way, and from the evil of their doings.

There will come a day when everyone will see and understand. Many today will read this and still walk away blind, but God did not send these prophets. Yet they ran around saying He did. God didn't speak to them, yet they spoke as if He had. If they had stood in His counsel and stuck to His Word, they wouldn't have caused the people to err.

Jeremiah 23:25- 27
I have heard what the prophets said, that prophesy lies in my name, saying, I have dreamed, I have dreamed.
How long shall *this* be in the heart of the prophets that prophesy lies? yea, *they are* prophets of the deceit of their own heart;
Which think to cause my people to forget my name by their dreams which they tell every man to his neighbour, as their fathers have forgotten my name for Baal.

I have a dream. Well, if my dream doesn't help people to know God's name or to know God's Word, what good is it? To proclaim "I have a dream" doesn't necessarily mean it is a good dream or that God had a hand in it.

Jeremiah 23:32, 33
Behold, I *am* against them that prophesy false dreams, saith the LORD, and do tell them, and cause my people to err by their lies, and by their lightness; yet I sent them not, nor commanded them: therefore they shall not profit this people at all, saith the LORD.
And when this people, or the prophet, or a priest, shall ask thee, saying, What *is* the burden of the LORD? thou shalt then say unto them, What burden? I will even forsake you, saith the LORD.

When people move away from the Word, the religion which follows becomes a burden on people. God and His Word are never a burden to the people. It's only error and falsehood and the low esteem of God and His Word which burdens people. God and His Word are never a burden.

Jeremiah 23:36
And the burden of the LORD shall ye mention no more: for every man's word shall be his burden; for ye have perverted the words of the living God, of the LORD of hosts our God.

If you feel weighed down by religion, then maybe it is time to change your religion. Actually, it would be better to get rid of religion all together and just come back to God and His Word. Religion by definition is always that which man has made, while Christianity by definition is that which God has wrought in Christ. There may be a lot of religion in Christianity today. This is why I said that it would be better just to come back to the Word and God and leave all the religion behind. Simply look at what God has wrought in Christ.

Romans 3:21- 26
But now the righteousness of God without the law is manifested, being witnessed by the law and the prophets;
Even the righteousness of God *which is* by faith of Jesus Christ unto all and upon all them that believe: for there is no difference:
For all have sinned, and come short of the glory of God;
Being justified freely by his grace through the redemption that is in Christ Jesus:
Whom God hath set forth *to be* a propitiation through faith in his blood, to declare his righteousness for the remission of sins that are past, through the forbearance of God;
To declare, *I say*, at this time his righteousness: that he might be just, and the justifier of him which believeth in Jesus.

Now the righteousness of God is opened to us. It is available to us, even that which was attested to by the law and the prophets. Jeremiah spoke of the Lord our righteousness, the righteous branch or sprout which would come out of the root of David. It is by him that the righteousness of God is available to us today. It came through Jesus Christ's believing. God's righteousness is now upon all who believe in Jesus Christ. We have been justified, which is to be made just as if you'd never sinned. It was done freely, which is at no cost to you. By God's grace because He wanted to, through the redemption that is in Christ Jesus. Jesus paid for us with his life. Now if we are willing to place our believing in his blood, we have remission of sins. By believing in Jesus Christ, we also have his righteousness. This is the work of Christ. Do you want it? Then place your believing in Jesus Christ, and accept what is freely given to you through the payment of his blood.

Ephesians 1:12, 13
That we should be to the praise of his glory, who first trusted in Christ.
In whom ye also *trusted*, after that ye heard the word of truth, the gospel of your salvation: in whom also after that ye believed, ye

were sealed with that holy Spirit of promise.

We accept what Christ has done for us when we believe in him. When we believe in Christ, we praise God in His glory because He first trusted in Christ. God trusted in Christ. He trusted that Christ would do all that was prophesied of him. God knew the red thread would prove to be our salvation. We also then trusted in that word of truth, the gospel or good news of our salvation. Once we heard and then believed, we were sealed with that holy spirit of promise.

Ephesians 1:15- 20
Wherefore I also, after I heard of your faith [believing] **in the Lord Jesus, and love unto all the saints,**
Cease not to give thanks for you, making mention of you in my prayers;
That the God of our Lord Jesus Christ, the Father of glory, may give unto you the spirit of wisdom and revelation in the knowledge of him:
The eyes of your understanding being enlightened; that ye may know what is the hope of his calling, and what the riches of the glory of his inheritance in the saints,
And what *is* **the exceeding greatness of his power to us-ward who believe, according to the working of his mighty power,**
Which he wrought in Christ, when he raised him from the dead, and set *him* **at his own right hand in the heavenly** *places*,
Far above all principality, and power, and might, and dominion, and every name that is named, not only in this world, but also in that which is to come.

Paul said, *when I heard of your believing in the Lord Jesus, I continued to give thanks for you and to pray for you that the eyes of your understanding be enlightened.* It is important for us to know what we have in Christ. Righteousness gives us the ability to stand in the very presence of God without any sense of sin, fear, guilt or condemnation. We have been made right with the return of the holy spirit. Now it is just a matter of living up to our righteousness. The spirit of wisdom and revelation in the knowledge of him is now available. We have the spirit, and we are able to receive revelation providing wisdom and knowledge in Him. Put aside the burden of religion and have your eyes enlightened to all that is available to you in Christ. Look for that which God wrought when He raised Christ from the dead and set him at His own right hand. We do not need to live in condemnation with a negative judgment hanging over our head. We have been made free in the Lord our righteousness.

Romans 8:1, 2
There is **therefore now no condemnation to them which are in Christ Jesus, who walk not after the flesh, but after the Spirit.**
For the law of the Spirit of life in Christ Jesus hath made me free from the law of sin and death.

There is no condemnation to them who are in Christ Jesus. We now live under the law of the spirit of life that we have in Christ Jesus. We have been made free.

II Corinthians 3:17, 18
Now the Lord is that Spirit: and where the Spirit of the Lord *is*, **there** *is* **liberty.**
But we all, with open face beholding as in a glass the glory of the Lord, are changed into the same image from glory to glory, *even* **as by the Spirit of the Lord.**

"Where the spirit of the Lord is, there is liberty." This is righteousness when we are his and he is ours. This is what God had in mind all along. With the spirit of the Lord, we are able to see with an open face as beholding in a mirror the glory that we are in the Lord, and thereby be changed into that same image from glory to glory. This is the red thread in the book of Jeremiah, the Lord our righteousness.

The Red Thread of Jeremiah

The Comforter

In the book of Lamentations, the lamentation is that there is no comforter. Jerusalem had lost her children. They had all gone into captivity, and the city lay in the hands of the enemy. The city speaks for the people because the people are gone. The city therefore weeps "because the comforter that should relieve my soul is far from me." She spreads forth her hands, but there is none to comfort her. This is the lamentation: what would it take to span the chasm and repair the breach? Who can heal thee? The red thread in the book of Lamentations has to do with the comforter. Here in Lamentations, it was lamented that there was no comforter. But when the comforter came, he healed the breach and spanned the chasm and provided yet another comforter when he himself had to go.

Lamentations 1:1-3
How doth the city sit solitary, *that was* full of people! *how* is she become as a widow! she *that was* great among the nations, *and* princess among the provinces, *how* is she become tributary!
She weepeth sore in the night, and her tears *are* on her cheeks: among all her lovers she hath none to comfort *her*: all her friends have dealt treacherously with her, they are become her enemies.
Judah is gone into captivity because of affliction, and because of great servitude: she dwelleth among the heathen, she findeth no rest: all her persecutors overtook her between the straits.

The city is empty of its people. There is none to comfort her. Judah is gone into captivity. This is the situation: her children are gone into captivity, and she lay naked before her enemy.

Lamentations 1:8-10
Jerusalem hath grievously sinned; therefore she is removed: all that honoured her despise her, because they have seen her nakedness: yea, she sigheth, and turneth backward.
Her filthiness *is* in her skirts; she remembereth not her last end; therefore she came down wonderfully: she had no comforter. O LORD, behold my affliction: for the enemy hath magnified *himself*.
The adversary hath spread out his hand upon all her pleasant things: for she hath seen *that* the heathen entered into her sanctuary,

whom thou didst command *that* **they should not enter into thy congregation.**

Jerusalem was raped and violated. She had willingly run to her lovers, but they were deceiving her. They were her enemy. Her uncleanliness remained in her, and she didn't remember what she was before this. Therefore the enemy was magnified, and she came apart utterly.

Lamentations 1:16- 18
For these *things* **I weep; mine eye, mine eye runneth down with water, because the comforter that should relieve my soul is far from me: my children are desolate, because the enemy prevailed.**
Zion spreadeth forth her hands, *and there is* **none to comfort her: the LORD hath commanded concerning Jacob,** *that* **his adversaries** *should be* **round about him: Jerusalem is as a menstruous woman among them.**
The LORD is righteous; for I have rebelled against his commandment: hear, I pray you, all people, and behold my sorrow: my virgins and my young men are gone into captivity.

The comforter had not yet come, and Jerusalem had not kept herself to that day. It appeared the enemy had won. Jerusalem had lost her children. Jerusalem was as a woman during menstruation and therefore was considered unclean.

Lamentations 1:21, 22
They have heard that I sigh: *there is* **none to comfort me: all mine enemies have heard of my trouble; they are glad that thou hast done** *it*: **thou wilt bring the day** *that* **thou hast called, and they shall be like unto me.**
Let all their wickedness come before thee; and do unto them, as thou hast done unto me for all my transgressions: for my sighs *are* **many, and my heart** *is* **faint.**

Everyone could hear the sigh and see the exasperation of the desolation and discomfort. Her enemies were glad. Yet there will be a day when the tables are turned and their wickedness will be brought upon their own heads. God is faithful, and God is just. Even though the heart is faint, God knows what it will take to heal thee.

Lamentations 2:13, 14
What thing shall I take to witness for thee? what thing shall I liken to thee, O daughter of Jerusalem? what shall I equal to thee, that I may comfort thee, O virgin daughter of Zion? for thy breach *is* great like the sea: who can heal thee?

Thy prophets have seen vain and foolish things for thee: and they have not discovered thine iniquity, to turn away thy captivity; but have seen for thee false burdens and causes of banishment.

What will it take to witness to thee? God asks the question, what can I do or what can I use as a witness that you will accept? To what can I liken it that you will understand? What shall I equal to thee? What can I measure out to tip the scales that I may comfort you? Thy breach is great; the chasm between us is wide. As sung in the old hymn, "O the mighty gulf that God did span."[2] God had a plan to heal them.

Lamentations 3:21- 26
This I recall to my mind, therefore have I hope.
***It is of* the LORD'S mercies that we are not consumed, because his compassions fail not.**
***They are* new every morning: great *is* thy faithfulness.**
The LORD *is* my portion, saith my soul; therefore will I hope in him.
The LORD *is* good unto them that wait for him, to the soul *that* seeketh him.
***It is* good that *a man* should both hope and quietly wait for the salvation of the LORD.**

Oh people, come back to the promise of God. The comforter has come, and we have the witness with us even to this day. We no longer have to wait for the salvation of the Lord. Salvation is here and with us today.

John 14:1
Let not your heart be troubled: ye believe in God, believe also in me.

---

2 At Calvary. Words by: William R. Newell, 1895. Music by: Daniel B. Towner

Jesus said, if you believe in God, believe also in me. Not because I am God, but because I am the promised salvation and the comforter who shall repair the breach. In my name, the Father will send the holy spirit, who shall be another comforter to you forever.

John 14:15- 18
If ye love me, keep my commandments.
And I will pray the Father, and he shall give you another Comforter, that he may abide with you for ever;
***Even* the Spirit of truth; whom the world cannot receive, because it seeth him not, neither knoweth him: but ye know him; for he dwelleth with you, and shall be in you.**
I will not leave you comfortless: I will come to you.

Jesus came as a comforter, and he healed the people who would accept it. He came to heal the world, if they only knew it. Jesus made it available for the Father to give us another comforter, even the spirit of truth. The spirit that would dwell with us forever.

John 14:25, 26
These things have I spoken unto you, being *yet* present with you.
But the Comforter, *which is* the Holy Ghost [holy spirit], **whom the Father will send in my name, he shall teach you all things, and bring all things to your remembrance, whatsoever I have said unto you.**

The comforter, which is the holy spirit, is sent by God in Christ's name. We are told to believe in Christ. We are baptized in the name of Jesus Christ. It is Christ in you, the hope of glory. We have the new birth in Jesus Christ. Jesus had to leave so that he could finish the work which is in his name.

John 16:16, 17
But because I have said these things unto you, sorrow hath filled your heart.
Nevertheless I tell you the truth; It is expedient for you that I go away: for if I go not away, the Comforter will not come unto you; but if I depart, I will send him unto you.

Jesus said he had to go, and those who loved him were sorrowful. But he said that it is needful for him to go in order to send the comforter, which is the holy spirit unto you.

John 16:20
Verily, verily, I say unto you, That ye shall weep and lament, but the world shall rejoice: and ye shall be sorrowful, but your sorrow shall be turned into joy.

The world for the most part will reject the comforter, because they can't see it. They won't accept the witness of the holy spirit. Most people were glad to see Jesus Christ go, because they didn't accept his comfort. But those of us who love him will have our sorrow turned into joy by the comfort of the holy spirit and the witness thereof.

Acts 1:5
For John truly baptized with water; but ye shall be baptized with the Holy Ghost [holy spirit] not many days hence.

Just before he left, Jesus told them of the baptism of the holy spirit, which would be available soon. Jesus told them of the power of the holy spirit which they would manifest.

Acts 1:8, 9
But ye shall receive power, after that the Holy Ghost [holy spirit] is come upon you: and ye shall be witnesses unto me both in Jerusalem, and in all Judaea, and in Samaria, and unto the uttermost part of the earth.
And when he had spoken these things, while they beheld, he was taken up; and a cloud received him out of their sight.

Jesus left this earth with a promise of his return. What Jesus had promised concerning the holy spirit was all fulfilled just ten short days later. On the day of Pentecost that particular year, all the waiting was over and the holy spirit was poured out. The holy spirit was now available for all who would believe on that day and every day since.

Acts 2:1, 4
And when the day of Pentecost was fully come, they were all with one accord in one place.
And they were all filled with the Holy Ghost [holy spirit], and began to speak with other tongues, as the Spirit gave them utterance.

They had been waiting for this. They received the holy spirit, and they spoke in tongues. Speaking in tongues is the witness of the internal reality of the power and the presence of the holy spirit to everyone who is born again.

Acts 2:32, 33, 39
This Jesus hath God raised up, whereof we all are witnesses.
Therefore being by the right hand of God exalted, and having received of the Father the promise of the Holy Ghost [holy spirit], **he hath shed forth this, which ye now see and hear.**
For the promise is unto you, and to your children, and to all that are afar off, *even* **as many as the Lord our God shall call.**

In the book of Lamentations, Jerusalem lamented that there was no comforter. Today, Jerusalem still laments because of the rejection of the comforter. The people of Israel were in bondage in the time of the book of Lamentations, and they will continue to be so until they accept the work which was accomplished in Christ. Jesus Christ is the comforter prophesied in Lamentations, who gave another comforter in the holy spirit. This was done so that we could be delivered from bondage and be reunited with God. The comfort comes through the spirit of the Lord, the red thread, the comforter, the Lord of glory, Jesus Christ.

II Corinthians 3:17
Now the Lord is that Spirit: and where the Spirit of the Lord *is*, **there** *is* **liberty.**

Now the Lord is that spirit. It is all in Christ, through Christ, by Christ, and in the name of Christ Jesus our Lord that we enjoy the spirit we have in us. Where the spirit of the Lord is, there is liberty. This liberty is not a cause for banishment, but a cause for salvation, reconciliation, and atonement with God. This is how the red thread in the book of Lamentations was fulfilled. Jesus Christ as the comforter came to offer comfort by leaving another comforter. We now have the comfort of the holy spirit in us forever.

The Son of Man

The book of Ezekiel is marked by the number thirteen, the number for rebellion. The red thread can be found in the phrase "the son of man." The son of man stands in the midst of rebellion. The son of man is the son of God to those who believe. He is also the son of man when he stands in the midst of a rebellious house. As the red thread, Jesus Christ is the son of man, for he is a descendant of man. As such, he stood in the midst of man's rebellion. He is also the son of God to all those who believe. The son of man was made for suffering and rejection, but not without glory and regeneration in the end.

Ezekiel 1:1
Now it came to pass in the thirtieth year, in the fourth *month*, in the fifth *day* of the month, as I *was* among the captives by the river of Chebar, *that* the heavens were opened, and I saw visions of [from] God.

Ezekiel 2:1- 8
And he said unto me, Son of man, stand upon thy feet, and I will speak unto thee.

And the spirit entered into me when he spake unto me, and set me upon my feet, that I heard him that spake unto me.

And he said unto me, Son of man, I send thee to the children of Israel, to a rebellious nation that hath rebelled against me: they and their fathers have transgressed against me, *even* unto this very day.

For *they are* impudent children and stiffhearted. I do send thee unto them; and thou shalt say unto them, Thus saith the Lord GOD.

And they, whether they will hear, or whether they will forbear, (for they *are* a rebellious house,) yet shall know that there hath been a prophet among them.

And thou, son of man, be not afraid of them, neither be afraid of their words, though briers and thorns *be* with thee, and thou dost dwell among scorpions: be not afraid of their words, nor be dismayed at their looks, though they *be* a rebellious house.

And thou shalt speak my words unto them, whether they will hear, or whether they will forbear: for they *are* most rebellious.

But thou, son of man, hear what I say unto thee; Be not thou rebellious like that rebellious house: open thy mouth, and eat that I give thee.

You get the idea early on that we are dealing with rebellion. Israel is a rebellious nation; it was then and still is today. The son of man was sent to a rebellious house to speak the Word to them. Whether they were willing to hear or not, there was no doubt there was a prophet among them.

In the first verse, we open with the number thirteen, but we also see the number four, which is the number for the world and the number five, which is the number for grace. Even though we open with rebellion in the world, we will end with the world in grace, and it is all because of the red thread, Jesus Christ, the son of man.

Ezekiel 36:22- 28
Therefore say unto the house of Israel, Thus saith the Lord GOD; I do not *this* for your sakes, O house of Israel, but for mine holy name's sake, which ye have profaned among the heathen, whither ye went.

And I will sanctify my great name, which was profaned among the heathen, which ye have profaned in the midst of them; and the heathen shall know that I *am* the LORD, saith the Lord GOD, when I shall be sanctified in you before their eyes.

For I will take you from among the heathen, and gather you out of all countries, and will bring you into your own land.

Then will I sprinkle clean water upon you, and ye shall be clean: from all your filthiness, and from all your idols, will I cleanse you.

A new heart also will I give you, and a new spirit will I put within you: and I will take away the stony heart out of your flesh, and I will give you an heart of flesh.

And I will put my spirit within you, and cause you to walk in my statutes, and ye shall keep my judgments, and do *them*.

And ye shall dwell in the land that I gave to your fathers; and ye shall be my people, and I will be your God.

The question has always been, when will this happen? Some say that Israel has been returned to their land, and their struggle is common to God's people. But Israel has yet to see the fulfillment of this prophecy, which was spoken by Ezekiel.

Ezekiel 36:33, 35
Thus saith the Lord GOD; In the day that I shall have cleansed you from all your iniquities I will also cause *you* to dwell in the cities, and the wastes shall be builded.

And they shall say, This land that was desolate is become like the garden of Eden; and the waste and desolate and ruined cities *are become* fenced, *and* are inhabited.

In the day that I shall have cleansed you, even the land will become like the garden of Eden. For this to occur for the whole house of Israel, it will require the coming of the son of man and the resurrection.

Ezekiel 37:1- 14
The hand of the LORD was upon me, and carried me out in the spirit of the LORD, and set me down in the midst of the valley which *was* full of bones,
And caused me to pass by them round about: and, behold, *there were* very many in the open valley; and, lo, *they were* very dry.
And he said unto me, Son of man, can these bones live? And I answered, O Lord GOD, thou knowest.
Again he said unto me, Prophesy upon these bones, and say unto them, O ye dry bones, hear the word of the LORD.
Thus saith the Lord GOD unto these bones; Behold, I will cause breath to enter into you, and ye shall live:
And I will lay sinews upon you, and will bring up flesh upon you, and cover you with skin, and put breath in you, and ye shall live; and ye shall know that I *am* the LORD.
So I prophesied as I was commanded: and as I prophesied, there was a noise, and behold a shaking, and the bones came together, bone to his bone.
And when I beheld, lo, the sinews and the flesh came up upon them, and the skin covered them above: but *there was* no breath in them.
Then said he unto me, Prophesy unto the wind, prophesy, son of man, and say to the wind, Thus saith the Lord GOD; Come from the four winds, O breath, and breathe upon these slain, that they may live.
So I prophesied as he commanded me, and the breath came into them, and they lived, and stood up upon their feet, an exceeding great army.
Then he said unto me, Son of man, these bones are the whole house of Israel: behold, they say, Our bones are dried, and our hope is lost: we are cut off for our parts.
Therefore prophesy and say unto them, Thus saith the Lord GOD; Behold, O my people, I will open your graves, and cause you to come up out of your graves, and bring you into the land of Israel.

And ye shall know that I *am* the LORD, when I have opened your graves, O my people, and brought you up out of your graves,

And shall put my spirit in you, and ye shall live, and I shall place you in your own land: then shall ye know that I the LORD have spoken *it*, and performed *it*, saith the LORD.

When will this happen? In the resurrection. Some say there is no resurrection. Some say that the resurrection is past already. Some claim you go to heaven without waiting for the resurrection, but all of these claims are contradictory to what God declares to be true. Christ will come for Israel and there will be a resurrection.

Matthew 9:4- 6

And Jesus knowing their thoughts said, Wherefore think ye evil in your hearts?

For whether is easier, to say, *Thy* sins be forgiven thee; or to say, Arise, and walk?

But that ye may know that the Son of man hath power on earth to forgive sins, (then saith he to the sick of the palsy,) Arise, take up thy bed, and go unto thine house.

Jesus came as the son of man knowing the evil that was in people's hearts, yet he had the power on earth to forgive sins and heal them.

Matthew 13:36- 43

Then Jesus sent the multitude away, and went into the house: and his disciples came unto him, saying, Declare unto us the parable of the tares of the field.

He answered and said unto them, He that soweth the good seed is the Son of man;

The field is the world; the good seed are the children of the kingdom; but the tares are the children of the wicked *one*;

The enemy that sowed them is the devil; the harvest is the end of the world; and the reapers are the angels.

As therefore the tares are gathered and burned in the fire; so shall it be in the end of this world.

The Son of man shall send forth his angels, and they shall gather out of his kingdom all things that offend, and them which do iniquity;

And shall cast them into a furnace of fire: there shall be wailing and gnashing of teeth.

Then shall the righteous shine forth as the sun in the kingdom of

their Father. Who hath ears to hear, let him hear.

Jesus knew that he had come to find a rebellious house and that the world lay in wickedness. The son of man came as the parable indicates, sowing the good seed and knowing that in the end, righteousness would shine forth.

Matthew 16:27
For the Son of man shall come in the glory of his Father with his angels; and then he shall reward every man according to his works.

The son of man shall come in glory. The son of man was rejected when he came to the house of Israel the first time, but the next time around, he will be handing out the rewards for what every man has done.

Matthew 17:22, 23
And while they abode in Galilee, Jesus said unto them, The Son of man shall be betrayed into the hands of men:
And they shall kill him, and the third day he shall be raised again. And they were exceeding sorry.

Jesus Christ was betrayed and killed, but he rose again. The son of man was made for suffering and death, but not without a purpose. He suffered for all men.

Matthew 18:11
For the Son of man is come to save that which was lost.

What the son of man did was needful. Not for himself, but for all who are lost. Jesus Christ did not suffer and die for himself, but for you and me. Men have rebelled against God, but the son of man was willing to come, even in the midst of a rebellious house, and save all who are lost.

Matthew 19:28
And Jesus said unto them, Verily I say unto you, That ye which have followed me, in the regeneration when the Son of man shall sit in the throne of his glory, ye also shall sit upon twelve thrones, judging the twelve tribes of Israel.

When Jesus spoke of the regeneration and the throne of glory, he spoke of that which Ezekiel prophesied. Ezekiel spoke of all the dried bones of the house of Israel being brought back to life, and Israel dwelling in a land like the garden of Eden.

Matthew 24:3
And as he sat upon the mount of Olives, the disciples came unto him privately, saying, Tell us, when shall these things be? and what *shall be* **the sign of thy coming, and of the end of the world?**

The disciples wanted to know about the end of the world and were concerned about when things were going to happen. What do we look for; how do we know when it will occur? The world had waited this long for Jesus to come. Now Jesus was talking about dying and being raised from the dead. He was speaking of coming again and regeneration, and his disciples wanted to know what to look for.

Matthew 24:6- 8
And ye shall hear of wars and rumours of wars: see that ye be not troubled: for all *these things* **must come to pass, but the end is not yet.**
For nation shall rise against nation, and kingdom against kingdom: and there shall be famines, and pestilences, and earthquakes, in divers places.
All these *are* **the beginning of sorrows.**

Jesus told the people they were going to hear of wars and rumors of wars. People will see nations rise and fall. There will be famines and plagues and earthquakes. You are going to hear of these things too, but don't be deceived. These are only the beginning of sorrows. The end is not yet come.

Matthew 24:15- 21
When ye therefore shall see the abomination of desolation, spoken of by Daniel the prophet, stand in the holy place, (whoso readeth, let him understand:)
Then let them which be in Judaea flee into the mountains:
Let him which is on the housetop not come down to take any thing out of his house:
Neither let him which is in the field return back to take his clothes.
And woe unto them that are with child, and to them that give suck in those days!

> But pray ye that your flight be not in the winter, neither on the sabbath day:
> For then shall be great tribulation, such as was not since the beginning of the world to this time, no, nor ever shall be.

Jesus speaks of the abomination of desolation spoken of by Daniel. This abomination of desolation will be a man exalting himself as God, standing in the holy place and proclaiming himself to be God. This type of iniquity and deception has already been put to work preparing men for that very day.

Matthew 24:23- 31
> Then if any man shall say unto you, Lo, here *is* Christ, or there; believe *it* not.
> For as the lightning cometh out of the east, and shineth even unto the west; so shall also the coming of the Son of man be.
> For wheresoever the carcase is, there will the eagles be gathered together.
> Immediately after the tribulation of those days shall the sun be darkened, and the moon shall not give her light, and the stars shall fall from heaven, and the powers of the heavens shall be shaken:
> And then shall appear the sign of the Son of man in heaven: and then shall all the tribes of the earth mourn, and they shall see the Son of man coming in the clouds of heaven with power and great glory.
> And he shall send his angels with a great sound of a trumpet, and they shall gather together his elect from the four winds, from one end of heaven to the other.

When the day arrives that this abomination occurs, those who are here upon the earth will believe the lie and will be living under strong delusion. There will be many lying signs and wonders. When someone says, "Lo here is Christ, or there," don't believe it. Many will believe that this abomination is Christ, but if you happen to be on the earth at this time, know that this is not the Christ. The son of man shall come, and no one will mistake him when it happens. Before the son of man comes, there will be only carcasses remaining.

The eagle referred to here is a scavenger that feeds on carrion. Immediately after the tribulation of those days, the son of man shall appear, but who will be around to see it? The answer lies in the resurrection, for every man that ever lived will be around to see it. Then shall the angels gather together God's elect, who are Israel, from the four winds to a place that will be like the garden of Eden. When the son of man was here the first time, he told of these things. But when he spoke to a rebellious house, they did not see him as the son of God. He was perceived as one guilty of death.

Matthew 26:62- 66
And the high priest arose, and said unto him, Answerest thou nothing? what *is it which* these witness against thee?
But Jesus held his peace. And the high priest answered and said unto him, I adjure thee by the living God, that thou tell us whether thou be the Christ, the Son of God.
Jesus saith unto him, Thou hast said [you figure it out]: **nevertheless I say unto you, Hereafter shall ye see the Son of man sitting on the right hand of power, and coming in the clouds of heaven.**
Then the high priest rent his clothes, saying, He hath spoken blasphemy; what further need have we of witnesses? behold, now ye have heard his blasphemy.
What think ye? They answered and said, He is guilty of death.

When the high priest said he wanted to know if Jesus was the Christ, the son of God, his mind was already made up as to who he thought Jesus was. Jesus said, you figure it out. Everyone will figure it out sooner or later, because the son of man will fulfill all that God has said concerning him. He will be all that God has said he will be, and he will do all that God has said he will do. The son of man was never guilty of death. Even though he gave his life, he took it up again and is now sitting on the right hand of power, and he will be coming back. Today he has left for us the world in grace and by the grace of God we can see him for who he is. As the red thread in the book of Ezekiel, Jesus Christ is the son of man. Even though he came bearing that name, he is also the Son of God. It would be good to figure that out sooner rather than later.

The Messiah

In the book of Daniel, the red thread is found in the Messiah. Later the Messiah would also be known as the Christ, which is the interpretation of the name. In a vision, Daniel saw things leading up to the end. In these things we find the Messiah being cut off, and we find tribulation because of the abomination which will make all things desolate. We also see the son of man coming, being given dominion and glory, and a kingdom which shall not pass away.

Daniel 7:1
In the first year of Belshazzar king of Babylon Daniel had a dream and visions of his head upon his bed: then he wrote the dream, *and* told the sum of the matters.

What did Daniel see in his dream? He saw four beasts, and one of them was very different from the others, very dreadful and terrible. Daniel described three of the beasts, but the fourth beast was different and very troubling. Daniel watched until all these beasts were cast down, and the Ancient of days, who is the everlasting one, was set for the judgment.

Daniel 7:7-10
After this I saw in the night visions, and behold a fourth beast, dreadful and terrible, and strong exceedingly; and it had great iron teeth: it devoured and brake in pieces, and stamped the residue with the feet of it: and it *was* diverse from all the beasts that *were* before it; and it had ten horns.
I considered the horns, and, behold, there came up among them another little horn, before whom there were three of the first horns plucked up by the roots: and, behold, in this horn *were* eyes like the eyes of man, and a mouth speaking great things.
I beheld till the thrones were cast down, and the Ancient of days did sit, whose garment *was* white as snow, and the hair of his head like the pure wool: his throne *was like* the fiery flame, *and* his wheels *as* burning fire.
A fiery stream issued and came forth from before him: thousand thousands ministered unto him, and ten thousand times ten thousand stood before him: the judgment was set, and the books were opened.

Daniel saw this fourth beast reaping havoc on the residue or remainder of the inhabitants of the world. Daniel heard the beast speaking great things, so he watched the beast until it was destroyed by the burning flame. There is a time in the end reserved for the judgment, and in this time there will also be the resurrection. This will all come on the heels of this fourth beast, which shall devour the whole earth and stamp out the residue of its inhabitants with his feet. This beast is an abomination and will make all things desolate.

Daniel 7:11
I beheld then because of the voice of the great words which the horn spake: I beheld *even* till the beast was slain, and his body destroyed, and given to the burning flame.

This beast likes to blow his own horn. He speaks great words, swelling words, boastful words. His words are way out there. Even though the beast will be so far out there, people will listen to him. The words of the beast will prove to be a strong or powerful delusion.

Daniel 7:13, 14
I saw in the night visions, and, behold, *one* like the Son of man came with the clouds of heaven, and came to the Ancient of days, and they brought him near before him.
And there was given him dominion, and glory, and a kingdom, that all people, nations, and languages, should serve him: his dominion *is* an everlasting dominion, which shall not pass away, and his kingdom *that* which shall not be destroyed.

Daniel was grieved, and his visions troubled him. He saw one like the son of man come with the clouds of heaven and receive the dominion and glory and the kingdom that shall not pass away. But there was also the beast that spoke these great words and stamped the residue with his feet and made war with the saints and prevailed against them. Daniel wanted to know the truth of all this which he saw, so one that stood by told him the interpretation.

Daniel 7:17, 18
These great beasts, which are four, *are* four kings, *which* shall arise out of the earth.
But the saints of the most High shall take the kingdom, and possess the kingdom for ever, even for ever and ever.

It was told to Daniel that these great beasts are four; four kings shall rise out of the earth. The number four is the world's number. These kings will be worldly and do a great deal to destroy the earth, but the saints of the most High shall take the kingdom and possess it for ever. This was the long and short of it, but Daniel said, *wait a minute, what about that fourth beast?*

Daniel 7:19- 22
Then I would [wanted to know] **know the truth of the fourth beast, which was diverse from all the others, exceeding dreadful, whose teeth** *were of* **iron, and his nails** *of* **brass;** *which* **devoured, brake in pieces, and stamped the residue with his feet;**
And of the ten horns that *were* **in his head, and** *of* **the other which came up, and before whom three fell; even** *of* **that horn that had eyes, and a mouth that spake very great things, whose look** *was* **more stout than his fellows.**
I beheld, and the same horn made war with the saints, and prevailed against them;
Until the Ancient of days came, and judgment was given to the saints of the most High; and the time came that the saints possessed the kingdom.

This fourth beast was different. This beast devoured everything. Daniel saw him wage war against the saints, and he was winning. Nothing was left in his wake. This beast was stamping out the residue of the inhabitants of the earth.

Daniel 7:23- 27
Thus he said, The fourth beast shall be the fourth kingdom upon earth, which shall be diverse from all kingdoms, and shall devour the whole earth, and shall tread it down, and break it in pieces.
And the ten horns out of this kingdom *are* **ten kings** *that* **shall arise: and another shall rise after them; and he shall be diverse from the first, and he shall subdue three kings.**
And he shall speak *great* **words against the most High, and shall wear out the saints of the most High, and think to change times and laws: and they shall be given into his hand until a time and times and the dividing of time.**
But the judgment shall sit, and they shall take away his dominion, to consume and to destroy *it* **unto the end.**
And the kingdom and dominion, and the greatness of the

kingdom under the whole heaven, shall be given to the people of the saints of the most High, whose kingdom *is* an everlasting kingdom, and all dominions shall serve and obey him.

This was the end of the matter concerning the beast. Yet Daniel's cogitations still troubled him, so he kept the matter in his heart. Then three years later, Daniel had another vision where he saw a ram and a goat.

Daniel 8:9- 12
And out of one of them came forth a little horn, which waxed exceeding great, toward the south, and toward the east, and toward the pleasant *land*.
And it waxed great, *even* to the host of heaven; and it cast down *some* of the host and of the stars to the ground, and stamped upon them.
Yea, he magnified *himself* even to the prince [ruler] of the host, and by him the daily *sacrifice* was taken away, and the place of his sanctuary was cast down.
And an host was given *him* against the daily *sacrifice* by reason of transgression, and it cast down the truth to the ground; and it practiced, and prospered.

The little horn represents an individual in a position of power. This individual is going to magnify himself or compare himself to God. He is going to claim to be God, causing the sacrifice which God has instituted to be taken away. The sacrifice will no longer be available, and the sanctuary God has provided will be cast down. This will be allowed because the truth concerning the sacrifice will be cast aside. This perversion will be allowed to be practiced and to prosper, but only for a time. For this one claiming to be God will come to an end, and the sanctuary shall be cleansed. Daniel saw all of this, and again he sought to know the meaning of the things that he had seen in the vision. Then Gabriel came and helped Daniel to understand the vision.

Daniel 8:19
And he said, Behold, I will make thee know what shall be in the last end of the indignation: for at the time appointed the end *shall be.*

Daniel was looking at the time of the end, the time which we will come to call the end of the world. This is the time in the gospel of Matthew when the disciples came and asked Jesus about the end of the world. Jesus also mentions some of these visions from Daniel when he tells them of the end.

Daniel 8:23-27

And in the latter time of their kingdom, when the transgressors are come to the full, a king of fierce countenance, and understanding dark sentences, shall stand up.

And his power shall be mighty, but not by his own power: and he shall destroy wonderfully, and shall prosper, and practice, and shall destroy the mighty and the holy people.

And through his policy also he shall cause craft [deception] to prosper in his hand; and he shall magnify *himself* in his heart, and by peace shall destroy many: he shall also stand up against the Prince of princes; but he shall be broken without hand.

And the vision of the evening and the morning which was told *is* true: wherefore shut thou up the vision; for it *shall be* for many days.

And I Daniel fainted, and was sick *certain* days; afterward I rose up, and did the king's business; and I was astonished at the vision, but none understood *it*.

This individual of whom Daniel speaks will stand up against the prince of princes. He will be the antichrist. Christ is the Messiah, the prince, the one who God has chosen and anointed, but this individual will set himself against all that Christ is and has done. All this which Daniel saw astonished him and made him sick just at the thought. After this Daniel was praying and lamenting over all the sins and transgressions of his people, Israel. He was considering the state they were now in when again Gabriel showed up and had a little talk with Daniel.

Daniel 9:24

Seventy weeks [sevens] are determined upon thy people and upon thy holy city, to finish the transgression, and to make an end of sins, and to make reconciliation for iniquity, and to bring in everlasting righteousness, and to seal up the vision and prophecy, and to anoint the most Holy.

"Seventy weeks" should literally be translated "seventy sevens." This term "seventy sevens" does not mean the days of the week, but rather refers to the significance of the biblical meaning of numbers found in the scriptures.

When Jesus was teaching Peter the importance of forgiveness, Peter asked how many times he was to forgive an individual. Peter queried, *seven times?* Jesus answered and said, *seventy times seven.* Jesus told him to forgive until the perfect end or the perfect outcome could be obtained. Gabriel showed Daniel that God's plan had to wait until the perfect time and the perfect outcome can be obtained. Then Gabriel showed Daniel something else. This is where the red thread is truly unveiled in the book of Daniel, and what a prophecy it is.

Daniel 9:25- 27
Know therefore and understand, *that* **from the going forth of the commandment to restore and to build Jerusalem unto the Messiah the Prince** *shall be* **seven weeks [sevens], and threescore and two weeks [sevens]: the street shall be built again, and the wall, even in troublous times.**

And after threescore and two weeks [sevens] shall Messiah be cut off, but not for himself: and the people of the prince that shall come shall destroy the city and the sanctuary; and the end thereof *shall be* **with a flood, and unto the end of the war desolations are determined.**

And he shall confirm the covenant with many for one week [seven]: and in the midst of the week [seven] he shall cause the sacrifice and the oblation to cease, and for the overspreading of abominations he shall make *it* **desolate, even until the consummation, and that determined shall be poured upon the desolate.**

Looking back, we can perhaps now figure out some of this prophesy, because part of it has been fulfilled. The Messiah has come, and he gave his life upon the tree. He was cut off; his life was ended, but he didn't do it for himself. He did it for you and me. In Daniel's time, it had been twenty-one years since Israel had gone into captivity. It would be another forty-nine years before all those who wanted to return to Jerusalem would all be allowed to go back. The time of Ezra and Nehemiah had not even happened at this point, the time when the captives of Israel were allowed to go and begin rebuilding the walls and the city. The prophecy stated that from the time the commandment which would allow Jerusalem to be restored was issued, there would be these seven sevens and sixty two sevens unto the Messiah. Figuring these numbers as representing years, they define a specific amount of time. This amount of time works out to be accurate in figuring when the Messiah came. It is only looking back that we can now define these numbers as years. Before the time of Daniel, Jeremiah prophesied of the seventy years of Israel's captivity. He told that it would take seventy years before those who wanted to were allowed to move back to Jerusalem. This was when the commandment went forth. It proved to be another four hundred and thirty four years until the Messiah came and more specifically until he was cut off.

We have seen prophesies of the Messiah in Daniel. He is the primary focus of our study dealing with the red thread, but there is another element running throughout the prophecy of Daniel. This opposing element has to do with the one who stands in opposition to the Messiah. The one who will do much harm and destruction to the residue of the people in the end.

Daniel 10:14
Now I am come to make thee understand what shall befall thy people in the latter days: for yet the vision *is* for *many* days [for days untold].

Gabriel again told Daniel what was going to happen to Israel in this time of the end. He talks of certain kings and kingdoms rising up in these last times. He relays that the one who will cause the most harm will rise out of obscurity, a little horn yet speaking great things. He will arrive not by merit or morals. He won't come with high standards or goodness, but by smooth talking, by cajolery, by sycophancy. This is how he will take the place of the one who came before him.

Daniel 11:21, 22
And in his estate [the one who was before him] **shall stand up a vile person, to whom they shall not give the honour of the kingdom: but he shall come in peaceably, and obtain the kingdom by flatteries.**
And with the arms of a flood shall they be overflown from before him, and shall be broken; yea, also the prince of the covenant.

"With the arms of a flood," with the strength of the flood of his flatteries. His smooth talking will overwhelm them like a flood. Everyone will be swept up by his deceit and swept away by this strong delusion. The truth of the prince of the covenant will also be swept away from the eyes of the world, and they will only be left with a lie.

Daniel 11:31- 33
And arms [the powers that be] **shall stand on his part, and they shall pollute the sanctuary of strength, and shall take away the daily *sacrifice*, and they shall place the abomination that maketh desolate.**
And such as do [such as want to do or are willing to do] **wickedly against the covenant shall he corrupt by flatteries: but the people that**

do know their God shall be strong, and do *exploits*.
And they that understand among the people shall instruct many: yet they shall fall by the sword, and by flame, by captivity, and by spoil, *many* days.

The deception will be so great that you will not find many who will know God, but there will be a few who figure it out. The few who do figure it out will do what is required of them to be saved, knowing it will mean the end of them in this life. The abomination that maketh desolate is this one that will come in by flatteries, this vile person that will come in on the arms of a flood. The strong arm of the law will be behind him. They will pollute; they will water down the strength of the sanctuary and take away the daily sacrifice. With the sacrifice gone, people will languish under the hand of the one magnifying himself above God.

Daniel 11:35, 36
And *some* [some is in italics it must be removed] **of them of understanding shall fall** [by the means stated in the previous verse], **to try them, and to purge, and to make *them* white, *even* to the time of the end: because *it is* yet for a time appointed.**
And the king shall do according to his will; and he shall exalt himself, and magnify himself above every god, and shall speak marvellous things against the God of gods, and shall prosper till the indignation be accomplished: for that that is determined shall be done.

There will be no mistaking this time when it happens, for this man will exalt himself and lay claim that he is God. He is the abomination that maketh desolate.

Daniel 12:1- 4
And at that time shall Michael stand up, the great prince which standeth for the children of thy people: and there shall be a time of trouble, such as never was since there was a nation *even* to that same time: and at that time thy people shall be delivered, every one that shall be found written in the book.
And many of them that sleep in the dust of the earth shall awake, some to everlasting life, and some to shame *and* everlasting contempt.
And they that be wise shall shine as the brightness of the firmament; and they that turn many to righteousness as the stars for ever and ever.
But thou, O Daniel, shut up the words, and seal the book, *even* to

the time of the end: many shall run to and fro, and knowledge shall be increased.**

Daniel spoke of the end times. Looking ahead from his day, he was not allowed to see all that lay ahead. Certain things were sealed, and some things remain sealed even today. This time of trouble Daniel spoke of is yet to come. The resurrection for Israel has not arrived yet. In the day it happens all will be clear and the prophecy will be proven. With the coming of the Messiah more has been revealed concerning the end, yet much of the timing still remains unknown. In the end many will be running every which way looking for the truth, and knowledge will increase. Few will actually see what is taking place around them, because the deception will be so great. We can be thankful, because today when it comes to the red thread, we can know it. Even the prophecy that has been fulfilled and the Word of God that attests to the truth of it can be known. There are deceivers in the world today, but the Word of God still stands and the integrity of the Word still speaks to those of us who have ears to hear and a desire to know the truth.

John 1:40- 42a
One of the two which heard John *speak*, and followed him, was Andrew, Simon Peter's brother.
He first findeth his own brother Simon, and saith unto him, We have found the Messias, which is, being interpreted, the Christ. And he brought him to Jesus.

Jesus is the Christ, which is by interpretation the Messiah. Daniel prophesied of this man. This is the truth: Jesus is the Christ, the Messiah. Jesus also spoke of the abomination of desolation. When Jesus spoke of the end time, he referred to the prophecy in Daniel.

Matthew 24:15, 16, 21
When ye therefore shall see the abomination of desolation, spoken of by Daniel the prophet, stand in the holy place, (whoso readeth, let him understand:)
Then let them which be in Judaea flee into the mountains:
For then shall be great tribulation, such as was not since the beginning of the world to this time, no, nor ever shall be.

Even today in our time, we can understand what Daniel spoke of and see the truth of what is to come. We can see that Jesus is the Christ and that there are those who work against the Messiah to prepare the world to receive this abomination which is to come.

I John 2:18, 22
Little children, it is the last time: and as ye have heard that antichrist shall come, even now are there many antichrists; whereby we know that it is the last time.
Who is a liar but he that denieth that Jesus is the Christ? He is antichrist, that denieth the Father and the Son.

It is the last time, the time before the end time. The antichrist shall come. The one who is against Christ. He is the antithesis of the Christ. The many antichrists John refers to are those who are against Christ, because they deny that Jesus is the Christ. The many who are against Christ deny who the Father is and who the son is.

II John 1:7
For many deceivers are entered into the world, who confess not that Jesus Christ is come in the flesh. This is a deceiver and an antichrist.

Many deceivers are in the world today who try to deny that Jesus came in the flesh. They try to make him out to be something more than the man that he was or that he is something other than the son of God. There is a spirit at work today setting the stage for the deception that is to follow. The deception that places a man on the throne claiming that he is God. People will believe a man to be God, because they have already been brought up believing that Jesus is somehow or other God in the flesh. This is a lie that has been perpetrated and propounded in the Christian church for many years. But we as Christians can still see through this lie today and know Christ for who he really is. When this day is done and those that are Christ's are gathered together unto him, the son of perdition shall be revealed. This word perdition means complete and irreparable ruin. Christ offers us a way to salvation, but if we reject the truth of who he is and what he has done, we seal our own perdition. When we are gone and the man of sin is revealed, the delusion which remains will be so strong people will gladly believe a lie.

II Thessalonians 2:1-8
Now we beseech you, brethren, by the coming of our Lord Jesus Christ, and *by* our gathering together unto him,
That ye be not soon shaken in mind, or be troubled, neither by spirit, nor by word, nor by letter as from us, as that the day of Christ is

at hand.

Let no man deceive you by any means: for *that day shall not come*, **except there come a falling away** [a departure] **first, and that man of sin be revealed, the son of perdition;**

Who opposeth and exalteth himself above all that is called God, or that is worshipped; so that he as God sitteth in the temple of God, showing himself that he is God.

Remember ye not, that, when I was yet with you, I told you these things?

And now ye know what withholdeth that he might be revealed in his time.

For the mystery of iniquity doth already work: only he who now letteth *will let*, **until he be taken out of the way.**

And then shall that Wicked be revealed, whom the Lord shall consume with the spirit of his mouth, and shall destroy with the brightness of his coming.

Christ is the Messiah, the son of God, the son of man, the one whom God anointed to be man's salvation. This Jesus Christ is the red thread all the way through the Word of God. There will be those that deny Christ. This is no secret. The day of Christ is at hand, yet the time of the end will remain shut up until we are gone. Believe what you will, but in the end, it can be just the end for you, or simply the beginning.

The Red Thread of Daniel

The Head

Have you ever lost your head? The children of Israel did. They rejected God's rule over them, and God made Saul the head of the tribes of Israel. God told them from the very start that Saul would not prove to be the best man for the job. The children of Israel continued to move away from God and eventually split into two nations: the nation of Israel and the nation of Judah. God's mercy continued to be extended to them, but they continued to reject God and His mercy and His salvation. In the book of Hosea, God speaks of the one head who shall come, and all the children of Israel and the children of Judah shall be gathered together under this one head. As the red thread, Jesus Christ will prove to be the head of the prophesy in the book of Hosea. Israel and Judah will once again have extended to them the mercy and salvation that they had spurned.

Hosea 1:11
Then shall the children of Judah and the children of Israel be gathered together, and appoint themselves one head, and they shall come up out of the land: for great *shall be* the day of Jezreel.

The children of Israel and the children of Judah shall be gathered together, and one head shall be appointed over them. This is the testimony of Hosea in the prophecy of the word of the Lord which was given to him.

Hosea 1:2- 4
The beginning of the word of the LORD by Hosea. And the LORD said to Hosea, Go, take unto thee a wife of whoredoms and children of whoredoms: for the land hath committed great whoredom, *departing* from the LORD.
So he went and took Gomer the daughter of Diblaim; which conceived, and bare him a son.
And the LORD said unto him, Call his name Jezreel.

God told Hosea to take a wife of whoredoms, one who did not believe in God, one who had been led away to love other gods. So Hosea took Gomer as his wife. The meaning of her name is 'heat,' and she was full of sexual passion. Gomer was the daughter of Diblaim, and her name carries the meaning of 'a double cake of figs,' which is symbolic of sensual pleasure. Diblaim was really into the pleasure of the senses. Now, when

Hosea and Gomer had a son, they named him Jezreel, which has two meanings. The first meaning is 'may God scatter,' and the second is 'may God sow.' Israel shall be scattered to the four winds, but the promise has always been that Israel shall be sown in the promised land again.

Hosea 1:6
And she conceived again, and bare a daughter. And *God* said unto him, Call her name Lo-ruhamah: for I will no more have mercy upon the house of Israel; but I will utterly take them away.

The name Lo-ruhamah means 'no mercy.' The name is also rendered as 'not beloved' and 'not having obtained mercy,' but the idea is clear. God said: *I will no more have mercy upon the house of Israel*. The Old Testament is defined by mercy, just as the Church Epistles are defined by grace and the future administration yet to come will be defined by glory. Even though God's mercy was withheld from Israel for awhile and Israel was scattered, God's mercy will yet again be extended to the children of Israel.

Hosea 1:8-11
Now when she had weaned Lo-ruhamah, she conceived, and bare a son.
Then said *God*, Call his name Lo-ammi: for ye *are* not my people, and I will not be your *God*.
Yet the number of the children of Israel shall be as the sand of the sea, which cannot be measured nor numbered; and it shall come to pass, *that* in the place where it was said unto them, Ye *are* not my people, *there* it shall be said unto them, *Ye are* the sons of the living God.
Then shall the children of Judah and the children of Israel be gathered together, and appoint themselves one head, and they shall come up out of the land: for great *shall be* the day of Jezreel.

Gomer bore another child and called him Lo-ammi, which means 'not my people.' It is clear that the children of Israel turned away from God and were no longer God's people. They had gone off and sought out other gods, thereby committing whoredoms. Yet the number of the children of Israel shall be as the sand of the sea. It shall come to pass that it shall be said of Israel, "Ye are now the sons of the living God." God had always said that He would not withhold His mercy forever.

Hosea 2:1
Say ye unto your brethren, **Ammi** [My people]; and to your sisters, **Ruhamah** [mercy].

Moving into our day and looking for the fulfillment of the red thread in the book of Hosea, we see Jesus Christ is the head of the church. The church is comprised of Jews and Gentiles. We are sons of God not by joining the children of Israel, nor are the Jews sons by joining the Gentiles. Both Jews and Gentiles are one in Christ and form a new body, the body of Christ.

Romans 9:24- 26
Even us, whom he hath called, not of the Jews only, but also of the Gentiles.
As he saith also in Osee [Hosea]**, I will call them my people, which were not my people; and her beloved, which was not beloved.**
And it shall come to pass, *that* **in the place where it was said unto them, Ye** *are* **not my people; there shall they be called the children of the living God.**

God's plan is that in the administration of the fullness of time[3], He might gather all things together in Christ, and it starts here and now in the body of Christ. Christ is set to be the head over all things in the church.

Ephesians 1:10 and 20- 23
That in the dispensation of the fulness of times he might gather together in one all things in Christ, both which are in heaven, and which are on earth; *even* **in him:**
Which he [God] **wrought** [worked] **in Christ, when he raised him from the dead, and set** *him* **at his own right hand in the heavenly** *places*,
Far above all principality, and power, and might, and dominion, and every name that is named, not only in this world, but also in that which is to come:
And hath put all *things* **under his feet, and gave him** *to be* **the head over all** *things* **to the church,**
Which is his body, the fulness of him that filleth all in all.

---

[3] There are periods of time defined in the Bible. The word *dispensation* is used in the church epistles but the word *administration* would better define the Greek word *oikonomia*, meaning the administration of a house or period. The age or administration that we live in today is identified as the grace administration. There are future ages yet to come in which we will see all things gathered together in Christ.

God did a beautiful work when He raised Christ from the dead. He made him to be the head over all the church. Today it is the church of the body, and we are complete in him.

Colossians 1:19, 2:9, 10 and 3:4
For it pleased *the Father* that in him [Christ] **should all fulness dwell;**
For in him dwelleth all the fulness of the Godhead bodily.
And ye are complete in him, which is the head of all principality and power:
When Christ, *who is* our life, shall appear, then shall ye also appear with him in glory.

Today we have the promise of glory already being in the body of Christ. He is already our head. The children of Israel who lived before Christ also have a promise made to them in the makeup of the church. But the promise is through marriage, not through birth.

Matthew 16:18
And I say also unto thee, That thou art Peter [*petros,* a tiny grain of sand]**, and upon this rock** [*petra,* an immovable object] **I will build my church; and the gates of hell shall not prevail against it.**

Jesus said that he would build his church upon this rock, referring to himself. "I will build my church." Jesus said this to Israel in the Gospels. Israel still has this promise awaiting them.

Hebrews 11:13, 39 and 40
These all [all the Old Testament believers listed here] **died in faith** [believing]**, not having received the promises, but having seen them afar off, and were persuaded of *them*, and embraced *them*, and confessed that they were strangers and pilgrims on the earth.**
And these all, having obtained a good report through faith [believing]**, received not the promise:**
God having provided some better thing for us, that they without us should not be made perfect.

Christ is the head of the church's body now, but the promise to Israel shall be fulfilled in marriage when the church of the bride is joined to the church of the body.

Revelation 19:6- 9
And I heard as it were the voice of a great multitude, and as the voice of many waters, and as the voice of mighty thunderings, saying, Alleluia: for the Lord God omnipotent reigneth.
Let us be glad and rejoice, and give honour to him: for the marriage of the Lamb is come, and his wife hath made herself ready.
And to her was granted that she should be arrayed in fine linen, clean and white: for the fine linen is the righteousness of saints.
And he saith unto me, Write, Blessed *are* they which are called unto the marriage supper of the Lamb. And he saith unto me, These are the true sayings of God.

The book of Revelation speaks of a marriage which is yet to come, a marriage of the Lamb and his wife. It goes on to tell who the wife will be and where the marriage will take place.

Revelation 21:9- 12
And there came unto me one of the seven angels which had the seven vials full of the seven last plagues, and talked with me, saying, Come hither, I will show thee the bride, the Lamb's wife.
And he carried me away in the spirit to a great and high mountain, and showed me that great city, the holy Jerusalem, descending out of heaven from God, having the glory of God:
And her light *was* like unto a stone most precious, even like a jasper stone, clear as crystal;
And had a wall great and high, *and* had twelve gates, and at the gates twelve angels, and names written thereon, which are *the names* of the twelve tribes of the children of Israel.

God shows us the bride who is the Lamb's wife. The bride is made up of the twelve tribes of the children of Israel. So it is that the bride is always connected with Israel. We will also see the Lamb connected with Jesus Christ.

John 1:29
The next day John seeth Jesus coming unto him, and saith, Behold the Lamb of God, which taketh away the sin of the world.

When John saw Jesus coming, he said, "Behold the Lamb of God which taketh away the sin of the world." Jesus Christ is the Lamb; and as the bridegroom, he is able to take away the sin that so plagued Israel. The law which governs marriage states that when two are joined together, they become one flesh. This is how the bride of Israel receives her salvation. All those who make up the church of the bride will rejoice greatly when they hear the voice of the bridegroom.

John 3:27- 29
John answered and said, A man can receive nothing, except it be given him from heaven.
Ye yourselves bear me witness, that I said, I am not the Christ, but that I am sent before him.
He that hath the bride is the bridegroom: but the friend of the bridegroom, which standeth and heareth him, rejoiceth greatly because of the bridegroom's voice: this my joy therefore is fulfilled.

John the Baptist openly admitted that he was not the Christ. John stated, "He that hath the bride is the bridegroom." John was only the friend of the bridegroom. He rejoiced greatly, because the bridegroom was now here. In Hosea we find a marriage of which was prophesied between Israel and her true Lord.

Hosea 2:2
Plead with your mother [speaking of Israel]**, plead: for she *is* not my wife, neither *am* I her husband: let her therefore put away her whoredoms out of her sight, and her adulteries from between her breasts.**

God said this concerning Israel: She was not His wife and even though she was spoken for, she went off and pursued others.

Hosea 2:5
For their mother hath played the harlot: she that conceived them hath done shamefully: for she said, I will go after my lovers, that give *me* my bread and my water, my wool and my flax, mine oil and my drink.

She didn't know what she had until it was gone. Many of us do the same thing. At times, the grass is greener on the other side of the fence. God, in His infinite mercy, was willing to take her back even after she treated Him so poorly.

Hosea 2:14-17
Therefore, behold, I will allure her, and bring her into the wilderness, and speak comfortably unto her.

And I will give her her vineyards from thence, and the valley of Achor [trouble] **for a door of hope: and she shall sing there, as in the days of her youth, and as in the day when she came up out of the land of Egypt.**

And it shall be at that day [referring to the Lord's day], **saith the LORD,** *that* **thou shalt call me Ishi** [my husband]**; and shalt call me no more Baali** [my lord]**.**

For I will take away the names of Baalim [many lords] **out of her mouth, and they shall no more be remembered by their name.**

Israel is going to meet her Lord, and she is going to get to know him as her husband. Israel will also be reunited with God, being betrothed in righteousness and Judgment.

Hosea 2:19, 20, 23
And I will betroth thee unto me for ever; yea, I will betroth thee unto me in righteousness, and in judgment, and in loving kindness, and in mercies.

I will even betroth thee unto me in faithfulness: and thou shalt know the LORD.

And I will sow her unto me in the earth; and I will have mercy upon her that had not obtained mercy; and I will say to *them which were* **not my people, Thou** *art* **my people; and they shall say,** *Thou art* **my God.**

Christ is the head now, and he will be the head of the children of Israel and of the children of Judah as prophesied in the book of Hosea. Christ will be the head over Israel and will bring God's people back to Him. God will sow her, Israel, in the earth, and they will obtain mercy. They which were not My people shall be My people, and they shall say, "Thou art my God." This is how Christ is woven in as the red thread in the book of Hosea. The children of Israel and Judah will be made one flesh in marriage to the Lamb of God, which taketh away the sin of the world. They will then be a part of his body, the fullness of him that filleth all in all.

The Red Thread of Hosea

The Vine

In the book of Joel God said, "My vine is laid waste." Who would lay waste to God's vine, because in the book of Joel, the red thread is the vine.

Joel 1:1-4
The word of the LORD that came to Joel the son of Pethuel.
Hear this, ye old men, and give ear, all ye inhabitants of the land. Hath this been in your days, or even in the days of your fathers?
Tell ye your children of it, and *let* your children *tell* their children, and their children another generation.
That which the palmerworm hath left hath the locust eaten; and that which the locust hath left hath the cankerworm eaten; and that which the cankerworm hath left hath the caterpillar eaten.

Something is definitely wrong here. Things have gotten way out of balance. The destruction described by these insects amount to small things left unchecked which in turn causes great devastation.

Joel 1:6, 7
For a nation is come up upon my land, strong, and without number, whose teeth *are* the teeth of a lion, and he hath the cheek teeth of a great lion.
He [the one referred to as a great lion] **hath laid my vine waste, and barked my fig tree: he hath made it clean bare, and cast *it* away; the branches thereof are made white.**

There is one here referred to as a great lion, and God said, "He hath laid My vine waste, and barked My fig tree." There is another place in the Word where one is referred to as a lion, looking for those whom he may devour.

I Peter 5:8
Be sober, be vigilant; because your adversary the devil, as a roaring lion, walketh about, seeking whom he may devour.

In the book of Joel, the great lion is also the devil, looking to destroy God's vine and God's fig tree. God's vine is Jesus Christ, and God's fig tree refers to God's people, Israel. There is another place in the Bible which will give us some additional information regarding this matter and how such a thing could happen.

Jeremiah 2:12, 13
Be astonished, O ye heavens, at this, and be horribly afraid, be ye very desolate, saith the LORD.
For my people have committed two evils; they have forsaken me the fountain of living waters, *and* **hewed them out cisterns, broken cisterns, that can hold no water.**

Jeremiah says, "My people," for God is talking about His people, Israel. They have committed two evils. They have forsaken God, who is likened here to a fountain which is ever issuing forth with an unending supply. And they have hewed them out their own broken cisterns. A cistern, on the other hand, is a container that has a limited supply. This shows God's abundance and resource as opposed to the inability of men to provide for themselves. These cisterns of men were broken as well. When they put in the water, it would run out a crack and leave it empty at just the time they needed it. Without God's supply, men are most vulnerable. The devil is always looking for someone to devour, and who better than God's people?

Jeremiah 2:20, 21
For of old time I [God] have broken thy yoke, *and* **burst thy bands; and thou saidst, I will not transgress; when upon every high hill and under every green tree thou wanderest, playing the harlot.**
Yet I had planted thee a noble vine, wholly a right seed: how then art thou turned into the degenerate plant of a strange vine unto me?

Even from the time of Israel's beginning, God broke the yoke and the bands which bond them. He planted a noble vine, a wholly right seed, yet they wandered from what God had planted and turned into a degenerate plant of a strange vine.

Jeremiah 2:31, 32
O generation, see ye the word of the LORD. Have I been a wilderness unto Israel? a land of darkness? wherefore say my people, We are lords; we will come no more unto thee?
Can a maid forget her ornaments, *or* **a bride her attire? yet my people have forgotten me days without number.**

God was never a wilderness to Israel. He never left them in the dark, yet they wanted to be their own lords. They no longer sought out God.

Isaiah 5:1-4
Now will I sing to my wellbeloved a song of my beloved touching his vineyard. My wellbeloved hath a vineyard in a very fruitful hill:

And he fenced it, and gathered out the stones thereof, and planted it with the choicest vine, and built a tower in the midst of it, and also made a winepress therein: and he looked that it should bring forth grapes, and it brought forth wild grapes.

And now, O inhabitants of Jerusalem, and men of Judah, judge, I pray you, betwixt me and my vineyard.

What could have been done more to my vineyard, that I have not done in it? wherefore, when I looked that it should bring forth grapes, brought it forth wild grapes?

God planted the choicest vine you will ever find in His vineyard. Yet when He saw the wild sour grapes that His vineyard brought forth, He wondered what more He could have done. He asked those inhabitants of Jerusalem, those who were the sour grapes, what more could He have done? Now we are going to meet that choice vine, that noble vine, that wholly right seed. You tell me if there is anything more that God could have done.

John 15:1-7
I am the true vine, and my Father is the husbandman.

Every branch in me that beareth not fruit he taketh away: and every *branch* that beareth fruit, he purgeth it, that it may bring forth more fruit.

Now ye are clean through the word which I have spoken unto you.

Abide in me, and I in you. As the branch cannot bear fruit of itself, except it abide in the vine; no more can ye, except ye abide in me.

I am the vine, ye *are* the branches: He that abideth in me, and I in him, the same bringeth forth much fruit: for without me ye can do nothing.

If a man abide not in me, he is cast forth as a branch, and is withered; and men gather them, and cast *them* into the fire, and they are burned.

If ye abide in me, and my words abide in you, ye shall ask what ye will, and it shall be done unto you.

Jesus said, "I am the vine." He is the true vine. Jesus Christ is the vine that the devil wanted to lay to waste in the book of Joel. Without Jesus Christ we could do nothing. We need to abide in him and he in us. The devil has always wanted to get rid of Jesus Christ, so when he was given a chance he jumped on it. This is why the prophet Joel said, *Lament like a virgin who lost the husband of her youth.*

Joel 1:8
Lament like a virgin girded with sackcloth for the husband of her youth.

The virgin's husband was taken from her before they came together in marriage. Jesus Christ was also taken before Israel joined him in marriage. Therefore, when Joel speaks of the day of the Lord, he said, "Alas for the day!"

Joel 1:15
Alas for the day! for the day of the LORD *is* at hand, and as a destruction from the Almighty shall it come.

When the Lord comes back, it is going to be as a destruction from the Almighty. All those who had a hand in laying God's vine to waste are going to answer for what they did.

Joel 2:1- 3
Blow ye the trumpet in Zion, and sound an alarm in my holy mountain: let all the inhabitants of the land tremble: for the day of the LORD cometh, for *it is* nigh at hand;
A day of darkness and of gloominess, a day of clouds and of thick darkness, as the morning spread upon the mountains: a great people and a strong; there hath not been ever the like, neither shall be any more after it, *even* to the years of many generations.
A fire devoureth before them; and behind them a flame burneth: the land *is* as the garden of Eden before them, and behind them a desolate wilderness; yea, and nothing shall escape them.

When the day of the Lord comes, he will come with a great people. Those of us who are in Christ are part of this army. There will be a flame which devours, and it will clean things up. Before we see the land once again restored like the garden of Eden, it will be a desolate wilderness.

Joel 2:10, 11
The earth shall quake before them; the heavens shall tremble: the sun and the moon shall be dark, and the stars shall withdraw their shining:
And the LORD shall utter his voice before his army: for his camp *is* very great: for *he is* strong that executeth his [God's] word: for the day of the LORD *is* great and very terrible; and who can abide it?

Do you really want to be a part of laying waste to My vine? God asks the question, because the day of the Lord is going to be great and very terrible; who can abide it? You can be sure of this: the Lord will win, and in the end he will restore what was devoured.

Joel 2:25- 27
And I will restore to you the years that the locust hath eaten, the cankerworm, and the caterpillar, and the palmerworm, my great army which I sent among you [will restore].
And ye shall eat in plenty, and be satisfied, and praise the name of the LORD your God, that hath dealt wondrously with you: and my people shall never be ashamed.
And ye shall know that I *am* in the midst of Israel, and *that* I *am* the LORD your God, and none else: and my people shall never be ashamed.

All of God's people have a promise made unto them so that they need never be disappointed in their expectations. The Lord will be the hope of all His people and the strength of the children of Israel. God has always desired to restore Israel to her former glory, although it is evident the children of Israel had gotten to the point of rejecting all God had done for them. Even today, they are rejecting what God is doing. When it comes to Jesus Christ, just how many realize and accept that he is the Lord? Despite all of this, in the end not one of God's people will ever be ashamed of their believing in Jesus Christ the Lord.

Joel 3:16
The LORD also shall roar out of Zion, and utter his voice from Jerusalem; and the heavens and the earth shall shake: but the LORD *will be* the hope of his people, and the strength of the children of Israel.

Joel also speaks of something taking place in the last days which affects us today. Peter made reference to it on the day of Pentecost. God has made holy spirit available to all of us, if we are willing to abide in the vine. To abide in Christ begins with us today along with the promise to Israel, which is yet to come. Your sons and your daughters shall be inspired to prophesy, because they will have the spirit. God will once again be able to freely communicate with them. Your young men shall be able to perceive and see things like they never could before, amazing things which God will show them. Your old men shall dream dreams; they will begin to see the vast possibilities we have in Christ, the vast potential that the body of Christ holds for all of us.

Acts 2:16- 21

But this is that which was spoken by the prophet Joel;

And it shall come to pass in the last days, saith God, I will pour out of my Spirit upon all flesh: and your sons and your daughters shall prophesy, and your young men shall see visions, and your old men shall dream dreams:

And on my servants and on my handmaidens I will pour out in those days of my Spirit; and they shall prophesy:

And I will show wonders in heaven above, and signs in the earth beneath; blood, and fire, and vapour of smoke:

The sun shall be turned into darkness, and the moon into blood, before that great and notable day of the Lord come:

And it shall come to pass, *that* **whosoever shall call on the name of the Lord shall be saved.**

Whosoever shall call on the name of the Lord shall be saved. We will never be ashamed nor disappointed in our expectations when we believe in the Lord Jesus. If we abide in him, we can ask what we will, and it shall be done. When we get to the point of believing what is written in Romans chapter ten, we will not be disappointed. Salvation is ours, and we begin to abide in him and he in us.

Romans 10:8- 13

But what saith it? The word is nigh thee, *even* **in thy mouth, and in thy heart: that is, the word of faith** [believing], **which we preach;**

That if thou shalt confess with thy mouth the Lord Jesus, and shalt believe in thine heart that God hath raised him from the dead, thou shalt be saved.

For with the heart man believeth unto righteousness; and with the mouth confession is made unto salvation.

For the scripture saith, Whosoever believeth on him shall not be ashamed.

For there is no difference between the Jew and the Greek: for the same Lord over all is rich unto all that call upon him.

For whosoever shall call upon the name of the Lord shall be saved.

We can put things back in balance in our lives and not prove to be sour grapes or those who would lay waste to God's vine. For it is written, "whosoever believeth on him shall not be ashamed." We can bear fruit by abiding in the vine. Our lives will be fruitful. The palmer worm need not strip us bare. We do not have to be swarmed by the locust and live in the wake of their destruction. We need not stand helpless while the canker worm sucks the life out of us, nor are we destined to be consumed by the caterpillar, that worm-like larva whose sole purpose is to eat you out of house and home. God said: *My vine is a choice vine; it is a noble vine.* We are of a whole right seed, and we abide in the true vine Jesus Christ. The day of the Lord is coming, but to what end is it going to be for you? God has promised so much and provided a vine in which we can flourish. Are we willing to believe in him or not? We all have a decision to make. Let us make it wisely.

Joel 3:13, 14
Put ye in the sickle, for the harvest is ripe: come, get you down; for the press is full, the vats overflow; for their wickedness *is* great.

Multitudes, multitudes in the valley of decision: for the day of the LORD *is* near in the valley of decision.

In the book of Joel, the red thread is the vine. God said that the one who is referred to as a lion has laid waste to My vine. We have come to know God's vine. For those of us who are willing to believe, he is the true vine. If we abide in him, he will abide in us, and we shall produce fruit. Otherwise, we will wither and become white and end up cast into the fire. The decision is always ours.

The Red Thread of Joel

The Lord of Glory

In the book of Amos, God again turns to the stars in defining the red thread. Amos was a herdsman and spent many starry nights under the heavens with his sheep. He knew of the houses of heaven which were entrusted to the children of Israel. Amos knew of the witness of the stars. God turns our attention to the house of Joseph, and more specifically to the constellation of Orion. Orion is the glorious one, the one coming as light, the coming prince, the Lord of glory. This Lord of glory is coming in judgment, and he is coming triumphant. In his left hand is the head of the roaring lion and his left foot is over the constellation Lepus, which means 'the confounded and failing.' Amos wrote, "Seek the Lord and ye shall live; lest he break out like fire in the house of Joseph and devour it." Amos looks to this sign of Taurus to see what it is made of and what we can learn from this witness of the stars. This is our study of the red thread in the book of Amos. Israel was told to return to the Lord. Israel needed to prepare to meet God, because at this point they had moved far away from the truth of what was promised to them. Even for those who desired the day of the Lord, this time when Christ would come would prove to be a day of darkness and not light on their present course.

Amos 5:1, 2
Hear ye this word which I take up against you, *even* **a lamentation, O house of Israel.**
The virgin of Israel is fallen; she shall no more rise: she is forsaken upon her land; *there is* **none to raise her up.**

When speaking of the witness of the stars, the virgin can be none other than Virgo, the one who would bear the promised seed. Amos takes up a lamentation against the house or the whole family of the sons of Israel. Amos said the virgin is fallen and there is no helping her up. No one cares anymore what she is witness to. The virgin is forsaken upon the land. Her witness is still true, but no one cares to raise her up anymore.

Amos 5:4, 6
For thus saith the LORD unto the house of Israel, Seek ye me, and ye shall live:
Seek the LORD, and ye shall live; lest he break out like fire in

the house of Joseph, and devour *it,* **and** *there be* **none to quench** *it* **in Bethel.**

"Seek the Lord and ye shall live; lest [unless] he break out like a fire in the house of Joseph and devour *it.*" The house of Joseph was given the sign of Taurus for its keeping, and within the sign of Taurus is a constellation called Eridanus. This constellation is known as the river of the judge. It flows forth from before the glorious Orion and is associated with fire. It is a river of fire, not of water. The river goes forth in judgment and fire. Fire is a cleaning agent just as water is, but water carries away the filth whereas fire devours it. Fire burns it up so that it is no more.

Amos 5:7, 8
Ye who turn judgment to wormwood, and leave off righteousness in the earth,
***Seek him* that maketh the seven stars and Orion, and turneth the shadow of death into the morning, and maketh the day dark with night: that calleth for the waters of the sea, and poureth them out upon the face of the earth: The LORD** *is* **his name.**

"Ye who turn judgment into wormwood." This speaks of those who have become bitter toward God and His judgment. They have turned the time of judgment into a bitter, unpleasant, and mortifying experience for themselves. Being bitter toward God, they left off looking for the Lord of righteousness and went about establishing their own righteousness. No longer seeing what makes up the seven stars and Orion, they lost sight of judgment. They no longer see him who will turn the shadow of death into the morning, and the day of the Lord will now be as dark as the night for them. The seven stars are the Pleiades, a grouping of seven stars found in the neck of Taurus, the bull. The Pleiades means the congregation of the judge. If Israel would believe on the coming redeemer, they would ride with him in the congregation of the judge. When he comes in judgment, they would not be pushed out of the way and trampled under foot by him. Orion is the Lord of glory; this is Jesus Christ written in the stars, the prophecy of his coming in glory and in judgment. He comes holding the head of the lion triumphing over him. He shall come forth as light, a strong and mighty man, in judgment prevailing against his enemies.

Isaiah 42:13, 14
The LORD shall go forth as a mighty man, he shall stir up jealousy like a man of war: he shall cry, yea, roar; he shall prevail

against his enemies.

I have long time holden my peace; I have been still, *and* refrained myself: *now* will I cry like a travailing woman; I will destroy and devour at once.

Here Isaiah attests to the truth of the constellation of Orion with the written Word, establishing what we know to be in the witness of the stars.

Isaiah 60:1- 4

Arise, shine; for thy light is come, and the glory of the LORD is risen upon thee.

For, behold, the darkness shall cover the earth, and gross darkness the people: but the LORD shall arise upon thee, and his glory shall be seen upon thee.

And the Gentiles shall come to thy light, and kings to the brightness of thy rising.

Lift up thine eyes round about, and see: all they gather themselves together, they come to thee: thy sons shall come from far, and thy daughters shall be nursed at *thy* side.

This is Orion, the Lord of glory. He is going to bring light even though gross darkness will be upon the people. Amos says, *look to that which makes the seven stars and Orion.* For those of us who see Orion, it will turn the shadow of death into the morning. For others who do not see Orion, it will make the day dark with night. If we can see the red thread in Amos, we will see Orion for who he is.

Isaiah 60:5, 6

Then thou shalt see, and flow together, and thine heart shall fear, and be enlarged; because the abundance of the sea shall be converted unto thee, the forces of the Gentiles shall come unto thee.

The multitude of camels shall cover thee, the dromedaries of Midian and Ephah; all they from Sheba shall come: they shall bring gold and incense; and they shall show forth the praises of the LORD.

All the flocks of Kedar shall be gathered together unto thee, the rams of Nebaioth shall minister unto thee: they shall come up with acceptance on mine altar, and I will glorify the house of my glory.

Isaiah speaks of "The house of My glory," which is the house where Taurus and Orion abide. God said that He would glorify the house of His glory. Jesus Christ came, and God gave him His glory just as He had promised. We beheld his glory, the glory given to the only begotten of the Father.

John 1:14
And the Word was made flesh, and dwelt among us, (and we beheld his glory, the glory as of the only begotten of the Father,) full of grace and truth.

The Word was made flesh; God's Word was made flesh in the person of Jesus Christ. Moses gave us the law, but grace and truth came with Jesus Christ. The Lord of glory dwelt among us, and we beheld his glory. Yet the acceptance of him was not what you might think. God's Word was manifest to us in Jesus Christ, yet how many saw the light and believed in Jesus Christ? His own people, the children of Israel, put him to shame and crucified him. Orion also lets us know that this glorious one was once bruised. He was once sacrificed, but the cumulative testimony of Orion's stars is that he is coming and he is coming quickly. He is coming with a vengeance, swiftly crushing the enemy under foot.

II Thessalonians 1:7- 10
And to you who are troubled rest with us, when [the word when is the word in] **the Lord Jesus** [the word who could be supplied here] **shall be revealed from heaven with his mighty angels,**
In flaming fire taking vengeance on them that know not God, and that obey not the gospel of our Lord Jesus Christ:
Who shall be punished with everlasting destruction from the presence of the Lord, and from the glory of his power;
When he shall come to be glorified in his saints, and to be admired in all them that believe (because our testimony among you was believed) in that day.

If you find yourself troubled, rest with us in the Lord Jesus. He shall be revealed from heaven, because that's where he happens to be at the moment. Even the revelation of Orion is yet to be glorified in that day. We know it to be true. We have believed not only the witness of the stars, but also the witness of the Word, the good news of our Lord Jesus Christ. The day will reveal the proof of what we believe. He shall come to be glorified in his saints and admired in all them who believe. In the book of Amos, God speaks to His people Israel and warns them that on their present course, the day of the Lord shall be darkness and not light.

Amos 5:18- 20
Woe unto you that desire the day of the LORD! to what end *is* it for you? the day of the LORD *is* darkness, and not light.
As if a man did flee from a lion, and a bear met him; or went into the house, and leaned his hand on the wall, and a serpent bit him.
Shall not the day of the LORD *be* darkness, and not light? even very dark, and no brightness in it?

Israel was facing its end, and it was not a pretty sight. God's people no longer wanted Him. Yet God had made promises to Israel, and there was one who yet needed to arise out of Jacob. So God did the last thing that He could do before He stopped passing by them anymore.

Amos 7:7, 8
Thus he showed me: and, behold, the Lord stood upon a wall *made* by a plumbline, with a plumbline in his hand.
And the LORD said unto me, Amos, what seest thou? And I said, A plumbline. Then said the Lord, Behold, I will set a plumbline in the midst of my people Israel: I will not again pass by them any more.

This was all God could do. This was all they would allow, and He could not pass by them any more. God could not do the things He used to do. In the days of Moses, God passed by them all the time. In the days of Joshua, God visited all the time. While the prophets prophesied and the people held them in high regard, God was around. By the time Amos arrived, the prophets were being told not to speak anymore. So God set a plumb line so that anyone who cared to could line up their thinking with what was right and straight and true, and He left it hang in the midst of His people.

Amos 8:1, 2
Thus hath the Lord GOD showed unto me: and behold a basket of summer fruit.
And he said, Amos, what seest thou? And I said, A basket of summer fruit. Then said the LORD unto me, The end is come upon my people of Israel; I will not again pass by them any more.

Amos saw the end come upon the people of Israel. He saw the darkness overtake them as the night. God's promises would hold true, but Israel would suffer a famine that rivaled any famine the Gentiles experienced or could experience, a famine far greater than the lack of physical food.

Amos 8:7-12

The LORD hath sworn by the excellency of Jacob, Surely I will never forget any of their works.

Shall not the land tremble for this, and every one mourn that dwelleth therein? and it shall rise up wholly as a flood; and it shall be cast out and drowned, as *by* the flood of Egypt.

And it shall come to pass in that day, saith the Lord GOD, that I will cause the sun to go down at noon, and I will darken the earth in the clear day: [There would be a day that the sun would go down at noon.]

And I will turn your feasts into mourning, and all your songs into lamentation; and I will bring up sackcloth upon all loins, and baldness upon every head; and I will make it as the mourning of an only *son*, and the end thereof as a bitter day. [God would mourn the loss of an only son.]

Behold, the days come, saith the Lord GOD, that I will send a famine in the land, not a famine of bread, nor a thirst for water, but of hearing the words of the LORD:

And they shall wander from sea to sea, and from the north even to the east, they shall run to and fro to seek the word of the LORD, and shall not find *it*.

There was something excellent in Jacob, but it was not what Israel was doing here. God tells Amos of things that were going to take place in the future. Today some people still think Israel is still somehow privileged as God's chosen people. But the house of Israel has been sifted among all nations, and today God sees no difference between Jew and Gentile. Both Jew and Gentile are all under sin with the same salvation extended to the one as to the other.

Amos 9:7-10

Are ye not as children of the Ethiopians unto me, O children of Israel? saith the LORD. Have not I brought up Israel out of the land of Egypt? and the Philistines from Caphtor, and the Syrians from Kir?

Behold, the eyes of the Lord GOD *are* upon the sinful kingdom, and I will destroy it from off the face of the earth; saving that I will not utterly destroy the house of Jacob, saith the LORD.

For, lo, I will command, and I will sift the house of Israel among all nations, like as *corn* is sifted in a sieve, yet shall not the least grain

fall upon the earth.
All the sinners of my people shall die by the sword, which say, The evil shall not overtake nor prevent us.

The constellation of Orion speaks to us in the book of Amos as the red thread. Jesus Christ is the Lord of glory, and all who believe on him will be glorified together with him. Israel has always been told to believe on him. The seven stars in the neck of Taurus tell Israel that they were meant to ride with the redeemer in glory and not be pushed out of the way by him. Israel was failing in the days of Amos, yet God did not forsake them. God will not forget the Word written in the stars or the Word which is written in the scriptures. God will not forget the Word that came to us in the person of Jesus Christ, the Word of God in the flesh. God is always faithful to His Word, and the red thread is proof of that. We are to believe on the Lord Jesus Christ, the Lord of glory. Both Jews and Gentiles are to believe on Jesus Christ. There is no consideration of race when it comes to salvation. The rich and the poor all need the liberty found in Christ Jesus our Lord.

James 2:1
My brethren, have not the faith of our Lord Jesus Christ, *the Lord* of glory, with respect of persons.

James calls Jesus Christ the Lord of glory. If the Devil had known what God had prepared for us who love him, he never would have crucified the Lord of glory. The Devil can no longer hide from us in darkness. The light is on, and our eyes are open.

I Corinthians 2:8, 9
Which none of the princes of this world knew: for had they known *it*, they would not have crucified the Lord of glory.
But as it is written, Eye hath not seen, nor ear heard, neither have entered into the heart of man, the things which God hath prepared for them that love him.

Jesus Christ is a prince among princes. Jesus Christ is our light. Jesus Christ has the glory of the Father. He came the first time and some seemed not to notice. He is coming again as the fulfillment of the Lord of glory found in the constellation of Orion. He will be triumphant, and we will be with him in glory. This has been the red thread in the book of Amos.

The Red Thread of Amos

The Judgment of the Nations

The vision of Obadiah was the judgment of God upon the heathen. The heathens are known as the Gentiles or the nations. The nations are epitomized by Edom, because it was Esau that sold his birth right and was lifted up by pride to think that he did not need the salvation of the Lord. He thought he could escape the judgment to come and could live unaffiliated with God or the Devil. All the wisdom of the world is foolishness with God; for a man to think he can live without God is sheer folly. Those who determined not to drink of the cup will assuredly drink from it, and they shall not go unpunished. Jesus Christ is the red thread in the book of Obadiah as the judgment of the nations, in that God will judge the nations in him and by him.

Obadiah 1:1
The vision of Obadiah. Thus saith the Lord GOD concerning Edom; We have heard a rumour from the LORD, and an ambassador is sent among the heathen, Arise ye, and let us rise up against her in battle.

The vision of Obadiah is concerning Edom. Obadiah said, "We have heard a rumor." They heard a report that could not be substantiated at the time, although there was another who had heard the same report. This rumor was of an ambassador being sent among the Gentiles. The purpose for this ambassador is not stated. We do know an ambassador is sent with goodwill, and the Lord is sending this one before war breaks out.

Jeremiah 49:14
I have heard a rumour from the LORD, and an ambassador is sent unto the heathen, *saying*, Gather ye together, and come against her, and rise up to the battle.

Jeremiah also heard the report of an ambassador being sent to the heathen. Yet just what the message would contain was not apparent to Jeremiah, nor was it revealed to Obadiah. It had to do with the mystery still to be revealed.

Ephesians 3:4- 6
Whereby, when ye read, ye may understand my knowledge in

the mystery of Christ.
> Which in other ages was not made known unto the sons of men, as it is now revealed unto his holy apostles and prophets by the Spirit;
> That the Gentiles should be fellowheirs, and of the same body, and partakers of his promise in Christ by the gospel.

This mystery of Christ was not known in the days of Jeremiah and Obadiah, although they both heard a rumor of an ambassador being sent among the heathen.

II Corinthians 5:19, 20
> To wit, that God was in Christ, reconciling the world unto himself, not imputing their trespasses unto them; and hath committed unto us the word of reconciliation.
> Now then we are ambassadors for Christ, as though God did beseech *you* by us: we pray *you* in Christ's stead, be ye reconciled to God.

We are ambassadors for Christ, sent with the word of reconciliation. The prophets alluded to this time, for this is an acceptable time and the day of salvation for all the nations.

II Corinthians 6:2
> (For he saith, I have heard thee in a time accepted, and in the day of salvation have I succoured thee: behold, now *is* the accepted time; behold, now *is* the day of salvation.)

God told the prophets that there would be a time when He would visit the nations, a time when they should turn back to God and forsake the wisdom of this world. Those who think they can go on without God are not convinced by even their own destruction. Many keep right on going until they are no longer. In the judgment of God, those who think they can get away without drinking of the cup of salvation or the cup of wrath are sadly mistaken.

Jeremiah 49:7- 12
> Concerning Edom, thus saith the LORD of hosts; *Is* wisdom no more in Teman? is counsel perished from the prudent? is their wisdom vanished?
> Flee ye, turn back, dwell deep, O inhabitants of Dedan; for I will bring the calamity of Esau upon him, the time *that* I will visit him.

If grapegatherers come to thee, would they not leave *some* gleaning grapes? if thieves by night, they will destroy till they have enough.

But I have made Esau bare, I have uncovered his secret places, and he shall not be able to hide himself: his seed is spoiled, and his brethren, and his neighbours, and he *is* not.

Leave thy fatherless children, I will preserve *them* alive; and let thy widows trust in me.

For thus saith the LORD; Behold, they whose judgment *was* not to drink of the cup have assuredly drunken; and *art* thou he *that* shall altogether go unpunished? thou shalt not go unpunished, but thou shalt surely drink *of it*.

For those whose judgment was not to drink of the cup have assuredly drunken. We can chose to either drink of the cup of salvation or the cup of wrath, but to think that you can escape it altogether is not an option.

Psalms 116:12, 13
What shall I render unto the LORD *for* all his benefits toward me?
I will take the cup of salvation, and call upon the name of the LORD.

We can take the cup of salvation and stop drinking the dregs we have been choking down, even the cup of wrath and its bitter end.

Isaiah 51:21- 23
Therefore hear now this, thou afflicted, and drunken, but not with wine:
Thus saith thy Lord the LORD, and thy God *that* pleadeth the cause of his people, Behold, I have taken out of thine hand the cup of trembling, *even* the dregs of the cup of my fury; thou shalt no more drink it again:
But I will put it into the hand of them that afflict thee; which have said to thy soul, Bow down, that we may go over: and thou hast laid thy body as the ground, and as the street, to them that went over.

We've heard it said, "what goes around comes around," but is this really what we want coming our way? We can either drink of the cup of salvation or of the cup of wrath.

Jeremiah 25:27- 29
Therefore thou shalt say unto them, Thus saith the LORD of hosts, the God of Israel; Drink ye, and be drunken, and spue, and fall, and rise no more, because of the sword which I will send among you.
And it shall be, if they refuse to take the cup at thine hand to drink, then shalt thou say unto them, Thus saith the LORD of hosts; Ye shall certainly drink.
For, lo, I begin to bring evil on the city which is called by my name, and should ye be utterly unpunished? Ye shall not be unpunished: for I will call for a sword upon all the inhabitants of the earth, saith the LORD of hosts.

God begins with judgment in His own house. But when it comes to those who are not of God's house, dare they think they will go utterly unpunished?

Romans 1:18, 32
For the wrath of God is revealed from heaven against all ungodliness and unrighteousness of men, who hold the truth in unrighteousness;
Who knowing the judgment of God, that they which commit such things are worthy of death, not only do the same, but have pleasure in them that do them.

You can reject the judgment of God if you choose to, and you can even come up with your own judgments. Yet the judgment of God is sure according to the truth. The day of wrath will come, and every man will be judged according to his deeds.

Romans 2:1- 6
Therefore thou art inexcusable, O man, whosoever thou art that judgest: for wherein thou judgest another, thou condemnest thyself; for thou that judgest doest the same things.
But we are sure that the judgment of God is according to truth against them which commit such things.
And thinkest thou this, O man, that judgest them which do such things, and doest the same, that thou shalt escape the judgment of God?
Or despisest thou the riches of his goodness and forbearance and longsuffering; not knowing that the goodness of God leadeth thee to repentance?
But after thy hardness and impenitent heart treasurest up unto

thyself wrath against the day of wrath and revelation of the righteous judgment of God;
Who will render to every man according to his deeds.

Obadiah had said, "let us rise up against her in battle," and it will ultimately come to that because of pride. It is pride that deceives the heart into thinking that it can exalt itself above God and dwell unmolested.

Obadiah 1:1- 4

The vision of Obadiah. Thus saith the Lord GOD concerning Edom; We have heard a rumour from the LORD, and an ambassador is sent among the heathen, Arise ye, and let us rise up against her in battle.

Behold, I have made thee small among the heathen: thou art greatly despised.

The pride of thine heart hath deceived thee, thou that dwellest in the clefts of the rock, whose habitation *is* high; that saith in his heart, Who shall bring me down to the ground?

Though thou exalt *thyself* as the eagle, and though thou set thy nest among the stars, thence will I bring thee down, saith the LORD.

God said that the vision of Obadiah was concerning Edom, which is Esau. It was Esau's pride that deceived him. It was Esau who sold his birthright to Jacob for a bowl of lentil soup. He figured that he wasn't using it at the time and since he was hungry, why not? What was Esau's birthright anyway? It was more than the wealth of his father Isaac. It was the promised seed, Jesus Christ. This is what he despised, God's salvation, Jesus Christ. Esau was a good hunter and his father loved him best, yet he despised his birthright.

Genesis 25:30- 34

And Esau said to Jacob, Feed me, I pray thee, with that same red *pottage*; for I *am* faint: therefore was his name called Edom.

And Jacob said, Sell me this day thy birthright.

And Esau said, Behold, I *am* at the point to die: and what profit shall this birthright do to me?

And Jacob said, Swear to me this day; and he sware unto him: and he sold his birthright unto Jacob.

Then Jacob gave Esau bread and pottage of lentiles; and he did eat and drink, and rose up, and went his way: thus Esau despised *his* birthright.

Esau wasn't a fragile Southern belle with his hand on his forehead saying, "I am faint." He was a strong man, a cunning hunter, a man of the field. Nonetheless, he sold the promise of Jesus Christ for some lentil pottage. Why? He despised his birthright; he thought it to be worthless. Some say Jacob took advantage of his brother. However, Jacob realized the value of the birthright, whereas Esau despised it. That is why God said, "Behold, I have made thee small among the heathen: thou art greatly despised."

Romans 9:13
As it is written, Jacob have I loved, but Esau have I hated.

Why would God use such harsh language concerning Esau? Because he despised the judgment of God found in his birthright, the Lord Jesus Christ.

Obadiah 1:6
How are *the things* of Esau searched out! *how* are his hidden things sought up!

How are the things of Esau going to be searched out? Who is going to judge Edom in righteousness? All the hidden things of the heart will be sought out by the one who is set to judge the heathens, the one whom Esau despised, the Lord Jesus Christ.

Matthew 12:18
Behold my servant, whom I have chosen; my beloved, in whom my soul is well pleased: I will put my spirit upon him, and he shall show judgment to the Gentiles.

Who is God's servant, His beloved, the one whom He has chosen to show judgment to the Gentiles? Jesus Christ.

John 5:22
For the Father judgeth no man, but hath committed all judgment unto the Son.

It is the son of God to whom all judgment has been committed. Man's judging of others does not mean much if there is a failure to consider the red thread and who it is that will bring judgment to the nations. If we believe in Jesus Christ, we will have praise of God in the day of judgment.

I Corinthians 4:1 and 3- 5
Let a man so account of us, as of the ministers of Christ, and stewards of the mysteries of God.
But with me it is a very small thing that I should be judged of you, or of man's judgment: yea, I judge not mine own self.
For I know nothing by myself; yet am I not hereby justified: but he that judgeth me is the Lord.
Therefore judge nothing before the time, until the Lord come, who both will bring to light the hidden things of darkness, and will make manifest the counsels of the hearts: and then shall every man have praise of God.

This is man's judgment, man's day; today is the day man does the judging. You can choose to accept the salvation of the Lord or reject the Lord, but the day will come when the Lord will have his day. In the Lord's day, the hidden things will be judged, even the counsels of the heart. Men will tell you death is inevitable, but so also is the judgment.

Hebrews 9:27, 28
And as it is appointed unto men once to die, but after this the judgment:
So Christ was once offered to bear the sins of many; and unto them that look for him shall he appear the second time without sin unto salvation.

The day of the Lord is near upon all the heathen. As you have done, so it shall be done unto you. The day of the Lord can mean life or death. Even the heathen has a choice in the matter.

Obadiah 1:15
For the day of the LORD *is* near upon all the heathen: as thou hast done, it shall be done unto thee: thy reward shall return upon thine own head.

The day of the Lord is when all the judging will be done, all the secret and hidden things of men shall be made known. The Gentiles shall not escape the judgment of God for "as thou has done, it shall be done unto you." Everyone will receive a reward for all he has done.

Romans 2:16
In the day when God shall judge the secrets of men by Jesus Christ according to my gospel.

Jesus Christ holds the judgment of the nations. He is the red thread in the book of Obadiah. For the day of the Lord is near upon all the heathen. It is Jesus Christ who will deal out the fitting reward.

Romans 2:6- 9
Who will render to every man according to his deeds:
To them who by patient continuance in well doing seek for glory and honour and immortality, eternal life:
But unto them that are contentious, and do not obey the truth, but obey unrighteousness, indignation and wrath,
Tribulation and anguish, upon every soul of man that doeth evil, of the Jew first, and also of the Gentile.

It can go one of two ways for the Gentiles, but to think that you can get away from drinking of the cup is a false hope.

Obadiah 1:16
For as ye have drunk upon my holy mountain, *so* shall all the heathen drink continually, yea, they shall drink, and they shall swallow down, and they shall be as though they had not been.

It doesn't have to go this way for the nations, but it will if they choose not to accept the work that has been done in the red thread. There is a blessing in the judgment of the nations, if the desire is there.

Obadiah 1:21
And saviours shall come up on mount Zion to judge the mount of Esau; and the kingdom shall be the LORD'S.

The door is open and the way is there, but the judgment of the nations is clear. Obadiah is not a large book, but when it is taken in conjunction with the rest of the Word, it speaks volumes concerning the judgment of the Gentiles. When it comes to the red thread and the judgment of the nations, we can see the kingdom shall be the Lord's. In the day of the Lord, the judgment will be complete and all rewards will be handed out. God will judge all the secrets of men by Jesus Christ.

The Salvation of the Lord

Jonah is a book which again deals with people who are not of the nation of Israel. Jonah addresses the Gentiles, and in particular, the people who lived in the capital of Assyria. The Assyrians are the ones who ultimately brought an end to the nation of Israel when they led them away into captivity. The subject and the red thread of the book of Jonah is the salvation of the Lord. The book of Jonah shows the magnitude of God's mercy; it shows how God truly is no respecter of persons, that salvation is available to all. It also sets a sign, for as Jonah was three nights and three days in the belly of the fish, so shall the son of man be three nights and three days in the heart of the earth. Jesus Christ would be dead and entombed, just like Jonah was dead and entombed, only to be brought back to life again to bring salvation forth for all.

Jonah 1:1- 3
Now the word of the LORD came unto Jonah the son of Amittai, saying,
Arise, go to Nineveh, that great city, and cry against it; for their wickedness is come up before me.
But Jonah rose up to flee unto Tarshish from the presence of the LORD, and went down to Joppa; and he found a ship going to Tarshish: so he paid the fare thereof, and went down into it, to go with them unto Tarshish from the presence of the LORD.

Jonah was a prophet in Israel with a desire to help the children of Israel. The children of Israel were living under a king who did evil in the sight of the Lord, and the people followed him. Jonah knew that the children of Israel were flirting with disaster, and he could see the threat the Assyrians posed to God's people. This is why he was not very excited when God told him to go to Nineveh and preach. Jonah knew that if Nineveh believed, it would not play well for Israel.

II Kings 14:23- 25
In the fifteenth year of Amaziah the son of Joash king of Judah Jeroboam the son of Joash king of Israel began to reign in Samaria, *and reigned* **forty and one years.**
And he did *that which was* **evil in the sight of the LORD: he**

departed not from all the sins of Jeroboam the son of Nebat, who made Israel to sin.

[Yet] He restored the coast of Israel from the entering of Hamath unto the sea of the plain, according to the word of the LORD God of Israel, which he spake by the hand of his servant Jonah, the son of Amittai, the prophet, which *was* of Gathhepher.

Jonah was a prophet during the time of Jeroboam, the son of Joash, king of Israel. Jonah desired to help Israel, but the king and the kingdom were on the fast track to destruction. Nineveh, on the other hand, just happened to be a place were God could work. The people of Nineveh were ready to repent and believe God. So it was when God told Jonah to go on up to that place, he rose up and headed the opposite direction, toward Tarshish. Jonah figured if he moved far enough away from the presence of the Lord, God wouldn't know where to find him. Jonah hoped that He would change His mind about the whole Nineveh thing. Well, as you may have guessed, you can run but you can't hide.

Jonah 1:4
But the LORD sent out a great wind into the sea, and there was a mighty tempest in the sea, so that the ship was like to be broken.

While Jonah was sleeping in the ship, the mariners were up on deck. They started telling everyone aboard to start praying to their gods, but Jonah slept on until somebody came down and woke him up. Then the men on the ship started questioning why all this was happening and they looked to Jonah and said to him, tell us who you are and where you are from and what your occupation is.

Jonah 1:9, 10
And he said unto them, I *am* an Hebrew; and I fear [I work for] the LORD, the God of heaven, which hath made the sea and the dry *land*.
Then were the men exceedingly afraid, and said unto him, Why hast thou done this? For the men knew that he fled from the presence of the LORD, because he had told them.

Then Jonah told them that the only way for them to calm things down would be to throw him overboard. The sailors tried to row hard for awhile, but they saw it was to no avail. They reluctantly took Jonah and cast him into the sea. Here is a sign to all those who are looking for the salvation of the Lord. God had a great fish prepared to swallow Jonah. Jonah was entombed for three nights and three days before the fish spit him back out again. Jesus Christ was also three nights and three days in the heart of the earth, entombed until God raised him from the dead.

Matthew 12:38- 41
Then certain of the scribes and of the Pharisees answered, saying, Master, we would see a sign from thee.
But he [Jesus] answered and said unto them, An evil and adulterous generation seeketh after a sign; and there shall no sign be given to it, but the sign of the prophet Jonas:
For as Jonas was three days and three nights in the whale's belly; so shall the Son of man be three days and three nights in the heart of the earth.
The men of Nineveh shall rise in judgment with this generation, and shall condemn it: because they repented at the preaching of Jonas; and, behold, a greater than Jonas *is* here.

This is the sign of the salvation of the Lord. If you're looking for the salvation of the Lord, look for the one who died and was dead for three nights and three days before God raised him up. Jesus Christ has a greater salvation to offer than Jonah did. Jonah only gave Nineveh a brief pardon, while Jesus Christ gives remission of sins. Jonah prayed to the Lord his God before his soul fainted, and his life left him. Not wanting to forsake his own mercy, Jonah said that he would pay his vow and do the job which God had given him, being a prophet of the Lord.

Jonah 2:9
But I will sacrifice unto thee with the voice of thanksgiving; I will pay *that* that I have vowed. Salvation *is* of the LORD.

Jonah did not want to forsake the salvation of the Lord, even if it meant extending salvation to the people of Nineveh. Jonah still wanted the salvation of the Lord for Israel, but he was also willing to do what God had asked of him concerning the Gentiles as well.

Jonah 2:10- 3:5
And the LORD spake unto the fish, and it vomited out Jonah upon the dry *land*.
And the word of the LORD came unto Jonah the second time, saying,

Arise, go unto Nineveh, that great city, and preach unto it the preaching that I bid thee.
So Jonah arose, and went unto Nineveh, according to the word of the LORD. Now Nineveh was an exceeding great city of three days' journey.
And Jonah began to enter into the city a day's journey, and he cried, and said, Yet forty days, and Nineveh shall be overthrown.
So the people of Nineveh believed God, and proclaimed a fast, and put on sackcloth, from the greatest of them even to the least of them.

Jonah went to the Gentiles and told them that they had forty days left before Nineveh would be destroyed. The people of Nineveh did something that Israel had been failing to do for quite some time: they believed God. They turned from their evil way, and even their king proclaimed and published a decree to that end, and God saw it.

Jonah 3:10
And God saw their works, that they turned from their evil way; and God repented of the evil, that he had said that he would do unto them; and he did *it* not.

Jonah was not happy about this at all. To think that God would show mercy toward people like these was too much to bear. Jonah knew that God's people would suffer at the hands of the Assyrians. God's people had drifted away from Him before, but God always took them back. Now how was He going to work with this?

Jonah 4:1- 4
But it displeased Jonah exceedingly, and he was very angry.
And he prayed unto the LORD, and said, I pray thee, O LORD, *was* not this my saying, when I was yet in my country? Therefore I fled before unto Tarshish: for I knew that thou *art* a gracious God, and merciful, slow to anger, and of great kindness, and repentest thee of the evil.
Therefore now, O LORD, take, I beseech thee, my life from me; for *it is* better for me to die than to live.
Then said the LORD, Doest thou well to be angry?

When you have two groups, both doing evil, how do you choose which one to work with? You work with the one who is willing to believe and turn away from the evil.

Jonah 4:5, 6
So Jonah went out of the city, and sat on the east side of the city, and there made him a booth, and sat under it in the shadow, till he might see what would become of the city.
And the LORD God prepared a gourd, and made *it* to come up over Jonah, that it might be a shadow over his head, to deliver him from his grief. So Jonah was exceeding glad of the gourd.

God will always do what He can to bless you. Jonah was glad for the gourd, but he still remained angry. The next day when the gourd withered, his miserable state worsened. Now Jonah was angry that the gourd had died, and he wished that he might die also.

Jonah 4:9- 11
And God said to Jonah, Doest thou well to be angry for the gourd? And he said, I do well to be angry, *even* unto death.
Then said the LORD, Thou hast had pity on the gourd, for the which thou hast not laboured, neither madest it grow; which came up in a night, and perished in a night:
And should not I spare Nineveh, that great city, wherein are more than sixscore thousand persons that cannot discern between their right hand and their left hand; and *also* much cattle?

God said, *you didn't want to see the gourd die, and it was just a gourd. Why is it so hard to have the same compassion when it comes to the people of Nineveh?* At times, we look at other people who are but body and soul and think a stick would be more useful than these people. But if they are willing to accept the salvation of the Lord, how can we deny them? God told Jonah, if you cannot bring yourself to have compassion for the people, think of their animals. Most of the time we have more compassion for the animals than we do for the people anyway. Dumb animals win out over dumb people any day, especially when it comes to those dumb Gentiles. Praise God. He is no respecter of persons when it comes to salvation, because God knows we all need it.

Psalms 98:2, 3
The LORD hath made known his salvation: his righteousness hath he openly showed in the sight of the heathen.
He hath remembered his mercy and his truth toward the house

of Israel: all the ends of the earth have seen the salvation of our God.

God will not forget His mercy and His truth to the house of Israel, but He has also made known the salvation of the Lord even in the sight of the Gentiles. The salvation of the Lord will also be given to the Gentiles, because God knows how much we need it.

Isaiah 49:6
And he said, It is a light thing that thou shouldest be my servant to raise up the tribes of Jacob, and to restore the preserved of Israel: I will also give thee for a light to the Gentiles, that thou mayest be my salvation unto the end of the earth.

God's servant would not only raise up the tribes of Jacob and restore the preserved of Israel, but Jesus Christ will also be a light to the Gentiles, for he is the salvation of the Lord.

Isaiah 62:11
Behold, the LORD hath proclaimed unto the end of the world, Say ye to the daughter of Zion, Behold, thy salvation cometh; behold, his reward *is* with him, and his work before him.

Jonah could see the end of the nation of Israel coming, yet he knew as well as Isaiah that God had not forsaken Israel. The salvation of the Lord would come. The nation of Israel went into captivity at the hands of the Assyrians. Yet Jerusalem and the daughter of Zion were not forsaken.

Luke 2:25- 32
And, behold, there was a man in Jerusalem, whose name *was* Simeon; and the same man *was* just and devout, waiting for the consolation of Israel: and the Holy Ghost [the holy spirit] was upon him.
And it was revealed unto him by the Holy Ghost [the holy spirit], that he should not see death, before he had seen the Lord's Christ.
And he came by the Spirit into the temple: and when the parents brought in the child Jesus, to do for him after the custom of the law,
Then took he him up in his arms, and blessed God, and said, Lord, now lettest thou thy servant depart in peace, according to thy word:
For mine eyes have seen thy salvation, Which thou hast prepared before the face of all people; A light to lighten the Gentiles, and the glory of thy people Israel.

Jesus Christ was the salvation of Israel, and he came telling them so. Jesus Christ is the salvation of the Lord. He is a light to the Gentiles and the glory of the people of Israel.

Luke 19:9, 10
And Jesus said unto him, This day is salvation come to this house, forsomuch as he also is a son of Abraham.
For the Son of man is come to seek and to save that which was lost.

Jesus said, "This day is salvation come to this house," because Jesus Christ is the salvation of the Lord and the Lord of salvation. He came to seek and to save that which was lost.

Acts 4:12
Neither is there salvation in any other: for there is none other name under heaven given among men, whereby we must be saved.

There is only one thing that God tells anyone they must do, and that is to be saved. You will not find this salvation under any other name under heaven. It is only Jesus Christ who is the salvation of the Lord. Do not be disappointed in your expectations. Look to the good news in Christ, for in the gospel you will find the power of God unto salvation. This salvation is to everyone who believes, to the Jew first and also to the Gentile.

Romans 1:16
For I am not ashamed of the gospel of Christ: for it is the power of God unto salvation to every one that believeth; to the Jew first, and also to the Greek.

This is the salvation of the Lord. Jesus Christ is the salvation, and there is no other name given under heaven among men whereby you must be saved. Jesus Christ fulfills all the requirements of the Old Testament as the red thread.

The Red Thread of Jonah

The Red Thread of Micah

An Heir

In the book of Micah, both the cities of Samaria and Jerusalem were overrun with religion. Samaria was already destroyed by religion, and Jerusalem was infested. The problem is with how man had chosen to worship God. Religion is always the work of men's hands. Religion can be any system of belief or worship. There was always contention between Israel and Judah as to who the true worshipers were and how to worship God. They both thought that they were God's heritage and heir to God's promises. When all is said and done, to be an heir of God will take more than just being of the lineage of Israel. It will involve being joint-heir with the heir of God, Jesus Christ. Only then will you see the true worshipers stepping forth to worship God, making their heritage sure in the Lord. God will bring an heir, and he shall be the glory of Israel. This heir is the red thread in the book of Micah.

Micah 1:1- 5
The word of the LORD that came to Micah the Morasthite in the days of Jotham, Ahaz, *and* Hezekiah, kings of Judah, which he saw concerning Samaria and Jerusalem.
Hear, all ye people; hearken, O earth, and all that therein is: and let the Lord GOD be witness against you, the Lord from his holy temple.
For, behold, the LORD cometh forth out of his place, and will come down, and tread upon the high places of the earth.
And the mountains shall be molten under him, and the valleys shall be cleft, as wax before the fire, *and* as the waters *that are* poured down a steep place.
For [because of] the transgression of Jacob *is* all this, and for [because of] the sins of the house of Israel. What *is* the transgression of Jacob? *is it* not Samaria? and what *are* the high places of Judah? *are they* not Jerusalem?

Today Judaism is a religion which has been developed over many years. It has very little, if anything, to do with what God intended for Israel. Already in Micah's day, the children of Israel had begun to develop this religion. By taking elements from pagan religions around them and traditions they themselves introduced, the religious doctrine took shape. They were overlooking and forgetting the statutes which God had set forth for them. Because of this transgression and the sins of the house of Israel, the Lord will come and stomp on the high places of the earth. The high places are where the temples were placed. Even God's holy mountain had become just another high place. Jerusalem was just another place of religious worship.

Micah 1:6, 7
Therefore I will make Samaria as an heap of the field, *and* as plantings of a vineyard: and I will pour down the stones thereof into the valley, and I will discover the foundations thereof.
And all the graven images thereof shall be beaten to pieces, and all the hires thereof shall be burned with the fire, and all the idols thereof will I lay desolate: for she gathered *it* of the hire of an harlot, and they shall return to the hire of an harlot.

Samaria had always been religious. Its foundations were built on religion. The ones hired as ministers and the graven images shall be eradicated. All their idols will come to nothing. It will all be destroyed.

Micah 1:9
For her wound *is* incurable; for it is come unto Judah; he is come unto the gate of my people, *even* to Jerusalem.

Religion produces an incurable wound for those who succumb to it. All religions think that they are right in their beliefs. Jerusalem was being enveloped in religion, and no one was taking notice that they were being robbed of their heritage. People may change gods or come up with different notions as to what they think about God, but the power of God is not thwarted by religion. It has been said that religion is the opiate of the people. This observation may be accurate, if you realize that God is not found in religion. God can only be found in the things which He has wrought. The question then remains, what does it take to be a true worshiper of God?

Micah 1:15
Yet will I bring an heir unto thee, O inhabitant of Mareshah: he shall come unto Adullam the glory of Israel.

God said that He would bring an heir to them. This heir is the red thread in the book of Micah. This heir would prove to be none other than Jesus Christ, the first begotten of the Father.

Hebrews 1:1, 2
God, who at sundry times and in divers manners spake in time past unto the fathers by the prophets,
Hath in these last days spoken unto us by *His* Son, whom he hath appointed heir of all things, by [for] whom also he made the worlds [ages].

God spoke of the coming of his son by the prophets. Many things were foretold about him. God had him in mind all along; all the ages were prepared with him in mind. He was appointed by God to be heir of all things. If we are going to be heir to anything which belongs to God, it will be though God's son. God always wanted sons and daughters, and He knew that out of Abraham's lineage, He would have a seed who could accomplish His desire. He even called Israel His firstborn and tied them to the law so they could carry on until the promised seed could be born. God knew that Jacob had some shortcomings and that Israel as a house would be an unruly lot. But through it all, there would be an heir who would make it available for the servants of God to become sons.

Galatians 4:6- 9
And because ye are sons, God hath sent forth the Spirit of his Son into your hearts, crying, Abba [a term of endearment that only a son would use]**, Father.**
Wherefore thou art no more a servant, but a son; and if a son, then an heir of God through Christ.
Howbeit then, when ye knew not God, ye did service unto them which by nature are no gods.
But now, after that ye have known God, or rather are known of God, how turn ye again to the weak and beggarly elements, whereunto ye desire again to be in bondage?

We are heirs of God through Christ not through some religious ritual. All religion is bondage, but the spirit of God brings freedom to all those who are joint heirs with Christ.

Romans 8:15- 17a
For ye have not received the spirit of bondage again to fear; but ye have received the Spirit of adoption, whereby we cry, Abba, Father.
The Spirit itself beareth witness with our spirit, that we are the children of God:

And if children, then heirs; heirs of God, and joint-heirs with Christ.

This spirit of adoption is literally translated, "a sonship spirit." We are God's children, His sons and daughters and joint-heirs with Christ when we receive this spirit. No religion in the world can produce this. Not even the law could bring this to a man. Only believing and the promise of the spirit could make a man an heir.

Romans 4:13, 14
For the promise, that he [Abraham] should be the heir of the world, *was* not to Abraham, or to his seed, through the law, but through the righteousness of faith [believing]**.**
For if they which are of the law *be* heirs, faith [believing] **is made void, and the promise made of none effect.**

There was a promise made to Abraham and to his seed through believing, not through the law. This promise of being an heir was made long before the law was given, and even the coming of the law did not make void the promise.

Galatians 3:14
That the blessing of Abraham might come on the Gentiles through Jesus Christ; that we might receive the promise of the Spirit [spirit] **through faith** [believing]**.**

This is what God has worked in Christ that this blessing might come on the Gentiles as well as the Jews through Jesus Christ. The promise of the spirit is through believing and no other way.

Galatians 3:21, 22
***Is* the law then against the promises of God? God forbid: for if there had been a law given which could have given life, verily righteousness should have been by the law.**
But the scripture hath concluded all under sin, that the promise by faith [the believing] **of Jesus Christ might be given to them that believe.**

We are to believe in Jesus Christ. That is how we become children of God. You cannot be a child of God without believing in His son. Even the children of Israel are required to believe in him in order to receive the promise and become an heir.

Galatians 3:23- 29
But before faith [believing] **came, we were kept under the law, shut up unto the faith** [believing] **which should afterwards be revealed.**
Wherefore the law was our schoolmaster *to bring us* **unto** [just read "until"] **Christ, that we might be justified by faith** [believing].
But after that faith [believing] **is come, we are no longer under a schoolmaster.**
For ye are all the children of God by faith [believing] **in Christ Jesus.**
For as many of you as have been baptized into Christ have put on Christ.
There is neither Jew nor Greek, there is neither bond nor free, there is neither male nor female: for ye are all one in Christ Jesus.
And if ye *be* **Christ's, then are ye Abraham's seed, and heirs according to the promise.**

It doesn't matter, Jew or Gentile, male or female, we all become God's children and heirs by believing in Christ Jesus. The law only kept Israel until Christ came. The Jews had made the law their religion. So when Christ came, they rejected him and chose their own way and their own traditions. The apostle Paul was acquainted with the Jews' religion and profited in it above many of his equals until he became a believer in Christ.

Galatians 1:13, 14
For ye have heard of my conversation in time past in the Jews' religion, how that beyond measure I persecuted the church of God, and wasted it:
And profited in the Jews' religion above many my equals in mine own nation, being more exceedingly zealous of the traditions of my fathers.

Religious traditions are held in higher esteem than the commandments of God. Once men get a hold of something God has said or done and change it into a religious dogma, they will adhere to that more than the Word of God.

Matthew 15:1- 3 and 7- 9
Then came to Jesus scribes and Pharisees, which were of

Jerusalem, saying,
> Why do thy disciples transgress the tradition of the elders? for they wash not their hands when they eat bread.
> But he answered and said unto them, Why do ye also transgress the commandment of God by your tradition?
> *Ye* hypocrites, well did Esaias prophesy of you, saying, This people draweth nigh unto me with their mouth, and honoureth me with *their* lips; but their heart is far from me.
> But in vain they do worship me, teaching *for* doctrines the commandments of men.

Men come up with many doctrines and religions. This is man's day, and it is in the power of his hands to do so. Men dream up a lot of things. Men may devise this and they practice that, but it only robs a man of his true heritage.

Micah 2:1-5
> Woe to them that devise iniquity, and work evil upon their beds! when the morning is light, they practice it, because it is in the power of their hand.
> And they covet fields, and take *them* by violence; and houses, and take *them* away: so they oppress a man and his house, even a man and his heritage.
> Therefore thus saith the LORD; Behold, against this family do I devise an evil, from which ye shall not remove your necks; neither shall ye go haughtily: for this time *is* evil.
> In that day shall *one* take up a parable against you, and lament with a doleful lamentation, *and* say, We be utterly spoiled: he hath changed the portion of my people: how hath he removed *it* from me! turning away he hath divided our fields.
> Therefore thou shalt have none that shall cast a cord by lot in the congregation of the LORD.

The children of Israel were divided as a nation and as a people by greed and by violence. From oppression within their own ranks they suffered. Their heritage was in jeopardy. As they allowed religion in, they were utterly spoiling the portion they had as God's people. They had come to think they could lay claim on the heritage of God by their station or lot in life, by their family pedigree. You cannot cast a cord, lay claim to a place in the congregation of the Lord by being anything other than an heir. Micah said that there would be one who would take up a parable against the ones who thought they could lay claim to the fields without being heirs themselves.

Luke 20:9-16

Then began he [Jesus] to speak to the people this parable; A certain man planted a vineyard, and let it forth to husbandmen, and went into a far country for a long time.

And at the season he sent a servant to the husbandmen, that they should give him of the fruit of the vineyard: but the husbandmen beat him, and sent *him* away empty.

And again he sent another servant: and they beat him also, and entreated *him* shamefully, and sent *him* away empty.

And again he sent a third: and they wounded him also, and cast *him* out.

Then said the lord of the vineyard, What shall I do? I will send my beloved son: it may be they will reverence *him* when they see him.

But when the husbandmen saw him, they reasoned among themselves, saying, This is the heir: come, let us kill him, that the inheritance may be ours.

So they cast him out of the vineyard, and killed *him*. What therefore shall the lord of the vineyard do unto them?

He shall come and destroy these husbandmen, and shall give the vineyard to others. And when they heard *it*, they said, God forbid.

Jesus spoke this parable to Israel, to the religious who thought they could receive the inheritance without the heir of God. Israel had been rejecting God's servants for a long time, and they still killed the heir despite the consequence. Micah was one of those servants. Were those of his day willing to hear him?

Micah 2:6-8a

Prophesy ye not, *say they to them that* prophesy: they shall not prophesy to them, *that* they shall not take shame.

O *thou that art* named the house of Jacob, is the spirit of the LORD straitened? *are* these his doings? do not my words do good to him that walketh uprightly?

Even of late my people is risen up as an enemy.

There was trouble in paradise. Someone did not want to hear what God had to say. A prophet is one who speaks for God. His words will do good for those who want to walk uprightly. But what about those who like to have it their own way? Religions need to look religious; religion likes to mimic what God does, but all the while, deny what God is doing.

Micah 2:11
If a man walking in the spirit and falsehood do lie, *saying,* **I will prophesy unto thee of wine and of strong drink; he shall even be the prophet of this people.**

Find a man with just any kind of spirit in him and say to him, "Prophesy according to my bidding. Tell me what I want to hear." Even today men can stand behind the pulpit and use the name of Jesus, but does this indicate the dogma of the religion to be pure?

Micah 3:8
But truly I am full of power by the spirit of the LORD, and of judgment, and of might, to declare unto Jacob his transgression, and to Israel his sin.

Micah was not a prophet of lies and falsehood. He was a prophet full of power by the spirit of the Lord. Micah spoke that which God spoke, making intercession for the people according to the will of God. Micah spoke of an heir. He even pointed to a specific place and made this claim, which if he wasn't speaking for God, how could he have known?

Micah 5:2, 4
But thou, Bethlehem Ephratah, *though* **thou be little among the thousands of Judah,** *yet* **out of thee shall he come forth unto me** *that is* **to be ruler in Israel; whose goings forth [whose coming]** *have been* **from of old, from everlasting.**
And he shall stand and feed in the strength of the LORD, in the majesty of the name of the LORD his God; and they shall abide: for now shall he be great unto the ends of the earth.

His coming has been from old, from everlasting. God had His heir in mind all along, and God said that he shall come forth out of Bethlehem. Today we know where Jesus was born, but Micah spoke long before the heir of God was born. This was all foretelling of the red thread, the heir of God, the one who shall stand in the majesty of the name of the Lord his God. When Jesus did come, he became great. His name is still known all over the earth. Jesus was talking to a woman of Samaria one day, and she brought up the subject of worshiping God when she perceived that he was a prophet.

John 4:19- 26
The woman saith unto him, Sir, I perceive that thou art a prophet.

Our fathers worshipped in this mountain; and *ye* say [I know what you're going to say], that in Jerusalem is the place where men ought to worship.

Jesus saith unto her, Woman, believe me, the hour cometh, when ye shall neither in this mountain, nor yet at Jerusalem, worship the Father.

Ye worship ye know not what: we [should] know what we worship: for salvation is of the Jews.

But the hour cometh, and now is, when the true worshippers shall worship the Father in spirit and in truth: for the Father seeketh such to worship him.

God *is* a Spirit: and they that worship him must worship *him* in spirit and in truth.

The woman saith unto him, I know that Messias cometh, which is called Christ: when he is come, he will tell us all things.

Jesus saith unto her, I that speak unto thee am *he*.

The people of Samaria and the people living in Jerusalem had been at odds over this matter for a long time, as to where and how to worship God. But Jesus came and said that it was time to worship God in spirit and in truth. This was only possible because of the heir. The spirit was made available through Jesus Christ. We are now able to know the truth. We have the ability to worship God in spirit and in truth. Jesus Christ was the heir that made it all possible. We have not been made a joint-heir to be religious, but to be children of God and believers in Christ.

Micah 6:1- 8
Hear ye now what the LORD saith; Arise, contend thou before the mountains, and let the hills hear thy voice.

Hear ye, O mountains, the LORD'S controversy, and ye strong foundations of the earth: for the LORD hath a controversy with his people, and he will plead with Israel.

O my people, what have I done unto thee? and wherein have I wearied thee? testify against me.

For I brought thee up out of the land of Egypt, and redeemed thee out of the house of servants; and I sent before thee Moses, Aaron, and Miriam.

O my people, remember now what Balak king of Moab

The Red Thread of Micah

consulted, and what Balaam the son of Beor answered him from Shittim unto Gilgal; that ye may know the righteousness of the LORD.

Wherewith shall I come before the LORD, *and* **bow myself before the high God? shall I come before him with burnt offerings, with calves of a year old?**

Will the LORD be pleased with thousands of rams, *or* **with ten thousands of rivers of oil? shall I give my firstborn** *for* **my transgression, the fruit of my body** *for* **the sin of my soul?**

He hath showed thee, O man, what *is* **good; and what doth the LORD require of thee, but to do justly, and to love mercy, and to walk humbly with thy God.**

Make your arguments for your places of worship; shout them from the rooftops for all to hear. The Lord is ready for the controversy. After considering all that God has done for us, what more can be said? Carry on in your religion for woe is me. On the other hand, consider for a moment that you don't have to come up with your own religious rites and rituals in order to redeem your soul. God has made the way for you to be an heir, and it is through His son, Jesus Christ. What's left then for you to do? Do justly and love mercy and walk humbly with your God. God's heritage is certain to an heir of God, which is what we find in the red thread here in the book of Micah.

Our Peace

The burden of Nineveh can be found in the book of Nahum. We all must bear a burden in what we believe and who we are going to trust. Nineveh had been visited by Jonah. They repented, turning away from their evil way. But it didn't last. You can see the same thing happen today. Something occurs and people turn to God, but shortly thereafter most people will return to what they were doing before. The vision of Nahum shows the vengeance of the Lord, but also proclaims peace. This then is the red thread in the book of Nahum, our peace.

Nahum 1:2, 3a
God *is* jealous, and the LORD revengeth; the LORD revengeth, and *is* furious [the Lord of wrath]; **the LORD will take vengeance on his adversaries, and he reserveth *wrath* for his enemies.**
The LORD *is* slow to anger, and great in power, and will not at all acquit *the wicked*.

God is a jealous God. This is no secret; this is nothing new. God had made this known a long time ago. If there is one thing God is not crazy about, it's when we start making up our own gods. Men have been doing this for a long time, as you well know. Men make three-in-one gods, mother gods, son gods, fish gods, animal gods. Men make gods out of wood and stone. People worship 'mother earth' and make water gods and fire gods. They worship the sun and the moon and the stars, even the host of heaven. It is people who make gods out of men, and most believe that in some way, they themselves are gods. But God is not mocked. God is still one God, the creator of the heaven and earth and the father of our Lord Jesus Christ. You might think, who would be so foolish as to be an adversary of the Lord? Who would want to be his enemy? This is a good question, because most of God's enemies do not think they are His enemies. God has always had to deal with this problem. Nevertheless, the Lord will not acquit the wicked.

Romans 1:18, 21, 22, 23, 25
For the wrath of God is revealed from heaven against all ungodliness and unrighteousness of men, who hold the truth in unrighteousness;
Because that, when they knew God, they glorified *him* not as God, neither were thankful; but became vain in their imaginations, and

their foolish heart was darkened.

Professing themselves to be wise, they became fools, And changed the glory of the uncorruptible God into an image made like to corruptible man, and to birds, and fourfooted beasts, and creeping things.

Who changed the truth of God into a lie, and worshipped and served the creature more than the Creator, who is blessed for ever. Amen.

It has always been men who have turned away from God and not God turning away from men. The truth is out there for all to know if one but cares to see it. However, people can be vain in their imaginations and their foolish hearts will be darkened. How many people today think a man can be God? Many today think that they are so wise, but the incorruptible God cannot be changed into an image, made like a corruptible man. Throughout His Word, God has told all of us who He is and who His son is, yet how many would trouble you over this matter or over many other things of the truth of God's Word for that matter?

II Thessalonians 1:6- 10

Seeing *it is* a righteous thing with God to recompense tribulation to them that trouble you;

And to you who are troubled rest with us, when the Lord Jesus shall be revealed from heaven with his mighty angels,

In flaming fire taking vengeance on them that know not God, and that obey not the gospel of our Lord Jesus Christ:

Who shall be punished with everlasting destruction from the presence of the Lord, and from the glory of his power;

When he shall come to be glorified in his saints, and to be admired in all them that believe (because our testimony among you was believed) in that day.

"Vengeance is mine; I will repay, saith the Lord."[4] And it is a good thing to leave up to him. Who else could judge what a man truly believes? We are responsible to believe the gospel of our Lord Jesus Christ. God is slow to anger and great in power, but to invoke His indignation is not something you want to take lightly.

---

4 Romans 12:19

Nahum 1:6- 9

Who can stand before his indignation? and who can abide in the fierceness of his anger? his fury is poured out like fire, and the rocks are thrown down by him.

The LORD *is* **good, a strong hold in the day of trouble; and he knoweth them that trust in him.**

But with an overrunning flood he will make an utter end of the place thereof, and darkness shall pursue his enemies.

What do ye imagine against the LORD? he will make an utter end: affliction shall not rise up the second time.

Imagine what you will against the Lord. Think what you want, but He will make an utter end of it all. People propound theories and teach them as the gospel truth. This darkness shall continue to pursue people, and they shall be consumed. The day of trouble is not a day in which you want to be wandering around in darkness. Even though we all are in the dark at times, it is a good thing the Lord knows them that are His and who it is that trust in him.

II Timothy 2:16- 21

But shun profane *and* **vain babblings: for they will increase unto more ungodliness.**

And their word will eat as doth a canker: of whom is Hymenaeus and Philetus;

Who concerning the truth have erred, saying that the resurrection is past already; and overthrow the faith [believing] of some.

Nevertheless the foundation of God standeth sure, having this seal, The Lord knoweth them that are his. And, Let every one that nameth the name of Christ depart from iniquity.

But in a great house there are not only vessels of gold and of silver, but also of wood and of earth; and some to honour, and some to dishonour.

If a man therefore purge himself from these, he shall be a vessel unto honour, sanctified, and meet for the master's use, *and* **prepared unto every good work.**

At times even those who know the truth can be drawn into error. Here we have Hymenaeus and Philetus teaching that the resurrection is past already, just as many today teach in one form or another. Some would have you believe that the resurrection has already occurred, and that Jesus returned some time ago. Others will tell you that when you die, you immediately go to heaven to be with Jesus, so why would you need a resurrection? There are yet others who take a whole different direction and tell you that when you die, you are reincarnated and just come back as something else. There are many different forms of error which veer off from the truth. But by its very definition, a resurrection has to do with raising from the dead. The Word says, "The Lord knows them that are his." God knows those who are in Christ. God knows what a man truly believes and who he trusts. Timothy says that in a great house, there are going to be some vessels to honor and some to dishonor. This is a horrendous translation here in the King James version. No one is completely without honor when they are born again because of the gift of holy spirit. It should read: some to honor and some to less honor. All the vessels are needful in the house. It is simply that some are better prepared for the master's use than others. Those which are full of error are not prepared for honor, but that does not mean they are not a needed vessel in the household. If we believe in Christ today, even if we prove to be a vessel of less honor, in the resurrection we will all be prepared for the master's use. Therefore we will become vessels of honor because of our sanctification in Christ. The Lord is good and a stronghold in the day of trouble.

I Thessalonians 5:1- 10

But of the times and the seasons, brethren, ye have no need that I write unto you.

For yourselves know perfectly that the day of the Lord so cometh as a thief in the night.

For when they shall say, Peace and safety; then sudden destruction cometh upon them, as travail upon a woman with child; and they shall not escape.

But ye, brethren, are not in darkness, that that day should overtake you as a thief.

Ye are all the children of light, and the children of the day: we are not of the night, nor of darkness.

Therefore let us not sleep, as *do* **others; but let us watch and be sober.**

For they that sleep sleep in the night; and they that be drunken are drunken in the night.

But let us, who are of the day, be sober, putting on the breastplate of faith [believing] **and love; and for an helmet, the hope of salvation.**

For God hath not appointed us to wrath, but to obtain salvation

by our Lord Jesus Christ,
Who died for us, that, whether we wake or sleep, we should live together with him.

There are those who will say all is well. There is no need to believe the Word of God. They cannot see their destruction is as a pregnant woman about to give birth. Darkness can blind a man to something even as obvious as this. Yet we don't have to be in darkness. We have obtained salvation by our Lord Jesus Christ. He is our peace. There will always be those who would try to steal our peace and replace it with a false sense of security. But such a wicked counselor as this shall be cut down and devoured as stubble fully dry.

Nahum 1:10- 12
For while *they be* folden together *as* thorns, and while they are drunken *as* drunkards, they shall be devoured as stubble fully dry.
There is *one* come out of thee, that imagineth evil against the LORD, a wicked counsellor.
Thus saith the LORD; Though *they be* quiet, and likewise many, yet thus shall they be cut down, when he shall pass through.

This is the burden of Nineveh as well as all those who imagine evil against the Lord or go along with wicked counsel. The Lord shall pass through, and he will either bring vengeance or he will be our peace. It is up to us to look for the one who brings good tidings and publishes peace.

Nahum 1:14, 15
And the LORD hath given a commandment concerning thee, *that* no more of thy name be sown: out of the house of thy gods will I cut off the graven image and the molten image: I will make thy grave; for thou art vile.
Behold upon the mountains the feet of him that bringeth good tidings, that publisheth peace! O Judah, keep thy solemn feasts, perform thy vows: for the wicked shall no more pass through thee; he is utterly cut off.

If peace is what you desire, then look for the feet of him who brings good tidings. Look for he who publishes peace. Many speak of peace, but this peace only one could bring. This peace is between God and man.

John 14:27
Peace I leave with you, my peace I give unto you: not as the world giveth, give I unto you. Let not your heart be troubled, neither let it be afraid.

Jesus had peace, and it was unlike anything the world had to offer. Jesus Christ is our peace, and he was willing to give of himself. It is only in him that we can truly have peace.

John 16:33
These things I have spoken unto you, that in me ye might have peace. In the world ye shall have tribulation: but be of good cheer; I have overcome the world.

To be in Christ as opposed to being in the world is what we must consider. In Christ we have peace, but in the world we have tribulation. In the world, when people speak of peace, they speak of peace time as opposed to war time. They speak of peace in their community as conformity to their social standard. Men are hired to keep the peace and are called peace officers. But what peace are they keeping? In reality they live above the very law that they are supposed to be enforcing on others. Does this not do more to cause tribulation than to cure it? In order to have a peace to keep, we must of necessity believe in the Lord Jesus Christ. For by his believing, he became our peace, and in him we have peace.

Romans 5:1
Therefore being justified by faith [believing], **we have peace with God through our Lord Jesus Christ.**

How could we hope to have peace among ourselves if we do not first have peace with God? Therefore being justified by the believing of Jesus Christ, we have peace with God through our Lord Jesus Christ, when we believe in him.

Romans 10:13- 15
For whosoever shall call upon the name of the Lord shall be saved.
How then shall they call on him in whom they have not believed? and how shall they believe in him of whom they have not heard? and how shall they hear without a preacher?
And how shall they preach, except they be sent? as it is written,

The Red Thread of Nahum

How beautiful are the feet of them that preach the gospel of peace, and bring glad tidings of good things!

Jesus Christ, who is our peace, came and preached peace. We ourselves can preach peace also because we have been sent. We have the gospel of peace. Once we have believed in him and have peace with God, then we can start thinking about having peace between one another.

Ephesians 2:13- 20
But now in Christ Jesus ye who sometimes were far off are made nigh by the blood of Christ.
For he is our peace, who hath made both one, and hath broken down the middle wall of partition *between us*;
Having abolished in his flesh the enmity, *even* **the law of commandments** *contained* **in ordinances; for to make in himself of twain one new man,** *so* **making peace;**
And that he might reconcile both unto God in one body by the cross, having slain the enmity thereby:
And came and preached peace to you which were afar off, and to them that were nigh.
For through him we both have access by one Spirit [spirit] unto the Father.
Now therefore ye are no more strangers and foreigners, but fellowcitizens with the saints, and of the household of God;
And are built upon the foundation of the apostles and prophets, Jesus Christ himself being the chief corner *stone.*

He is our peace. Jesus Christ is our peace. This is the red thread in the book of Nahum, and it is fulfilled in us who believe in the Lord Jesus Christ. Jews or Gentiles, it makes no difference. We have both been reconciled unto God by Jesus Christ. Therefore, we can have peace between ourselves as well. We all have access by one spirit unto the Father, and with that we become saints and are of the household of God. This is the foundation upon which we build, Jesus Christ himself being the chief corner, for he is our peace.

The Red Thread of Nahum

His Faith

What is faith? How is the book of Habakkuk connected with the New Testament concerning faith? These are points worthy of consideration as we open our study of the red thread in the book of Habakkuk. God said, "I will work a work in your days, which ye will not believe, though it be told you." It all has to do with the faith of Jesus Christ. It is recorded in Habakkuk, "the just shall live by his faith." His faith is therefore the red thread and the focus of our study.

Habakkuk 1:1- 5
The burden which Habakkuk the prophet did see.
O LORD, how long shall I cry, and thou wilt not hear! *even* **cry out unto thee** *of* **violence, and thou wilt not save!**
Why dost thou show me iniquity, and cause *me* **to behold grievance? for spoiling and violence** *are* **before me: and there are** *that* **raise up strife and contention.**
Therefore the law is slacked, and judgment doth never go forth: for the wicked doth compass about the righteous; therefore wrong judgment proceedeth.

Behold ye among the heathen, and regard, and wonder marvellously: for *I* **will work a work in your days,** *which* **ye will not believe, though it be told** *you.*

Israel languished in the time of Habakkuk the prophet. They had forsaken the law. It was a violent time. Israel was going to spend time among the heathen. Habakkuk cried unto the Lord, *how long?* The Lord said, "Behold," and God showed Habakkuk something which would be understood much more clearly after it had come to pass.

Acts 13:36- 41
For David, after he had served his own generation by the will of God, fell on sleep, and was laid unto his fathers, and saw corruption:
But he, whom God raised again, saw no [not] corruption.
Be it known unto you therefore, men *and* **brethren, that through this man is preached unto you the forgiveness of sins:**
And by him all that believe are justified from all things, from which ye could not be justified by the law of Moses.

The Red Thread of Habakkuk

Beware therefore, lest that come upon you, which is spoken of in the prophets;

Behold, ye despisers, and wonder, and perish: for I work a work in your days, a work which ye shall in no wise believe, though a man declare it unto you.

This passage in the book of Acts is speaking of Jesus Christ. The one whom God raised from the dead. It is through this man that forgiveness of sins is preached. The law could not justify a man, but Jesus Christ did. The Jews had difficulty believing Jesus Christ. Even though he was declared unto them, they struggled with it. This is how the red thread begins to unfold in the book of Habakkuk and how the red thread is exposed to us through the vision Habakkuk saw.

Habakkuk 1:6- 11
For, lo, I raise up the Chaldeans, *that* bitter and hasty nation, which shall march through the breadth of the land, to possess the dwelling places *that are* not theirs.
They *are* terrible and dreadful: their judgment and their dignity shall proceed of themselves.
Their horses also are swifter than the leopards, and are more fierce than the evening wolves: and their horsemen shall spread themselves, and their horsemen shall come from far; they shall fly as the eagle *that* hasteth to eat.
They shall come all for violence: their faces shall sup up *as* the east wind, and they shall gather the captivity as the sand.
And they shall scoff at the kings, and the princes shall be a scorn unto them: they shall deride every strong hold; for they shall heap dust, and take it.
Then shall *his* mind change, and he shall pass over [go too far], and offend, *imputing* this his power unto his god.

God spoke to Habakkuk about the Chaldeans. He revealed to him who they were and what they were going to do. It was not looking good for Israel through all this, so Habakkuk questioned what God was showing him.

Habakkuk 1:12
Art thou not from everlasting, O LORD my God, mine Holy One? we shall not die. O LORD, thou hast ordained them for judgment; and, O mighty God, thou hast established them for correction.

Habakkuk asked God if He knew about this before knowing that God has been around forever. Habakkuk said, "We, (meaning Israel), shall not die." We can't die like this; it can't all end like this for Israel. What about all the promises which were made? So Habakkuk waited for God's reply.

Habakkuk 2:1- 4
I will stand upon my watch, and set me upon the tower, and will watch to see what he will say unto me, and what I shall answer when I am reproved.
And the LORD answered me, and said, Write the vision, and make *it* plain upon tables, that he may run that readeth it.
For the vision *is* yet for an appointed time, but at the end it shall speak, and not lie: though it tarry, wait for it; because it will surely come, it will not tarry.

Behold, his soul *which* is lifted up is not upright in him: but the just shall live by his faith.

God answered Habakkuk, telling him to write the vision and make it clear so that he who reads it may run. I don't know if he is running for cover or running to the Lord for refuge, but I do know the vision is yet for a time appointed. When that time comes, it shall speak clearly. It will surely come, so God told Habakkuk to wait for it. God again says, "Behold." He is revealing the red thread to Habakkuk. God says, "Behold his soul." This is the soul of all who are lifted up and not upright. "But the just shall live by his faith." This faith is speaking of Jesus Christ.

Romans 1:16, 17
For I am not ashamed of the gospel of Christ: for it is the power of God unto salvation to every one that believeth; to the Jew first, and also to the Greek.
For therein is the righteousness of God revealed from faith to faith: as it is written, The just shall live by faith.

This statement, "the just shall live by faith," ties Jesus Christ to the prophecy of Habakkuk. It also says: "the righteousness of God is revealed from faith to faith." We must question the meaning of the word "faith." The word "faith" is only about six hundred years old and is most commonly linked to Christianity. This word came to the English language through the Old French and Latin languages. Faith held the idea of trust. When using this word in the Bible, the translators chose "faith" to convey the meaning of the Greek word *pistis*. The aspect most problematic with this word choice is that "faith" is a noun. When the translators were working on the Bible, they chose two words in translating *pistis*. The words "believing" and "faith" were equally used for this one word, *pistis*. The word "faith" is being used to describe an action, but it is not a verb. The righteousness of God is revealed through the believing of Jesus Christ to those who believe in Christ. It is revealed from an action taken by one, Jesus Christ. Righteousness is then revealed to us when we believe in Jesus Christ. "Believing" is a verb and thereby is able to describe the action present here. Today faith is commonly perceived as something people have. The true force or meaning behind faith is not something you have but rather something you do.

Romans 3:21- 26
But now the righteousness of God without the law is manifested, being witnessed by the law and the prophets;
Even the righteousness of God *which is* by faith [the believing] **of Jesus Christ unto all and upon all them that believe: for there is no difference:**
For all have sinned, and come short of the glory of God;
Being justified freely by his grace through the redemption that is in Christ Jesus:
Whom God hath set forth *to be* a propitiation through faith [believing] **in his blood, to declare his righteousness for the remission of sins that are past, through the forbearance of God;**
To declare, *I say*, at this time his righteousness: that he might be just, and the justifier of him which believeth in Jesus.

Today when we believe in Jesus Christ, we receive the righteousness of God, which came to us by the believing of Jesus Christ. We have justification through the redemption which is in Christ Jesus. Justification is being made just as if you had never sinned. The price of redemption has been paid through believing in his blood. This is how the soul of a man, even though it is lifted up and is not right within him, can be made righteous by believing. Even greater, it is free to us who believe, because it is by grace. Don't run from this. Run to the believing of Jesus Christ, for he was raised again for our justification.

Romans 4:25- 5:2
Who was delivered for our offences, and was raised again for

our justification.
Therefore being justified by faith [believing]**, we have peace with God through our Lord Jesus Christ:**
By whom also we have access by faith [believing] **into this grace wherein we stand, and rejoice in hope of the glory of God.**

Therefore being justified by faith, his faith, we have peace with God through our Lord Jesus Christ. Then we have access by his faith into this grace wherein we stand. The law could not accomplish what Christ did. Jesus Christ had to believe so we could believe in him and be justified by his believing. Believing is an on-going action as well as an accomplished work.

Galatians 2:16
Knowing that a man is not justified by the works of the law, but by the faith [believing] **of Jesus Christ, even we have believed in Jesus Christ, that we might be justified by the faith** [believing] **of Christ, and not by the works of the law: for by the works of the law shall no flesh be justified.**

Faith is not something that Jesus had, but rather something he did. Therefore it is something we do as well. We believe, and therefore we act upon what we believe.

Galatians 2:20
I am crucified with Christ: nevertheless I live; yet not I, but Christ liveth in me: and the life which I now live in the flesh I live by the faith [believing] **of the Son of God, who loved me, and gave himself for me.**

If I have life at all now, it is because of the believing of the son of God who loved me and gave himself for me. I can believe to live in the flesh or not, but it is not something I have, it is something I do.

Galatians 3:10- 14
For as many as are of the works of the law are under the curse: for it is written, Cursed *is* every one that continueth not in all things which are written in the book of the law to do them.
But that no man is justified by the law in the sight of God, *it is* evident: for, The just shall live by faith [believing]**.**
And the law is not of faith [believing]**: but, The man that doeth them shall live in them.**

Christ hath redeemed us from the curse of the law, being made a curse for us: for it is written, Cursed *is* every one that hangeth on a tree:
That the blessing of Abraham might come on the Gentiles through Jesus Christ; that we might receive the promise of the Spirit through faith [believing].

"The just shall live by faith." The word "faith" would better be served by the word "believing." The verb "believing" better describes the action in the verse. It is through Jesus Christ that we receive the promise of the spirit through believing.

Galatians 3:21- 28
Is **the law then against the promises of God? God forbid: for if there had been a law given which could have given life, verily righteousness should have been by the law.**
But the scripture hath concluded all under sin, that the promise [of the spirit] **by faith** [the believing] **of Jesus Christ might be given to them that believe.**
But before faith [believing] **came, we were kept under the law, shut up unto the faith** [believing] **which should afterwards be revealed.**
Wherefore the law was our schoolmaster *to bring us* **unto Christ, that we might be justified by faith** [believing].
But after that faith [that believing of Christ] **is come, we are no longer under a schoolmaster.**
For ye are all the children of God by faith [believing] **in Christ Jesus.**
For as many of you as have been baptized into Christ have put on Christ.
There is neither Jew nor Greek, there is neither bond nor free, there is neither male nor female: for ye are all one in Christ Jesus.

You will notice that you can replace the word "faith" with the word "believing" every place it is used, but you cannot exchange the word "believing" with the word "faith." This is important to note, because both English words are translated from the same Greek word in your version of the Bible.

Christ believed, now we can believe. We are all the children of God by believing in Christ Jesus. Yes, people believed before Christ came, but it was not the believing that we have in Christ today. We received the spirit, and with the spirit came a change in perspective. The translators could see that something had changed with regard to believing, and this is why the word faith was employed. It is still believing, but the difference lies in the man's ability. A man who is without spirit has to see first then believe. The man who has the spirit of God has the ability to receive information in a new way. He receives his information from the spirit and has the ability to perceive things spiritually. He believes that information, and then he sees the result in the senses. Using the word "faith" provided an element of trust, but you cannot deny the action. Believing requires information and action. The man of faith, or believing, must trust God to make good on His word. Even before he is saved, the senses man must trust God, because he must believe the Word first before he will receive the new birth. He does not get born again and then believe. With his mouth he confesses that Jesus Christ is Lord and believes in his heart that God has raised him from the dead, and only then is he saved. Not the other way around. You were born the first time and then you saw and believed. The spiritual man believes first and then he sees. The senses are merely an indicator of the effects. This is why we must always look to Christ and get a knowledge of him so we know what is available and what to believe.

Hebrews 12:2
Looking unto Jesus the author and finisher of *our* faith [believing]**; who for the joy that was set before him endured the cross, despising the shame, and is set down at the right hand of the throne of God.**

Jesus wrote the book on believing. Jesus taught his disciples to believe God. He showed them the potential that they had when they believed. Jesus knew that when you received information from God and you believed that information, you must act upon it. He also saw the joy and peace in believing, and he knew that we could abound in the hope through the power of the holy spirit.

Romans 15:13
Now the God of hope fill you with all joy and peace in believing, that ye may abound in hope, through the power of the Holy Ghost [holy spirit]**.**

We have joy and peace in believing. Now there is no more of the strife and contention which Habakkuk saw, because we now live in the spirit and with the power of the holy spirit in us. Christ believed. It was his faith, or more accurately, his believing which made it available for us to believe.

We now believe to live and to have joy and peace through the power of the holy spirit. Now we can think the way Jesus Christ thought, see what he saw, know what he knows, and most of all, believe the way he believed.

Romans 12:1- 3
I beseech you therefore, brethren, by the mercies of God, that ye present your bodies a living sacrifice, holy, acceptable unto God, *which is* your reasonable service.
And be not conformed to this world: but be ye transformed by the renewing of your mind, that ye may prove what *is* that good, and acceptable, and perfect, will of God.
For I say, through the grace given unto me, to every man that is among you, not to think *of himself* more highly than he ought to think; but to think soberly, according as God hath dealt to every man the measure of faith [believing].

How much is the measure of faith? A bushel or a peck? No, it is neither. Faith is not a thing that we have but something we do. Faith is inert while believing is active. We don't let our thinking get out of bounds, which is to think more highly than we ought to think. The boundaries for our believing is the Word of God. High and lofty thoughts take us outside of the safe haven of God's Word. We are to think soberly, according to the right information, the way Jesus Christ did. We believe what Christ believed, the way he believed, how he believed, and who he believed. We now present our bodies as a living sacrifice, not a dead one unto God. Christ had to die, but it was so that you and I could live. We don't die for Christ. We live today and everyday because God raised him from the dead. Do not be conformed to this world, but be ye transformed by the renewing of your mind, by believing the Word. We have the mind of Christ. We have the believing of Christ. We have the spirit and the ability to perceive things of the spirit. This is why the knowledge of the glory of the Lord is so vital to us today. God told Habakkuk about the knowledge of the Lord. In Habakkuk's prayer, he rejoiced in the Lord and said, "The Lord God is my strength, and He will make my feet like hind's feet, and He will make me to walk upon my high places."

Habakkuk 2:14
For the earth shall be filled with the knowledge of the glory of the LORD, as the waters cover the sea.

We have so much to believe today that we could spend a lifetime being filled with the knowledge of the glory of the Lord and believing it. The believing of Jesus Christ is the red thread found in the book of Habakkuk. There is a work that God has worked in our day which speaks clearly now. We can run to it or away from it. It can prove to be a work you will not believe even though it was explained to you. It can also prove to be a work which began in Christ and now continues in us. From believing to believing.

The Red Thread of Habakkuk

The Red Thread of Zephaniah

The King of Israel

The day of the Lord is when you see the red thread revealed in the book of Zephaniah. The king of Israel will be in the midst of thee. In that day, all things will be utterly consumed from the land. You may gasp, but do not be dismayed at the presence of the Lord. The day of the Lord's sacrifice will be there as well. The day of the Lord is a day of wrath. The trumpet shall sound, and the land shall be devoured by the fire of his jealousy. It would do a man good to consider these things before the day of the Lord's anger comes upon him. The Lord will be awesome. He will famish all the gods of the earth, and everyone will bow before him. He is a just Lord. He will not be unreasonable or wicked, but he will bring judgment to light. *Therefore wait upon me*, saith the Lord, *until the day I rise up. My determination is to gather the nations and to pour out my indignation, for all the earth shall be devoured.* Then He will return to the people who want to serve Him with one consent. Sing, O daughter of Zion, for the Lord hath taken away thy judgment. He has cast out the enemy, and the king of Israel is in the midst of thee, even the Lord. This is the red thread in the book of Zephaniah, which is set in the day of the Lord when Jesus Christ, who is the king of Israel, shall be in the midst of you. He will gather you and will make you a name and a praise among all the people of the earth.

Zephaniah 1:1- 6
The word of the LORD which came unto Zephaniah the son of Cushi, the son of Gedaliah, the son of Amariah, the son of Hizkiah, in the days of Josiah the son of Amon, king of Judah.
I will utterly consume all *things* from off the land, saith the LORD.
I will consume man and beast; I will consume the fowls of the heaven, and the fishes of the sea, and the stumblingblocks with the wicked; and I will cut off man from off the land, saith the LORD.
I will also stretch out mine hand upon Judah, and upon all the inhabitants of Jerusalem; and I will cut off the remnant [names] of Baal from this place, *and* the name of the Chemarims with the priests;
And them that worship the host of heaven upon the housetops; and them that worship *and* that swear by the LORD, and that swear by Malcham;
And them that are turned back from the LORD; and *those* that have not sought the LORD, nor inquired for him.

This is the word of the Lord which came unto Zephaniah. Everything and everyone will be utterly consumed from the land. Consider for a moment the names of Baal; Baal holds the meaning of 'my Lord.' People have lords in their lives, and here they called them by the name of Baal. All this Baal worship will be done away with, as well as the Chemarims who where ministers identified by their black robes. They were not ministers of God, but ministers of other lords. These ministers will also be consumed. Then you have those identified who swear by Malcham. Malcham refers to a king god or king idol. This title came from the Ammonites, who thought the king was a god who should be idolized and worshipped. All this perversion will be cut off from the land. But when will this take place? It will all take place in the day of the Lord which defines a period of time in which all of these things will happen.

Zephaniah 1:7- 9
Hold thy peace at the presence of the Lord GOD: for the day of the LORD *is* at hand: for the LORD hath prepared a sacrifice, he hath bid his guests.
And it shall come to pass in the day of the LORD'S sacrifice, that I will punish the princes, and the king's children, and all such as are clothed with strange apparel.
In the same day also will I punish all those that leap on [over] the threshold, which fill their masters' houses with violence and deceit.

Zephaniah speaks of the Lord God preparing a sacrifice and calling guests. The purpose for this is a wedding. There is going to be a wedding in the day of the Lord's sacrifice. There will be some who are punished for wearing strange clothes and some will be punished for leaping over the threshold. This all speaks of a wedding ceremony. Today we still know of this tradition of carrying the bride over the threshold after the wedding ceremony. The husband carries the wife over the threshold of their new home showing that she now has the right to be in the house and to come and go as she pleases. The bride has been given the rights of the house by her lord. Jesus spoke a parable concerning this wedding ceremony in the Gospels as well.

Matthew 22:1- 13
And Jesus answered and spake unto them again by parables, and said, The kingdom of heaven is like unto a certain king, which made a marriage for his son,

And sent forth his servants to call them that were bidden to the wedding: and they would not come.

Again, he sent forth other servants, saying, Tell them which are bidden, Behold, I have prepared my dinner: my oxen and *my* fatlings *are* killed, and all things *are* ready: come unto the marriage.

But they made light of *it*, and went their ways, one to his farm, another to his merchandise: And the remnant took his servants, and entreated *them* spitefully, and slew *them*.

But when the king heard *thereof*, he was wroth: and he sent forth his armies, and destroyed those murderers, and burned up their city.

Then saith he to his servants, The wedding is ready, but they which were bidden were not worthy.

Go ye therefore into the highways, and as many as ye shall find, bid to the marriage.

So those servants went out into the highways, and gathered together all as many as they found, both bad and good: and the wedding was furnished with guests.

And when the king came in to see the guests, he saw there a man which had not on a wedding garment:

And he saith unto him, Friend, how camest thou in hither not having a wedding garment? And he was speechless.

Then said the king to the servants, Bind him hand and foot, and take him away, and cast *him* into outer darkness; there shall be weeping and gnashing of teeth.

The slaying of the fatling would be the same as preparing the sacrifice in Zephaniah. The king would then bid his guests to come. When the king would invite his guests to the wedding, he would also send them the clothes they were to wear. If the guests came wearing some other garment, they would not be allowed in. This is why it says in Zephaniah that some would be punished for being clothed with strange apparel. Jesus also spoke of having legal access and the right to enter the sheep fold. This also relates to the idea of leaping over the threshold.

John 10:1, 2
Verily, verily, I say unto you, He that entereth not by the door into the sheepfold, but climbeth up some other way, the same is a thief and a robber.

But he that entereth in by the door is the shepherd of the sheep.

Jesus Christ is the shepherd, and he has the right to enter by the door.

If he carries you over the threshold, you have the right to be there as well. If you try jumping over the threshold or getting in by some other way or means, you are a thief and a robber.

John 10:6- 9
This parable spake Jesus unto them: but they understood not what things they were which he spake unto them.
Then said Jesus unto them again, Verily, verily, I say unto you, I am the door of the sheep.
All that ever came before me are thieves and robbers: but the sheep did not hear them.
I am the door: by me if any man enter in, he shall be saved, and shall go in and out, and find pasture.

Jesus told this parable to them so that they might understand, but they didn't. No one wants to be stuck on the outside when the day of the Lord comes. This is why we must understand that Jesus Christ is the door, and we have to enter by or through him. Then we shall be saved, and we can go out and come in and find good pasture.

John 14:1- 3 and 6
Let not your heart be troubled: ye believe in God, believe also in me.
In my Father's house are many mansions: if *it were* not *so*, I would have told you. I go to prepare a place for you.
And if I go and prepare a place for you, I will come again, and receive you unto myself; that where I am, *there* ye may be also.
Jesus saith unto him, I am the way, the truth, and the life: no man cometh unto the Father, but by me.

If you believe in God, believe also in Jesus Christ, for he is the way unto the Father. The bridegroom would prepare a house for his bride. He would carry her across the threshold after the wedding. This is what Jesus is telling the bride of Israel here in the gospel of John. This all fits with the events of which Zephaniah prophesied.

Zephaniah 3:8, 9
Therefore wait ye upon me, saith the LORD, until the day that I rise up to the prey: for my determination *is* to gather the nations, that I may assemble the kingdoms, to pour upon them mine indignation, *even* all my fierce anger: for all the earth shall be devoured with the fire of

my jealousy.
> For then will I turn to the people a pure language, that they may all call upon the name of the LORD, to serve him with one consent.

The Lord is telling Israel to wait upon him. This is also prophetic, speaking of the day of the Lord when Jesus Christ will come as king of kings and Lord of Lords. The day of the Lord will not be all fun and games. But for those who have found the way into the Father's house, they will be safe. Since we know the Lord's aim is to gather all the nations and pour out His indignation and devour the earth, it would be wise not only for Israel but for all of us to seek the Lord so we can be hidden in the day of the Lord's anger.

> **Zephaniah 2:1- 3**
> Gather yourselves together, yea, gather together, O nation not desired;
> Before the decree bring forth, *before* the day pass as the chaff, before the fierce anger of the LORD come upon you, before the day of the LORD'S anger come upon you.
> Seek ye the LORD, all ye meek of the earth, which have wrought his judgment; seek righteousness, seek meekness: it may be ye shall be hid in the day of the LORD'S anger.

It is good for all of us to understand what is written in Zephaniah, because the day of the Lord will not come upon Israel alone. We all need to find the way to righteousness and have the meekness to accept it before the day of the Lord's anger comes upon us. Israel must wait for the day when the Lord is in the midst of them as the king of Israel. They can rejoice and be glad with all their heart, because the Lord will take away their judgments and cast out their enemy. They will not see evil anymore, and this is what Zephaniah saw and prophesied of concerning the daughter of Zion.

> **Zephaniah 3:14, 15**
> Sing, O daughter of Zion; shout, O Israel; be glad and rejoice with all the heart, O daughter of Jerusalem.
> The LORD hath taken away thy judgments, he hath cast out thine enemy: the king of Israel, *even* the LORD, *is* in the midst of thee: thou shalt not see evil any more.

The king of Israel has taken away your judgments and has gotten rid of the enemy. Christ did not accomplish this for Israel the first time he was here upon earth. With his death and resurrection and in his ascension, the promise was made of his return. He still has a job to do as king, and he will yet reign and defeat the enemy.

I Corinthians 15:22- 28
For as in Adam all die, even so in Christ shall all be made alive.
But every man in his own order: Christ the firstfruits; afterward they that are Christ's at his coming.
Then *cometh* the end, when he shall have delivered up the kingdom to God, even the Father; when he shall have put down all rule and all authority and power.
For he must reign, till he hath put all enemies under his feet.
The last enemy *that* shall be destroyed *is* death.
For he hath put all things under his feet. But when he saith all things are put under *him, it is* manifest that he is excepted, which did put all things under him.
And when all things shall be subdued unto him, then shall the Son also himself be subject unto him that put all things under him, that God may be all in all.

As in Adam, all die. Even so in Christ shall all be made alive, but every man in his own order. Today we become the first fruits in Christ when we are born again. If the first fruits were only talking about Christ himself, the first fruits wouldn't be plural. We become the first fruits with Christ when we are born again. We are in Christ and from that moment on, we have eternal life. After this time of the mystery in which you and I live, Christ will return and gather the first fruits. The day of the Lord will be a continuation of the first time that he was here upon the earth. When Christ was here the first time, he was born and grew up and did the work of the Father that was set before him. He never claimed to be king of Israel nor did he reign. Even in the end when Pilate asked him if he was the king of the Jews, he did not lay claim to the title. Jesus knew that it was not yet time for that to be fulfilled. When he comes back, he will come with his kingdom, and everyone that ever lived will live again to see that day. Christ will then gather all those who are his. This is part of the job of the king of Israel in that day.

John 18:33- 38
Then Pilate entered into the judgment hall again, and called Jesus, and said unto him, Art thou the King of the Jews?
Jesus answered him, Sayest thou this thing of thyself, or did

others tell it thee of me?

Pilate answered, Am I a Jew? Thine own nation and the chief priests have delivered thee unto me: what hast thou done?

Jesus answered, My kingdom is not of this world: if my kingdom were of this world, then would my servants fight, that I should not be delivered to the Jews: but now is my kingdom not from hence.

Pilate therefore said unto him, Art thou a king then? Jesus answered, Thou sayest that I am a king. To this end was I born, and for this cause came I into the world, that I should bear witness unto the truth. Every one that is of the truth heareth my voice.

Pilate saith unto him, What is truth? And when he had said this, he went out again unto the Jews, and saith unto them, I find in him no fault *at all*.

Pilate asked Jesus, *are you the king of the Jews?* Jesus answered him with a question of his own, saying, *how did you come up with that idea?* Jesus went on to say, *my kingdom is not of this world. If it were, my servants would fight, but now my kingdom is not from hence.* Pilate again said, *are you a king then?* Jesus still just turned it back on him and said, *that's what you have said. I never said I was a king.* Jesus knew it wasn't his time to be called a king. He knew there was more to his life and more to come of the day of the Lord, a time in which he would be called the king of Israel.

Revelation 19:11- 16
And I saw heaven opened, and behold a white horse; and he that sat upon him *was* called Faithful and True, and in righteousness he doth judge and make war.

His eyes *were* as a flame of fire, and on his head *were* many crowns; and he had a name written, that no man knew, but he himself.

And he *was* clothed with a vesture dipped in blood: and his name is called The Word of God.

And the armies *which were* in heaven followed him upon white horses, clothed in fine linen, white and clean.

And out of his mouth goeth a sharp sword, that with it he should smite the nations: and he shall rule them with a rod of iron: and he treadeth the winepress of the fierceness and wrath of Almighty God.

And he hath on *his* vesture and on his thigh a name written, **KING OF KINGS, AND LORD OF LORDS.**

John's revelation again takes place in the Lord's day, and it is then that we see the marriage of the Lamb and the bride, which is Israel. It is in that day that the Lord Jesus Christ is called king. The Lord Jesus Christ needs to deliver up all things unto the Lord God. When he comes the next time, he will do just that. He will put down all rule and insurrection, and he will reign until he delivers the kingdom to the Father.

Zephaniah 3:16- 20
   In that day it shall be said to Jerusalem, Fear thou not: *and to* Zion, Let not thine hands be slack.
   The LORD thy God in the midst of thee *is* **mighty; he will save, he will rejoice over thee with joy; he will rest in his love, he will joy over thee with singing.**
   I will gather *them that are* sorrowful for the solemn assembly, *who* are of thee, *to whom* the reproach of it *was* a burden.
   Behold, at that time I will undo all that afflict thee: and I will save her that halteth, and gather her that was driven out; and I will get them praise and fame in every land where they have been put to shame.
   At that time will I bring you *again*, **even in the time that I gather you: for I will make you a name and a praise among all people of the earth, when I turn back your captivity before your eyes, saith the LORD.**

   The whole idea is to get God back in the midst of his people. Jesus Christ came to bring people back to God. All he is and all he has done is to fulfill that purpose. He will reign as the king of Israel in the day of the Lord so that he can bring you and gather you and "make you a name and a praise among all people of the earth." God desires to rest in His love toward you, O Israel. This then is the red thread in the book of Zephaniah, when the Lord Jesus Christ reigns as the king of Israel and is once again in the midst of you in the day of the Lord.

The Red Thread of Haggai

As a Signet

After the captivity, the children of Israel who had moved back to Jerusalem were dwelling in their own finished houses. Meanwhile the Lord's house still lay waste and was not rebuilt. The Lord of hosts said by Haggai the prophet, "consider your ways." The Lord of hosts, otherwise known as the Lord of the Sabbath, is Jehovah Zeba'oth. In considering their way, God directs the children of Israel to look at specific things. You have sown a lot, and yet you bring in a little. You eat, but you do not have enough. You drink, but it doesn't satisfy your thirst. You have clothes, but you're not warm. You earn money, but your pockets have holes in them; it's gone before you get it. Is there something wrong with this picture? At times we all get too busy living and forget God. We just don't have time for Him. When the children of Israel came out of Egypt, God made a covenant with them, and He was still with them. He speaks to them by Haggai the prophet as the Lord of the Sabbath, the one who had asked for a little bit of their time to think of Him and worship Him. It was the Lord of the Sabbath who wanted them to rebuild His house, which was the temple. Jehovah Zeba'oth also said that He would fill this house with glory, and it would be in this place that He would give peace. God was going to shake things up a little and bring the desire of the nations, even though they had no idea what that was. Even though Jesus Christ would prove to be the desire of the nations, the red thread in the book of Haggai has to do with Jesus Christ as a signet. A signet is a seal. Something was going to be done in the temple which required an authenticating stamp.

Haggai 1:2- 7
Thus speaketh the LORD of hosts, saying, This people say, The time is not come, the time that the LORD'S house should be built.
Then came the word of the LORD by Haggai the prophet, saying,
***Is it* time for you, O ye, to dwell in your ceiled houses, and this house *lie* waste?**
Now therefore thus saith the LORD of hosts; Consider your ways.
Ye have sown much, and bring in little; ye eat, but ye have not enough; ye drink, but ye are not filled with drink; ye clothe you, but there is none warm; and he that earneth wages earneth wages *to put it* into a bag with holes.

The Red Thread of Haggai

Thus saith the LORD of hosts; Consider your ways.

The Lord of hosts is Jehovah Zeba'oth, one of the ten redemptive names of Jehovah. It was He who spoke to Haggai concerning the Lord's house. God's house was the temple in the days of the Old Testament. It was the place where God's people could find Him, a place where they could go and worship and have their prayers heard. God's house still had a purpose to serve, and God's people still needed to know God was there. So Haggai spoke to the people about rebuilding the temple.

Haggai 1:12- 14
Then Zerubbabel the son of Shealtiel, and Joshua the son of Josedech, the high priest, with all the remnant of the people, obeyed the voice of the LORD their God, and the words of Haggai the prophet, as the LORD their God had sent him, and the people did fear before the LORD.
Then spake Haggai the LORD'S messenger in the LORD'S message unto the people, saying, I *am* with you, saith the LORD.
And the LORD stirred up the spirit of Zerubbabel the son of Shealtiel, governor of Judah, and the spirit of Joshua the son of Josedech, the high priest, and the spirit of all the remnant of the people; and they came and did work in the house of the LORD of hosts, their God.

We are introduced to a couple of individuals in the book of Haggai. Their names become important to us in our study of the red thread. Zerubbabel and Shealtiel were both of the lineage of king David and would play a part in the bloodline and family tree of the Lord Jesus Christ. Yet it is the meaning of their names that is significant here. The name Zerubbabel means 'sown in Babylon.' Zerubbabel was the royal seed carried through the sowing in Babylon. Shealtiel means 'asked for from God.' This points to the one chosen of God. These are the meanings of these two names, and what follows builds for us the body of the red thread here in the book of Haggai.

Haggai 2:4- 7
Yet now be strong, O Zerubbabel, saith the LORD; and be strong, O Joshua, son of Josedech, the high priest; and be strong, all ye people of the land, saith the LORD, and work: for I *am* with you, saith the LORD of hosts:
***According to* the word that I covenanted with you when ye came**

out of Egypt, so my spirit remaineth among you: fear ye not.
> For thus saith the LORD of hosts; Yet once, it *is* a little while, and I will shake the heavens, and the earth, and the sea, and the dry *land*;
> And I will shake all nations, and the desire of all nations shall come: and I will fill this house with glory, saith the LORD of hosts.

God established His pact with the children of Israel when they came out of Egypt, but God's covenant has always been man's redemption. God's spirit remained among them and was put upon certain individuals throughout the Old Testament, but God had something greater in mind. He was going to shake things up, the likes of which the world had never known. It would shake all the nations, and it would fulfill the desire of all people who hunger and seek after God. It would be this house, the one Zerubabbel and the remnant of the children of Israel would build which God would fill with glory. It would be in this house that God would give peace to the world.

Haggai 2:9
> The glory of this latter house shall be greater than of the former, saith the LORD of hosts: and in this place will I give peace, saith the LORD of hosts.

This would all occur not while Jesus was here upon the earth, but after he was ascended into heaven and was seated at the right hand of God. It would prove to be on the day of Pentecost recorded in the book of Acts. The outpouring of the holy spirit would take place in God's house.

Acts 2:1-4
> And when the day of Pentecost was fully come, they were all with one accord in one place.
> And suddenly there came a sound from heaven as of a rushing mighty wind, and it filled all the house [God's house, the temple] where they were sitting.
> And there appeared unto them cloven tongues like as of fire, and it sat upon each of them.
> And they were all filled with the Holy Ghost [holy spirit], and began to speak with other tongues, as the Spirit gave them utterance.

This fulfilled the prophecy of Haggai concerning God's house. God's house was instrumental, but it was Jesus Christ who was as a signet.

This seal was fulfilled in and with the outpouring of the holy spirit.

> **John 14:23-27**
> Jesus answered and said unto him, If a man love me, he will keep my words: and my Father will love him, and we will come unto him, and make our abode with him.
> He that loveth me not keepeth not my sayings: and the word which ye hear is not mine, but the Father's which sent me.
> These things have I spoken unto you, being *yet* present with you.
> But the Comforter, *which is* the Holy Ghost [holy spirit], whom the Father will send in my name, he shall teach you all things, and bring all things to your remembrance, whatsoever I have said unto you.
> Peace I leave with you, my peace I give unto you: not as the world giveth, give I unto you. Let not your heart be troubled, neither let it be afraid.

Jesus spoke these words while he was here, but he knew it would not take place while he was present with them. After he was gone the holy spirit would come. The Father would send the spirit in Jesus Christ's name. You have to ask yourself, what's in a name?

> **II Corinthians 1:20-22**
> For all the promises of God in him [Christ] *are* yea, and in him Amen, unto the glory of God by us.
> Now he which stablisheth us with you in Christ, and hath anointed us, *is* God;
> Who hath also sealed us, and given the earnest of the Spirit in our hearts.

All the promises of God are in Christ. It is God who establishes us in Christ. God has anointed us and sealed us and given us the spirit. A signet seals things. God has sealed us in Christ. Christ being as a signet leaves an impression on our heart. Christ is stamped in the holy spirit which God has put in our hearts.

> **II Corinthians 3:17, 18**
> Now the Lord is that Spirit: and where the Spirit of the Lord *is*, there *is* liberty.
> But we all, with open face beholding as in a glass the glory of the Lord, are changed into the same image from glory to glory, *even* as by the Spirit of the Lord.

It says, "now the Lord is that spirit," because the spirit we received from God was given in the name of the Lord Jesus Christ. This is the authentic stamp of approval. Don't accept a spirit given under any other name.

Haggai 2:23
In that day, saith the LORD of hosts, will I take thee, O Zerubbabel, my servant, the son of Shealtiel, saith the LORD, and will make thee as a signet: for I have chosen thee, saith the LORD of hosts.

At times in the Bible you will want to ask, what's in a name? In the name of Zerubbabel, we find the one who would be of the royal seed. In the name of Shealtiel, we find the one asked for of God. The one chosen by God to be as a signet. In the name of Jesus Christ, we find all the promises of God fulfilled and delivered. Here Christ is the one who as a signet sealed us. For in the name of Jesus Christ, God sealed us with holy spirit. This made Jesus Christ as a signet and the red thread in the book of Haggai the prophet.

The Red Thread of Haggai

The Branch

The book of Zechariah is written at the end of Israel's seventy-year captivity in Babylon. Jesus Christ is the red thread in the book of Zechariah as the branch, a term best defined as an offspring or sprout. In the book of Zechariah, God uses a good deal of symbolism. When dealing with figures of speech, the biblical usage of numbers, and other symbolism, God must always be the one who defines and explains their meaning. We dare not guess at the meaning. When looking at the branch as a division of a family tree, there are four divisions. You are first introduced to the servant and the man and then to the king and the lord. With regard to time, the branch splits off into two major divisions, noting Christ's first coming and also Christ's second coming. To see the incredible symbolism of the branch, we must recognize that Jesus Christ is the offspring of God as well as the sprout off of King David's family tree.

Zechariah 3:8- 10
Hear now, O Joshua the high priest, thou, and thy fellows that sit before thee: for they *are* men wondered at: for, behold, I will bring forth my servant the BRANCH.
For behold the stone that I have laid before Joshua; upon one stone *shall be* seven eyes: behold, I will engrave the graving thereof, saith the LORD of hosts, and I will remove the iniquity of that land in one day.
In that day, saith the LORD of hosts, shall ye call every man his neighbour under the vine and under the fig tree.

Zechariah turns to Joshua the high priest and to the other priests who sit before him and says, "For they are men wondered at." These would either be those high priests who came before Joshua, or it could also be the priests who would come after him. It all depends upon the way the translators handled the language as they were translating this into English. What would make men wonder about these priests? It could only be in terms of their acceptance or rejection of the branch. God showed them His servant the branch. God said, "Behold the stone that I have laid before Joshua." In terms of the red thread, who is the stone? God also said, "Upon this one stone shall be seven eyes." Here is some symbolism which needs to be understood. Seven is the number for spiritual perfection, and the eyes are set for sight. Therefore, the seven eyes indicate perfect spiritual sight or spiritual insight. Then upon that stone God engraved this: "I will remove the iniquity of that land in one day." In that day we shall call every man our neighbor under the vine and the fig tree. The vine and the fig tree speak of safety, prosperity, and good times. Calling every man your neighbor would indicate you do not harbor any ill will toward those around you. An additional interpretation could be that Jesus Christ is also known as the true vine, and the fig tree is representative of Israel. Therefore you could say that everyone of Israel who is under the true vine of Jesus is your neighbor.

We are being introduced to "my servant the branch," and the first fork of this branch is defined as a servant. This servant would have perfect spiritual insight and be someone who could remove iniquity from the land. Did Jesus Christ come in the form of a servant? If he is going to be "my servant the branch," he must have taken that form as well.

Philippians 2:5- 11
Let this mind be in you, which was also in Christ Jesus:
Who, being in the form of God, thought it not robbery to be equal with God:
But made himself of no reputation, and took upon him the form of a servant, and was made in the likeness of men:
And being found in fashion as a man, he humbled himself, and became obedient unto death, even the death of the cross.
Wherefore God also hath highly exalted him, and given him a name which is above every name:
That at the name of Jesus every knee should bow, of *things* in heaven, and *things* in earth, and *things* under the earth;
And *that* every tongue should confess that Jesus Christ *is* Lord, to the glory of God the Father.

To be a servant is a frame of mind more than anything. The true idea of a servant is for the servant to become so like his master that they think the same way, desire the same things, and share the same purpose. The servant and his master would most assuredly love and respect each other. Jesus had the form of God because he was mindful of the things of God. Jesus had the form of a servant because he was obedient to the plans and desires of his father. God gave him a name which is above every name and exalted him because of it.

Matthew 10:24, 25a
The disciple is not above *his* master, nor the servant above his lord.

It is enough for the disciple that he be as his master, and the servant as his lord.

Jesus' sole desire was to be like his father, and he taught this to his disciples as well. Jesus knew that it was not wrong to strive to be equal with his father. It is not wrong for us who are in Christ to be of this mindset also. As a servant, we must become familiar then with the plans, desires, and thoughts of our Lord.

There is a benefit to service, a benefit in believing and being obedient to the word of God. You will look past the flesh and into the spirit. Jesus Christ had perfect spiritual sight as prophesied by Zechariah.

Luke 10:25- 29
And, behold, a certain lawyer stood up, and tempted him, saying, Master, what shall I do to inherit eternal life?

He said unto him, What is written in the law? how readest thou?

And he answering said, Thou shalt love the Lord thy God with all thy heart, and with all thy soul, and with all thy strength, and with all thy mind; and thy neighbour as thyself.

And he said unto him, Thou hast answered right: this do, and thou shalt live.

But he, willing to justify himself, said unto Jesus, And who is my neighbour?

We read previously in Zechariah that in that day you shall call every man your neighbor. But who is your neighbor? You have to understand what a neighbor is before you can know who your neighbor is. Jesus had an understanding that baffled this lawyer, because Jesus did not look at who his neighbor was before he could see what God defined a neighbor to be. Therefore, Jesus spoke to him of a certain man who was traveling from one city to another, and he happened upon a man who was hurt. Two others who lived close to the injured man had already passed by and did nothing to help him. The traveling man had stopped to help. Then Jesus asked, *which of these three do you think was his neighbor?* The lawyer then said, *I suppose it was the one that showed mercy* and Jesus said, *go and do likewise.* Jesus looked at things the way God would. God said that He would bring forth "my servant the branch." We now leave the servant and look to the man.

Zechariah 6:9- 13
And the word of the LORD came unto me, saying,
Take of *them of* the captivity, *even* of Heldai, of Tobijah, and of

Jedaiah, which are come from Babylon, and come thou the same day, and go into the house of Josiah the son of Zephaniah;

Then take silver and gold, and make crowns, and set *them* **upon the head of Joshua the son of Josedech, the high priest;**

And speak unto him, saying, Thus speaketh the LORD of hosts, saying, Behold the man whose name *is* **The BRANCH; and he shall grow up out of his place, and he shall build the temple of the LORD:**

Even he shall build the temple of the LORD; and he shall bear the glory, and shall sit and rule upon his throne; and he shall be a priest upon his throne: and the counsel of peace shall be between them both.

Now we read, "Behold the man whose name is the branch." Previously we saw my servant the branch, and now we see the man whose name is the branch. Jesus Christ was of the lineage of David, yet he was also God's son. This branch of David's family tree takes a unique split. Mary was of the lineage of David as well as her husband Joseph. Yet Jesus' father was God, for as you know, Mary became pregnant while she was yet a virgin. Mary and Joseph had not yet come together in marriage. As we behold the man whose name is the branch we see not only his royal lineage but also a priest. He was to be a priest in service to God, sacrificing for sin and reuniting mankind with the Lord God. At the time Zechariah received the word of the Lord, he went to Joshua, the high priest, and placed crowns upon his head. He then said, "Behold the man whose name is the branch." This shows a royal marking in the branch. The branch has another sprout and yet another condition to be fulfilled. "He shall grow up out of his place, and he shall build the temple of the Lord." Jesus was born in Bethlehem of Judea, which is the city of David, but he grew up in Nazareth of Galilee. You may agree that this is true, but argue that he never built a temple.

John 2:19- 22

Jesus answered and said unto them, Destroy this temple, and in three days I will raise it up.

Then said the Jews, Forty and six years was this temple in building, and wilt thou rear it up in three days?

But he spake of the temple of his body.

When therefore he was risen from the dead, his disciples remembered that he had said this unto them; and they believed the scripture, and the word which Jesus had said.

Some only saw the physical temple. Jesus spoke to them of the temple of his body. Jesus knew the scriptures and what was prophesied concerning him. Jesus knew what Zechariah had written about the temple. Jesus' disciples later believed the scripture and the word which Jesus spoke, but they didn't see it at first either. The scriptures in Zechariah also speak of a priest. You might think Jesus Christ couldn't possibly be a priest, let alone a high priest. From the days of Aaron on, there was a Levitical priesthood. Every priest, according to the law of Moses, had to come out of the tribe of Levi. Jesus was of the tribe of Judah. Jesus Christ's life and ministry branched out in many areas. Although Jesus could not be a high priest after the order of Aaron, there was provision made after the order of Melchisedec.

Hebrews 5:1- 9
For every high priest taken from among men is ordained for men in things *pertaining* **to God, that he may offer both gifts and sacrifices for sins:**

Who can have compassion on the ignorant, and on them that are out of the way; for that he himself also is compassed with infirmity.

And by reason hereof he ought, as for the people, so also for himself, to offer for sins.

And no man taketh this honour unto himself, but he that is called of God, as *was* **Aaron.**

So also Christ glorified not himself to be made an high priest; but he that said unto him, Thou art my Son, to day have I begotten thee.

As he saith also in another *place***, Thou** *art* **a priest for ever after the order of Melchisedec.**

Jesus Christ did something that the priests in the law could not do. He sacrificed himself for sin. Jesus Christ was not made high priest while he was here on earth. But his life goes on and his priesthood has not expired.

Hebrews 7:11- 19
If therefore perfection were by the Levitical priesthood, (for under it the people received the law,) what further need *was there* **that another priest should rise after the order of Melchisedec, and not be called after the order of Aaron?**

For the priesthood being changed, there is made of necessity a change also of the law.

For he of whom these things are spoken pertaineth to another tribe, of which no man gave attendance at the altar.

For *it is* **evident that our Lord sprang out of Juda; of which tribe Moses spake nothing concerning priesthood.**

And it is yet far more evident: for that after the similitude of

Melchisedec there ariseth another priest,
Who is made, not after the law of a carnal commandment, but after the power of an endless life.
For he testifieth, Thou *art* **a priest for ever after the order of Melchisedec.**

"The Lord sprang out of Judah." As the branch, we see Jesus Christ being portrayed as a sprout. As we read here in Hebrews, the Word declares he sprang out of Judah. Jesus was a sprout or an offspring of the family tree of Judah. Tell me the word of God isn't too cool. Jesus Christ was made a priest after the power of an endless life. He brought in a better hope, by which we now can draw nigh unto God. Jesus Christ has been made the high priest forever after the order of Melchisedec, and we reap the benefit of his priesthood.

Hebrews 7:25- 27
Wherefore he is able also to save them to the uttermost that come unto God by him, seeing he ever liveth to make intercession for them.
For such an high priest became us, *who is* **holy, harmless, undefiled, separate from sinners, and made higher than the heavens;**
Who needeth not daily, as those high priests, to offer up sacrifice, first for his own sins, and then for the people's: for this he did once, when he offered up himself.

Jesus died once for us. He doesn't need to do it every day. He is a perfect high priest, because he now lives forever to make intercession for us. Jesus Christ became the sacrifice, and then he was made the high priest. He obtained eternal redemption for us in that he put away sin by the sacrifice of himself. If we can reckon ourselves to be dead in Christ, we can also live in him knowing that God has purged even our conscience. We now serve the living God, and Christ is the mediator of this new testament.

Hebrews 9:24, 27, 28
For Christ is not entered into the holy places made with hands, *which are* **the figures of the true; but into heaven itself, now to appear in the presence of God for us:**
And as it is appointed unto men once to die, but after this the judgment:
So Christ was once offered to bear the sins of many; and unto them that look for him shall he appear the second time without sin unto

salvation.

We have the full assurance of this hope that when Christ comes again, whether we be alive or dead, we will be with him without sin. It is appointed unto men once to die, but for us who are in Christ, we have died already with Christ. We now live unto God as long as we are able to endure this world. We await the return of Jesus Christ and our eternal salvation which he holds for us in heaven. Our judgment is not of wrath, but of rewards. Some will find the day of judgment to be less than rewarding, but not for us who are in Christ. Our judgment will be rewarding, because we already have Christ in us, the hope of glory. All of us today who believe in Christ have this hope of his second coming. In Zechariah's day their hope consisted of his first coming. Zechariah foretold of the branch. He saw a separation in the branch, and how it would be split into two periods of time.

Zechariah 9:9
Rejoice greatly, O daughter of Zion; shout, O daughter of Jerusalem: behold, thy King cometh unto thee: he *is* just, and having salvation; lowly, and riding upon an ass, and upon a colt the foal of an ass.

Rejoice greatly, O daughter of Zion. "Behold thy king cometh unto thee." This prophecy spoken by Zechariah was partially fulfilled by Jesus in his first coming, although it will not be until his second coming that he will reign as king.

Matthew 21:1- 5
And when they drew nigh unto Jerusalem, and were come to Bethphage, unto the mount of Olives, then sent Jesus two disciples,
Saying unto them, Go into the village over against you, and straightway ye shall find an ass tied, and a colt with her: loose *them*, and bring *them* unto me.
And if any *man* say ought unto you, ye shall say, The Lord hath need of them; and straightway he will send them.
All this was done, that it might be fulfilled which was spoken by the prophet, saying,
Tell ye the daughter of Sion, Behold, thy King cometh unto thee, meek, and sitting upon an ass, and a colt the foal of an ass.

Jesus knew of the prophecy of Zechariah. When Jesus was here the first time, he fulfilled the prophesies concerning his first coming. But there is more to come.

Jeremiah 23:5, 6
Behold, the days come, saith the LORD, that I will raise unto David a righteous Branch, and a King shall reign and prosper, and shall execute judgment and justice in the earth.
In his days Judah shall be saved, and Israel shall dwell safely: and this *is* his name whereby he shall be called, THE LORD OUR RIGHTEOUSNESS.

In Jeremiah, we have already been introduced to the Lord our righteousness, as the red thread. Here Jeremiah tells of the branch as well. He speaks of the righteous branch of David, a king who shall reign and prosper. Jesus Christ did not fulfill this prophecy with his first coming. This yet remains for the next time we see him.

Isaiah 4:2
In that day shall the branch of the LORD be beautiful and glorious, and the fruit of the earth *shall be* excellent and comely for them that are escaped of Israel.

Isaiah tells of the branch of the lord in that day. The phrase "in that day" speaks of the time when Christ will come again and fulfill all the promises yet wanting for Israel.

Zechariah 12:9, 10
And it shall come to pass in that day, *that* I will seek to destroy all the nations that come against Jerusalem.
And I will pour upon the house of David, and upon the inhabitants of Jerusalem, the spirit of grace and of supplications: and they shall look upon me whom they have pierced, and they shall mourn for him, as one mourneth for *his* only *son*, and shall be in bitterness for him, as one that is in bitterness for *his* firstborn.

Zechariah saw something that separated the days of the branch. He could see the house of David would mourn as one mourns his only son. But Zechariah could also see this death would not be the end, only an interruption and a pause for Israel.

The Red Thread of Zechariah

Zechariah 13:6, 7
And *one* shall say unto him, What *are* these wounds in thine hands? Then he shall answer, *Those* with which I was wounded *in* the house of my friends.

Awake, O sword, against my shepherd, and against the man *that is* my fellow, saith the LORD of hosts: smite the shepherd, and the sheep shall be scattered: and I will turn mine hand upon the little ones.

Zechariah did not know the whole plan, but God knew what needed to be done. God showed Zechariah the wounds in his hands and how he would be wounded in the house of those who should have been his friends. God showed Zechariah the man who was His fellow and said of him, "smite the shepherd, and the sheep shall be scattered." The thing that amazes me is that Jesus read this, too. He knew what awaited him, but he also knew that it would not be the end.

Matthew 26:31, 32
Then saith Jesus unto them, All ye shall be offended because of me this night: for it is written, I will smite the shepherd, and the sheep of the flock shall be scattered abroad.
But after I am risen again, I will go before you into Galilee.

Jesus Christ could see the forks in the branch, yet he still chose to be the branch. Jesus knew all these things recorded of him. He saw the symbolism and was able to decipher the meanings. He had the ability and the willingness to be the red thread, and he knew only he could be the one in the prophesies.

Jeremiah 33:14- 16
Behold, the days come, saith the LORD, that I will perform that good thing which I have promised unto the house of Israel and to the house of Judah.
In those days, and at that time, will I cause the Branch of righteousness to grow up unto David; and he shall execute judgment and righteousness in the land.
In those days shall Judah be saved, and Jerusalem shall dwell safely: and this *is the name* wherewith she shall be called, The LORD our righteousness.

You can be assured that what God promises, God will also perform. He caused the branch to grow. Jesus Christ knew he could count on God, and we can trust Him as well. Jesus Christ shall execute judgment and righteousness in the land. At times, you may wonder if this could ever be possible, but God says it will happen. Continue to look for the lord, for the day of the lord has not passed you by.

Zechariah 14:1- 9

Behold, the day of the LORD cometh, and thy spoil shall be divided in the midst of thee.

And his feet shall stand in that day upon the mount of Olives, which *is* before Jerusalem on the east, and the mount of Olives shall cleave in the midst thereof toward the east and toward the west, *and there shall be* a very great valley; and half of the mountain shall remove toward the north, and half of it toward the south.

And ye shall flee *to* the valley of the mountains; for the valley of the mountains shall reach unto Azal: yea, ye shall flee, like as ye fled from before the earthquake in the days of Uzziah king of Judah: and the LORD my God shall come, *and* all the saints with thee.

And it shall come to pass in that day, *that* the light shall not be clear, *nor* dark:

But it shall be one day which shall be known to the LORD, not day, nor night: but it shall come to pass, *that* at evening time it shall be light.

And it shall be in that day, *that* living waters shall go out from Jerusalem; half of them toward the former sea, and half of them toward the hinder sea: in summer and in winter shall it be.

And the LORD shall be king over all the earth: in that day shall there be one LORD, and his name one.

The day of the lord cometh, the day when Jesus Christ comes back. During this period of time, he shall set foot upon the earth once again. The face of the landscape will change, but all the saints shall be there. It will most definitely be the lord's day. He will reign as king, and he will hold the title of lord as well. When all is done, the Lord Christ Jesus will turn it all over to the Lord his God, and there will be one Lord and His name one. The branch is the red thread in the book of Zechariah. As we see the symbolism of the branch, we quickly realize the complexity of Christ, and yet the simplicity of God's plan still shines through. God wants His people to be reunited with Him and to enjoy all that He has prepared for them in Christ, the lord, the king, the man, and the servant who is the branch.

The Lord

After the days of Malachi, the Jews had some four hundred years to perfect their religion. Malachi is the last of the prophets before John the Baptist came to prepare the way of the Lord. Religions are manmade; it is what man introduces in his vain attempt to draw closer to God. Israel carried the weight of this burden just as all who reject what God has wrought in Christ Jesus the Lord. The red thread in the book of Malachi is found in the title, "the Lord." All those who will respect the Lord Jesus Christ and delight in him will find what he truly is the Lord of.

Malachi 1:1, 2
The burden of the word of the LORD to Israel by Malachi.
I have loved you, saith the LORD. Yet ye say, Wherein hast thou loved us? *Was* **not Esau Jacob's brother? saith the LORD: yet I loved Jacob.**

Malachi opens with this burden to Israel. When God's Word becomes a burden to you, you just have to know something isn't right. The Word was a burden to Israel, because they did not believe God loved them. Yet God chose them to be His people. Jacob was chosen over Esau even for all his faults, because he believed God while Esau despised his birthright. God has always loved Israel and desired for them to be as sons. God wanted them to hold fast to the promise of the Lord.

Malachi 1:6
A son honoureth *his* **father, and a servant his master: if then I** *be* **a father, where** *is* **mine honour? and if I** *be* **a master, where** *is* **my fear? saith the LORD of hosts unto you, O priests, that despise my name. And ye say, Wherein have we despised thy name?**

A son is to honor his father and a servant is to honor or respect his lord. You see the word "fear" being used in the Bible. Many times fear has the meaning of honor or respect. God said to the priests, *you have lost all honor and respect for my name; you despise my name.* God had instituted the sacrifices in the law to cover for sins until the true sacrifice could be offered by Jesus Christ. All sacrifices in the law represented aspects of the sacrifice Christ would make. Whenever we lose sight of what God has wrought in Christ, we become susceptible to religious practices.

Malachi 1:12, 13
But ye have profaned it, in that ye say, The table of the LORD *is* polluted; and the fruit thereof, *even* his meat, *is* contemptible.
Ye said also, Behold, what a weariness *is it!* and ye have snuffed at it, saith the LORD of hosts; and ye brought *that which was* torn, and the lame, and the sick; thus ye brought an offering: should I accept this of your hand? saith the LORD.

Do not lose the purity and precision of the Word and what God has promised concerning the Lord Jesus Christ. When Malachi said, "ye have profaned it," he meant the spirit of God had been removed; the sacrifice held no spiritual meaning and significance to them any longer. The table of the Lord became polluted, because they added things in and deleted things out. The things of God became a weariness, and they snuffed at it and saw the offerings as lame and weak. Therefore it also showed up in the items they brought as offerings.

Malachi 2:7, 8
For the priest's lips should keep knowledge, and they should seek the law at his mouth: for he *is* the messenger of the LORD of hosts.
But ye are departed out of the way; ye have caused many to stumble at the law; ye have corrupted the covenant of Levi, saith the LORD of hosts.

The covenant of the priesthood was given to Levi, because he saw the way to life and peace. He had a respect for God, and he was able to discern the spirit of the law and the job of the priest. Levi saw the spirit behind it; he was aware of the spiritual essence of the sacrifices and the law. We know there was more to the law than being mindful of the flesh. The law only had a glimpse of good things to come and was not the very image of those things. The priest was set to be a messenger of the Lord of hosts in these things. The priests were supposed to keep this knowledge and communicate it to God's people. The spirit of the law and the spirit of prophecy has always been with Christ in mind.

Malachi 2:10, 11
Have we not all one father? hath not one God created us? why do we deal treacherously every man against his brother, by profaning the covenant of our fathers?
Judah hath dealt treacherously, and an abomination is

committed in Israel and in Jerusalem; for Judah hath profaned the holiness of the LORD which he loved, and hath married the daughter of a strange god.

Malachi saw what God wanted. God wanted to be a father, and He wanted to have a closeness with His people. Yet there was no closeness between God and His people. Judah profaned the holiness of the Lord by going out and marrying the daughter of a strange god. Why was it so important for Judah not to marry outside the children of Israel? Christ was to be born out of the ranks of Israel. He was to come out of the tribe of Judah.

Malachi 2:14- 16
Yet ye say, Wherefore? Because the LORD hath been witness between thee and the wife of thy youth, against whom thou hast dealt treacherously: yet *is* she thy companion, and the wife of thy covenant.
And did not he make one? Yet had he the residue of the spirit. And wherefore one? That he might seek a godly seed. Therefore take heed to your spirit, and let none deal treacherously against the wife of his youth.
For the LORD, the God of Israel, saith that he hateth putting away: for *one* covereth violence with his garment, saith the LORD of hosts: therefore take heed to your spirit, that ye deal not treacherously.

The Lord had witnessed something between the husband and the wife of his youth, treacherous dealings. You have violated and betrayed a trust between you and your companion. The Word speaks here of the wife of thy youth. At this time in history, marriages were prearranged. Parents would typically help pick out a companion for their son or daughter. This was done to help ensure that the families were both upstanding and, even more importantly, that the children had been raised in the nurture and admonition of the Lord. When the Word speaks of the wife of thy covenant, it speaks of their pact with God, knowing from the Word of God that marriage is a three-fold cord. Marriage holds a great deal of significance, for when two are come together, they are made one. A permanent bond exists which cannot be broken without ripping it apart. There was only a residue of the spirit left in the world, and it went to believers who also looked for that godly seed which God had promised. God wanted Israel to remain a believer line so Christ could come in his due time. The children of Israel were losing sight of the spirit of marriage and were falling prey to the violence and deceit of unbelief in their marriages. The idea of divorce was becoming all too common. There are far too many excuses and reasons for not believing the Word.

Malachi 2:17
Ye have wearied the LORD with your words. Yet ye say, Wherein have we wearied *him*? When ye say, Every one that doeth evil *is* good in the sight of the LORD, and he delighteth in them; or, Where *is* the God of judgment?

When you are no longer able or willing to distinguish between good and evil, logic becomes flawed. When evil becomes an accepted practice, how one views God changes. The tendency to blame God begins to surface. We begin to ask, why doesn't God fix all the things that are messed up in the world? Why doesn't God do something if He really exists? We lose sight of the message and the messenger.

Malachi 3:1- 6
Behold, I will send my messenger, and he shall prepare the way before me: and the Lord, whom ye seek, shall suddenly come to his temple, even the messenger of the covenant, whom ye delight in: behold, he shall come, saith the LORD of hosts.
But who may abide the day of his coming? and who shall stand when he appeareth? for he *is* like a refiner's fire, and like fullers' soap:
And he shall sit *as* a refiner and purifier of silver: and he shall purify the sons of Levi, and purge them as gold and silver, that they may offer unto the LORD an offering in righteousness.
Then shall the offering of Judah and Jerusalem be pleasant unto the LORD, as in the days of old, and as in former years.
And I will come near to you to judgment; and I will be a swift witness against the sorcerers, and against the adulterers, and against false swearers, and against those that oppress the hireling in *his* wages, the widow, and the fatherless, and that turn aside the stranger *from his right*, and fear not me, saith the LORD of hosts.
For I *am* the LORD, I change not; therefore ye sons of Jacob are not consumed.

God speaks as if the way had already been prepared. God gives something to live up to. This is how God deals with us even in the face of unbelief. He is always looking for a positive response. You know that you get a more harmonious outcome that way. God said He would send a messenger to prepare the way, and that messenger happened to be John the Baptist.

Matthew 11:7-10
And as they departed, Jesus began to say unto the multitudes concerning John, What went ye out into the wilderness to see? A reed shaken with the wind?
But what went ye out for to see? A man clothed in soft raiment? behold, they that wear soft *clothing* are in kings' houses.
But what went ye out for to see? A prophet? yea, I say unto you, and more than a prophet.
For this is *he*, of whom it is written, Behold, I send my messenger before thy face, which shall prepare thy way before thee.

John was the messenger who was prophesied of in Malachi, but he was not the Lord whom ye seek. The Lord of which Malachi speaks is the red thread. John the Baptist prepared the way for the Lord. Jesus Christ came as the Lord, but the Lord of what? God also holds the title of Lord, and He changes not. What defines the title of Lord for God and for Jesus Christ?

Luke 10:21
In that hour Jesus rejoiced in spirit, and said, I thank thee, O Father, Lord of heaven and earth, that thou hast hid these things from the wise and prudent, and hast revealed them unto babes: even so, Father; for so it seemed good in thy sight.

Jesus said to God, "O Father, Lord of heaven and earth." Jesus recognized God as the Lord of the heaven and earth. The Lord God is the creator of heaven and earth and the Lord of it. No one can take that title other than the Lord God.

Mark 12:29, 30
And Jesus answered him, The first of all the commandments *is*, Hear, O Israel; The Lord our God is one Lord:
And thou shalt love the Lord thy God with all thy heart, and with all thy soul, and with all thy mind, and with all thy strength: this *is* the first commandment.

"Hear, O Israel; The Lord our God is one Lord." There are some things God holds exclusively for Himself and the title of Lord God is one of them. No other Lord can be called our God, and moreover, we are to love the Lord our God. The Lord Jesus held this truth to be self-evident.

Luke 4:5- 8
And the devil, taking him up into an high mountain, showed unto him all the kingdoms of the world in a moment of time.
And the devil said unto him, All this power will I give thee, and the glory of them: for that is delivered unto me; and to whomsoever I will I give it.
If thou therefore wilt worship me, all shall be thine.
And Jesus answered and said unto him, Get thee behind me, Satan: for it is written, Thou shalt worship the Lord thy God, and him only shalt thou serve.

The Devil tried to get Jesus to worship him, but Jesus said, "Get thee behind me Satan: for it is written, Thou shalt worship the Lord thy God." God is also the Lord of worship, and you should not worship anyone or anything other than the Lord of worship.

John 4:23, 24
But the hour cometh, and now is, when the true worshippers shall worship the Father in spirit and in truth: for the Father seeketh such to worship him.
God *is* a Spirit: and they that worship him must worship *him* in spirit and in truth.

It is now available for us to worship God in spirit and in truth because of the work of our Lord, Jesus Christ. God holds the title of the Lord God, the Lord of the heaven and earth, the Lord who seeks our worship. What then is Jesus Christ the Lord of?

Luke 2:10, 11
And the angel said unto them, Fear not: for, behold, I bring you good tidings of great joy, which shall be to all people.
For unto you is born this day in the city of David a Saviour, which is Christ the Lord.

The angel brought good tidings of great joy to all the people, because a savior was born, which is Christ the Lord. Here we find our answer already, and it is so simple to see. Jesus Christ is the Lord of salvation.

Romans 10:8- 13
But what saith it? The word is nigh thee, *even* in thy mouth, and in thy heart: that is, the word of faith, which we preach;

That if thou shalt confess with thy mouth the Lord Jesus, and shalt believe in thine heart that God hath raised him from the dead, thou shalt be saved.

For with the heart man believeth unto righteousness; and with the mouth confession is made unto salvation.

For the scripture saith, Whosoever believeth on him shall not be ashamed.

For there is no difference between the Jew and the Greek: for the same Lord over all is rich unto all that call upon him.

For whosoever shall call upon the name of the Lord shall be saved.

If you confess with your mouth the Lord Jesus and believe in your heart God has raised him from the dead, thou shalt be saved. Jesus Christ is the Lord over all unto salvation.

Acts 4:10, 12
Be it known unto you all, and to all the people of Israel, that by the name of Jesus Christ of Nazareth, whom ye crucified, whom God raised from the dead, *even* by him doth this man stand here before you whole.

Neither is there salvation in any other: for there is none other name under heaven given among men, whereby we must be saved.

When it comes to salvation, there is no other name under heaven given among men whereby we must be saved.

Acts 2:36
Therefore let all the house of Israel know assuredly, that God hath made that same Jesus, whom ye have crucified, both Lord and Christ.

God is the one who has made Jesus to be both Lord and Christ. It is God who has given Jesus Christ this title of Lord, and he is the Lord of salvation. He is not the Lord we worship, for that title belongs to the Lord our God. This is the red thread in the book of Malachi. There is one other thing that God has to say to Israel. Malachi prophesies of Elijah the prophet.

Malachi 4:4-6
Remember ye the law of Moses my servant, which I commanded unto him in Horeb for all Israel, *with* the statutes and judgments.
Behold, I will send you Elijah the prophet before the coming of the great and dreadful day of the LORD:
And he shall turn the heart of the fathers to the children, and the heart of the children to their fathers, lest I come and smite the earth with a curse.

God said that He would send the prophet Elijah before the coming of the Lord, but how could this be? Elijah the prophet had been dead for quite some time. Elijah was a prophet who was known for his great zeal for the children of Israel and his desire to turn their hearts back to the Lord their God. In Elijah's example, you can see that God would have the heart of the fathers to turn to their children. God wants fathers to think about their children and how a father's belief or unbelief concerning the Word will affect his children. God also wants the hearts of the children to turn to their fathers, to respect them in their direction and admonition in the Lord and the truth of the Word. This matter of Elijah might seem hard to understand if we did not have Jesus Christ to explain it to us.

Matthew 11:11-15
Verily I say unto you, Among them that are born of women there hath not risen a greater than John the Baptist: notwithstanding he that is least in the kingdom of heaven is greater than he.
And from the days of John the Baptist until now the kingdom of heaven suffereth violence, and the violent take it by force.
For all the prophets and the law prophesied until John.
And if ye will receive *it*, this is Elias [Elijah], which was for to come.
He that hath ears to hear, let him hear.

Jesus said that from the days of John the Baptist until now, men have been trying to force their way into the kingdom of heaven. It has been a very violent time, as you can see by all the prophets and the law. If you are willing to receive it, Jesus said, John is this Elijah who was to come. He that hath ears to hear, let him hear. But if violence and force are still your preferred methods of entry, you most likely will not accept it. John the Baptist came with the baptism of repentance; he wanted to turn the hearts of the people to the Lord, clearing the path and having people's hearts open to the Lord of salvation. This book of Malachi is the last book of the prophets and of what we call the Old Testament. This is where we bring a close our search for the red thread, but what Christ has accomplished and has done for us does not end here. Christianity is not meant to be one of the major religions of the world. Christianity is what God has wrought in Christ and is an ongoing reality in each and every believer's life who knows Jesus Christ as the Lord of salvation.

The Red Thread of Malachi

Appendix I
References of the red thread in the book of Isaiah building to the namesake of God

The book of Isaiah is full of references to the red thread. Some references came before the book of Isaiah while others can be seen in the books following Isaiah. All of these references build to the overall theme of God's namesake, which is the red thread in Isaiah. I felt it would be worth our time to add this to our study of the red thread, since we are dealing with the identity of Jesus Christ.

Isaiah 1:2- 8
Hear, O heavens, and give ear, O earth: for the LORD hath spoken, I have nourished and brought up children, and they have rebelled against me.

The ox knoweth his owner, and the ass his master's crib: *but* Israel doth not know, my people doth not consider.

Ah sinful nation, a people laden with iniquity, a seed of evildoers, children that are corrupters: they have forsaken the LORD, they have provoked the Holy One of Israel unto anger, they are gone away backward.

Why should ye be stricken [corrected] any more? ye will revolt more and more: the whole head is sick, and the whole heart faint.

From the sole of the foot even unto the head *there is* no soundness in it; *but* wounds, and bruises, and putrifying sores: they have not been closed, neither bound up, neither mollified with ointment.

Your country *is* desolate, your cities *are* burned with fire: your land, strangers devour it in your presence, and *it is* desolate, as overthrown by strangers.

And the daughter of Zion is left as a cottage in a vineyard, as a lodge in a garden of cucumbers, as a besieged city.

Israel headed in the wrong direction, and they just never seemed to change course. Even years after Isaiah when Christ came, he had this to say to the Jews of his day:

Luke 4:18, 19 and 21- 23
The Spirit of the Lord *is* upon me, because he hath anointed me to preach the gospel to the poor; he hath sent me to heal the brokenhearted, to preach deliverance to the captives, and recovering of

Appendix I

sight to the blind, to set at liberty them that are bruised,
To preach the acceptable year of the Lord.
And he began to say unto them, This day is this scripture fulfilled in your ears.
And all bare him witness, and wondered at the gracious words which proceeded out of his mouth. And they said, Is not this Joseph's son?
And he said unto them, Ye will surely say unto me this proverb, Physician, heal thyself.

God sent Jesus Christ to the children of Israel. Yet when they saw him, they did not see him for who he was. Many thought he was Joseph's son, no one of any real importance. Therefore, many thought that he needed psychological help when he came to them as the son of God. Just who is Jesus Christ? It seems like we should all know his true identity. This name is spoken of worldwide, but do we really know him?

Isaiah 1:9
Except the LORD of hosts had left unto us a very small remnant, we should have been as Sodom, *and* **we should have been like unto Gomorrah.**

Isaiah starts us out with the promised seed. If we are going to know God's namesake, we must understand what was prophesied of him. This very small remnant of which Isaiah speaks is a seed. If the Lord of hosts had not left us a seed, we would have been as Sodom and Gomorrah, utterly destroyed.

Romans 9:29
And as Esaias [Isaiah] said before, Except the Lord of Sabaoth [hosts] had left us a seed, we had been as Sodoma, and been made like unto Gomorrha.

By the testimony of the scripture in the book of Romans we can see that the small remnant of Isaiah is a seed. This seed is Christ, the red thread in the book of Genesis. If God had not worked out a plan for redemption, we would have all been goners.

Isaiah 2:5
O house of Jacob, come ye, and let us walk in the light of the LORD.

Appendix I

The light of the Lord is the red thread in II Chronicles. How many still walk in darkness, even in the light of day?

Isaiah 2:10
Enter into the rock, and hide thee in the dust, for fear of the LORD, and for the glory of his majesty.

The rock, as you may remember, is the red thread in the book of Deuteronomy. Is there anything more firm and trustworthy upon which we can build?

Isaiah 3:12
***As for* my people, children *are* their oppressors, and women rule over them. O my people, they which lead thee cause thee to err, and destroy the way of thy paths.**

Jesus Christ is the way in the book of I Chronicles. God has always wanted His people to know the way, but which way were the people headed? They were headed down paths of error. They were without God; they did not know His name, and they were in no condition to figure it out on their own. They had turned away from God. Children were their oppressors, and women ruled over them. God has woven the red thread through the Word to keep us on track. Jesus Christ read these scriptures in Isaiah as well. Jesus saw himself in these prophecies of the red thread.

Isaiah 7:13, 14
And he said, Hear ye now, O house of David; *Is it* a small thing for you to weary men, but will ye weary my God also?
Therefore the Lord himself shall give you a sign; Behold, a virgin shall conceive, and bear a son, and shall call his name Immanuel.

Israel's ignorance was a shame. How could they not know? God gave a sign. A virgin, one who has never known a man, shall conceive. A woman is going to become pregnant and have a son without a man introducing seed into her womb. How is this possible? How could such a thing happen? It just isn't natural. God said that when the son of the virgin is born, call his name Immanuel. What does the name Immanuel mean? The name means 'God is with us,' but how is God with us? God had a hand in it. God is with us because God was involved in making this woman pregnant. Mary's child was not going to be God, but a son of God's making. As the red thread, this son can also be seen in the book of II Samuel.

Isaiah 7:15, 16
Butter and honey shall he eat, that he may know to refuse the evil, and choose the good.
For before the child shall know to refuse the evil, and choose the good, the land that thou abhorrest shall be forsaken of both her kings.

The child of whom Isaiah prophesies shall be like every child. He will grow up and have to learn to refuse the evil and choose the good.

Isaiah 8:14
And he shall be for a sanctuary; but for a stone of stumbling and for a rock of offence to both the houses of Israel, for a gin and for a snare to the inhabitants of Jerusalem.

This stone, which becomes a stone of stumbling, is the red thread in the book of Joshua. Christ should have been a sanctuary, but for many he has become a stumbling block which trips them up in their attempt to know God. The name of Jesus Christ is a name we can go to for refuge. In the name of Jesus Christ we find power and safety. In Jesus Christ we find freedom from sin.

Isaiah 9:2
The people that walked in darkness have seen a great light: they that dwell in the land of the shadow of death, upon them hath the light shined.

This light is greater than the light of the sun. This light is the light of the only begotten son of God. The light spoken of here in Isaiah is the red thread of the book of II Chronicles. With this light we are able to see all things clearly.

Isaiah 9:6, 7
For unto us a child is born, unto us a son is given: and the government shall be upon his shoulder: and his name shall be called Wonderful, Counsellor, The mighty God, The everlasting Father, The Prince of Peace.
Of the increase of *his* government and peace *there shall be* no end, upon the throne of David, and upon his kingdom, to order it, and to establish it with judgment and with justice from henceforth even for

Appendix I

ever. The zeal of the LORD of hosts will perform this.

We are building the namesake of God. Isaiah lays the foundation and then develops an appreciation of who this child is, this son who will carry God's name. He will show forth the essence of the name he bears. Therefore, his name shall be called wonderful counselor, because God is a wonderful counselor. His name shall be called the mighty God, because God is mighty in His works. His name shall be called the everlasting father. Why? Is it because Jesus was going to be the father? No. It is because he was going to show God as a father, an everlasting father. He is the prince of peace, because he would establish peace between God and man, something that had been lost way back with Adam.

Isaiah 11:1- 4
And there shall come forth a rod out of the stem of Jesse, and a Branch shall grow out of his roots:
And the spirit of the LORD shall rest upon him, the spirit of wisdom and understanding, the spirit of counsel and might, the spirit of knowledge and of the fear of the LORD;
And shall make him of quick understanding in the fear of the LORD: and he shall not judge after the sight of his eyes, neither reprove after the hearing of his ears:
But with righteousness shall he judge the poor, and reprove with equity for the meek of the earth: and he shall smite the earth with the rod of his mouth, and with the breath of his lips shall he slay the wicked.

The spirit of the Lord shall rest upon him, the spirit of counsel and might. His name shall be called the wonderful counselor, the mighty God. This is how Jesus would be able to do the wonderful things he did and have the wisdom to counsel. This is how the name of the mighty God would be manifest in him. This is how he would do many mighty works. Not because he was God, but because the spirit of God was upon him. This branch, which shall grow out of the root of Jesse, is the branch that is the red thread in the book of Zechariah.

Matthew 11:20, 21
Then began he to upbraid the cities wherein most of his mighty works were done, because they repented not:
Woe unto thee, Chorazin! woe unto thee, Bethsaida! for if the mighty works, which were done in you, had been done in Tyre and

Appendix I

Sidon, they would have repented long ago in sackcloth and ashes.

Jesus did do mighty works when he came. His life was a testament to the prophecies that went before him. Did it change people's minds about him? All the mighty works which the people witnessed did not seem to have a huge effect. But no one could deny the wisdom or the mighty works they saw.

Matthew 13:54- 57
And when he was come into his own country, he taught them in their synagogue, insomuch that they were astonished, and said, Whence hath this *man* this wisdom, and *these* mighty works?
Is not this the carpenter's son? is not his mother called Mary? and his brethren, James, and Joses, and Simon, and Judas?
And his sisters, are they not all with us? Whence then hath this *man* all these things?
And they were offended in him. But Jesus said unto them, A prophet is not without honour, save in his own country, and in his own house.

Jesus had this wisdom and these mighty works because he was God's son, the one of whom Isaiah had prophesied. He is God's son, and he has the spirit of God upon him. However, people who thought of him as simply the carpenter's son were offended by him. This brings up a good question. Who do you think Jesus is? Was he the carpenter's son or is he the son of God?

Matthew 21:9- 11
And the multitudes that went before, and that followed, cried, saying, Hosanna [Hosanna means, help has come] **to the son of David: Blessed *is* he that cometh in the name of the Lord; Hosanna in the highest.**
And when he was come into Jerusalem, all the city was moved, saying, Who is this?
And the multitude said, This is Jesus the prophet of Nazareth of Galilee.

There were some who realized that Jesus came in the name of the Lord, but not everyone held that opinion and not everyone was pleased about who he said he was. When Jesus came in the name of the Lord, was he only God's agent or was he God's namesake?

Appendix I

Matthew 21:15
And when the chief priests and scribes saw the wonderful things that he did, and the children crying in the temple, and saying, Hosanna to the son of David; they were sore displeased.

The religious leaders were the ones who were displeased with the wonderful things that he did and with who he was. Many religious leaders today are displeased as well when they find out who he is, because many today believe Jesus to be God. This is a grievous error.

Isaiah 17:10
Because thou hast forgotten the God of thy salvation, and hast not been mindful of the rock of thy strength, therefore shalt thou plant pleasant plants, and shalt set it with strange slips.

We cannot allow ourselves to forget the God of our salvation. We need to be mindful of the rock of our strength, who is Christ Jesus. It is when we forget that we start setting strange slips onto an otherwise pleasant plant. The red thread shows us who and what Jesus Christ is so we can avoid the error to which some have succumbed.

Isaiah 22:21- 25
And I will clothe him with thy robe, and strengthen him with thy girdle, and I will commit thy government into his hand: and he shall be a father to the inhabitants of Jerusalem, and to the house of Judah.
And the key of the house of David will I lay upon his shoulder; so he shall open, and none shall shut; and he shall shut, and none shall open.
And I will fasten him *as* a nail in a sure place; and he shall be for a glorious throne to his father's house.
And they shall hang upon him all the glory of his father's house, the offspring and the issue, all vessels of small quantity, from the vessels of cups, even to all the vessels of flagons.
In that day, saith the LORD of hosts, shall the nail that is fastened in the sure place be removed, and be cut down, and fall; and the burden that was upon it shall be cut off: for the LORD hath spoken *it*.

The nail spoken of here is again the red thread. We can see the nail upon which all man's hope is hung in the book of Ezra, where Jesus Christ is the nail fastened in a sure place.

Isaiah 28:15, 16
Because ye have said, We have made a covenant with death, and with hell are we at agreement; when the overflowing scourge shall pass through, it shall not come unto us: for we have made lies our refuge, and under falsehood have we hid ourselves:
Therefore thus saith the Lord GOD, Behold, I lay in Zion for a foundation a stone, a tried stone, a precious corner *stone*, a sure foundation: he that believeth shall not make haste [shall not be disappointed].

Isaiah speaks to those who thought they had it all figured out. They thought they had beaten death. They thought their religion would save them. They made their gods to fit their purpose, but when all is said and done, it comes back to God's foundation. This stone is a tried stone, a precious corner. He who believes in him shall not be disappointed. God has laid this stone, which is Jesus Christ.

Isaiah 40:10, 11
Behold, the Lord GOD will come with strong *hand*, and his arm shall rule for him: behold, his reward *is* with him, and his work before him.
He shall feed his flock like a shepherd: he shall gather the lambs with his arm, and carry *them* in his bosom, *and* shall gently lead those that are with young.

God's arm and strong hand is Jesus Christ. God is a spirit being. He is not a man like you and I. There is an old poem which goes something like this: God has no hands but our hands to feed the people bread; He has no feet but our feet with which to walk amongst the almost dead. Jesus Christ also is a man. Like a shepherd, he is able to gather the lambs. Jesus had a job to do. The job was of God's design, but Jesus did the work.

Isaiah 41:4
Who hath wrought and done *it*, calling the generations from the beginning? I the LORD, the first, and with the last; I *am* he.

As the red thread, Jesus Christ is the "I am" in the book of Esther. To a people whom God's name is not known, Jesus Christ will remain hidden in God. Jesus came to make God's name known; he came to reveal the

Appendix I

Father unto the sons of men. People today get hung up on the three-in-one God, but there is no three-in-one God. There is, however, God and His son Jesus Christ, and the holy spirit which God gave. The orthodox definition of the trinity states that the Father is God, the Son is God, the Holy Spirit is God; and together, not exclusively, they form one God. It goes on to state that the trinity is co-eternal, without beginning or end, and co-equal, having no part greater than another. This definition, however, does not fit the God to which Isaiah refers. God said that He is the first and He will be with the last; I am.

Isaiah 43:10
Ye *are* my witnesses, saith the LORD, and my servant whom I have chosen: that ye may know and believe me, and understand that I *am* he: before me there was no God formed, neither shall there be after me.

God said, *you are my witnesses, believe Me. There was no God formed before me and neither shall there be after me.*

Isaiah 43:12, 13
I have declared, and have saved, and I have showed, when *there was* no strange *god* among you: therefore ye *are* my witnesses, saith the LORD, that I *am* God.
Yea, before the day *was* I *am* he; and *there is* none that can deliver out of my hand: I will work, and who shall let it?

God was at work long before anyone came up with the three-in-one version of God or any other strange god for that matter.

Isaiah 44:6
Thus saith the LORD the King of Israel, and his redeemer the LORD of hosts; I *am* the first, and I *am* the last; and beside me *there is* no God.

God tells us, "Beside me there is no God." What does this mean? It means that there is no God besides Him. Can there be a co-equal God then?

Isaiah 44:8
Fear ye not, neither be afraid: have not I told thee from that time, and have declared *it*? ye *are* even my witnesses. Is there a God beside me? yea, *there is* no God; I know not *any*.

Appendix I

God tells us twice that there is no other God except Him, but He first asks the question: "Is there a God beside me?" Then He says, "I know not any." If God does not know of any other God besides Himself, what does that tell you?

Isaiah 45:5
I *am* the LORD, and *there is* none else, *there is* no God beside me: I girded thee, though thou hast not known me:

Now for the third time, "there is no God beside me." How could we miss it? Well, part of the problem might be right here in this verse: "thou hast not known me." God said that He girded you; He looked over you and took care of you, even though you did not know Him.

Isaiah 45:6
That they may know from the rising of the sun, and from the west, that *there is* none beside me. I *am* the LORD, and *there is* none else.

For the fourth time, the message is clear. "There is none beside Me. I am the Lord, and there is none else." Everyone from the east to the west should know this. Was it only the prophet Isaiah who possessed this information?

Isaiah 45:21
Tell ye, and bring *them* near; yea, let them take counsel together: who hath declared this from ancient time? *who* hath told it from that time? *have* not I the LORD? and *there is* no God else beside me; a just God and a Saviour; *there is* none beside me.

Now for the fifth time, "there is no God else beside Me." You might think once would be enough for God to tell us this. Just in case you are still in doubt, God reiterates for a sixth time in this verse, "there is none beside Me." God has been declaring this information even from ancient times. I know there will still be some who will hold to the trinity and proclaim Jesus is God, but God has something else to say.

Isaiah 45:18
For thus saith the LORD that created the heavens; God himself that formed the earth and made it; he hath established it, he created it

not in vain, he formed it to be inhabited: I *am* the LORD; and *there is* none else.

Isaiah 45:22
Look unto me, and be ye saved, all the ends of the earth: for I *am* God, and *there is* none else.

Isaiah 46:9
Remember the former things of old: for I *am* God, and *there is* none else; *I am* God, and *there is* none like me.

Isaiah 45:6
That they may know from the rising of the sun, and from the west, that *there is* none beside me. I *am* the LORD, and *there is* none else.

When it comes to God, the creator of the heavens and earth, there is none else. There is nobody like Him. Four times He tells us there is none else. You might get the idea that God is trying to make a point. Why? Because He knew men would do what they are doing still today. He knew there would be those who would confuse His namesake for Himself. God has declared his namesake even from the beginning. He has shown us things we did not know. God wanted us to see what He was up to even before it came to pass.

Isaiah 48:3
I have declared the former things from the beginning; and they went forth out of my mouth, and I showed them; I did *them* suddenly, and they came to pass.

Just because God told you something before it happened does not mean that it was there before it was there. God wants us to know His name. He does not want us to be confused about who He is or who Christ is.

Isaiah 52:10
The LORD hath made bare his holy arm in the eyes of all the nations; and all the ends of the earth shall see the salvation of our God.

Jesus Christ is an extension of God's arm; he did the work. All the ends of the earth shall see the salvation of our God, because Jesus Christ accomplished it.

Appendix I

Isaiah 53:1-12

Who hath believed our report? and to whom is the arm of the LORD revealed?

For he shall grow up before him as a tender plant, and as a root out of a dry ground: he hath no form nor comeliness; and when we shall see him, *there is* no beauty that we should desire him.

He is despised and rejected of men; a man of sorrows, and acquainted with grief: and we hid as it were *our* faces from him; he was despised, and we esteemed him not.

Surely he hath borne our griefs, and carried our sorrows: yet we did esteem him stricken, smitten of God, and afflicted.

But he *was* wounded for our transgressions, *he was* bruised for our iniquities: the chastisement of our peace *was* upon him; and with his stripes we are healed.

All we like sheep have gone astray; we have turned every one to his own way; and the LORD hath laid on him the iniquity of us all.

He was oppressed, and he was afflicted, yet he opened not his mouth: he is brought as a lamb to the slaughter, and as a sheep before her shearers is dumb, so he openeth not his mouth.

He was taken from prison and from judgment: and who shall declare his generation? for he was cut off out of the land of the living: for the transgression of my people was he stricken.

And he made his grave with the wicked, and with the rich in his death; because he had done no violence, neither *was any* deceit in his mouth.

Yet it pleased the LORD to bruise him; he hath put *him* to grief: when thou shalt make his soul an offering for sin, he shall see *his* seed, he shall prolong *his* days, and the pleasure of the LORD shall prosper in his hand.

He shall see of the travail of his soul, *and* shall be satisfied: by his knowledge shall my righteous servant justify many; for he shall bear their iniquities.

Therefore will I divide him *a portion* with the great, and he shall divide the spoil with the strong; because he hath poured out his soul unto death: and he was numbered with the transgressors; and he bare the sin of many, and made intercession for the transgressors.

Isaiah was a Prophet, and he spoke concerning Christ. He said, "Who has believed our report?" We should say, "We do." When he asks, "To whom is the arm of the Lord revealed?" It is revealed to us, for Christ has already come. Christ was given a job to do, and he did it. Our salvation was the result, and God glorified him for his effort.

Isaiah 56:1, 2
Thus saith the LORD, Keep ye judgment, and do justice: for my salvation *is* near to come, and my righteousness to be revealed.
Blessed *is* the man *that* doeth this, and the son of man *that* layeth hold on it; that keepeth the sabbath from polluting it, and keepeth his hand from doing any evil.

Jesus Christ is the son of man. He also shows up as the son of man in the red thread in the book of Ezekiel. Isaiah said that salvation was near to come. It was Jesus Christ, the son of man, who was able to lay hold of it and reveal it to the world.

Isaiah 60:9
Surely the isles shall wait for me, and the ships of Tarshish first, to bring thy sons from far, their silver and their gold with them, unto the name of the LORD thy God, and to the Holy One of Israel, because he hath glorified thee.

As the holy one, Jesus Christ is the red thread of the book of Psalms. There is glory in the holy one. People will come from far and wide unto the Lord God because of the Lord Jesus Christ.

Isaiah 62:11
Behold, the LORD hath proclaimed unto the end of the world, Say ye to the daughter of Zion, Behold, thy salvation cometh; behold, his reward *is* with him, and his work before him.

As the red thread, Christ is the salvation of the Lord presented in the book of Jonah. Here in the book of Isaiah, the Lord has proclaimed unto the end of the world His namesake. Behold, his reward is with him, and his reward is his name. His work was before him, which is our salvation. Who is the Lord? Well, only you can decide that, because there can be many lords in a man's life. If you are looking for the red thread, you will find the Lord Jesus Christ, who is the Lord of salvation. If you are looking for the Lord God, you will find my heavenly Father. This is how the book of Isaiah builds to the namesake of God.

Appendix I

Appendix II
The ten redemptive names of Jehovah

In our study of the red thread, we find that God makes known His name through His namesake, Jesus Christ. This study has to do with the name of Jehovah, translated as "Lord" in the Bible. This is one of the names used for God which carries with it the covenant that God has with man. The name of Jehovah holds the meaning of God's dealings with man. Jehovah can be seen in His relationship to man. The one who came in the name of the Lord revealed to us all there is in Jehovah's name.

Psalms 118:26
Blessed *be* he that cometh in the name of the LORD: we have blessed you out of the house of the LORD.

Psalms 8:9
O LORD our Lord, how excellent *is* thy name in all the earth!

Psalms 9:10
And they that know thy name will put their trust in thee: for thou, LORD, hast not forsaken them that seek thee.

Psalms 25:11
For thy name's sake, O LORD, pardon mine iniquity; for it *is* great.

Psalms 124:8
Our help *is* in the name of the LORD, who made heaven and earth.

Psalms 143:11
Quicken me, O LORD, for thy name's sake: for thy righteousness' sake bring my soul out of trouble.

In Psalms, we see one coming in the name of the Lord. Those who know God's name will put their trust in him. It is difficult though to trust someone if you do not know them. This is why it is so important for God's namesake to reveal His name. The psalmist said, "for thy name's sake, O Lord, pardon my iniquity." We had need of this pardon. The one who would come in Jehovah's name would spend his life as a ransom for our pardon.

Appendix II

We can see our help in the name of the Lord, the God who made the heaven and earth. In His infinite purpose and wisdom, God gives life through His namesake. He will bring righteousness and save our soul from trouble.

God is known as the Lord by the name Jehovah. There are ten redemptive names of Jehovah. Christ would exemplify all of these as God's namesake. Jesus never claimed to be God, but he did carry the name of the Lord and has shown us all that is in Jehovah's name.

Exodus 6:3
And I appeared unto Abraham, unto Isaac, and unto Jacob, by *the name of* God Almighty, but by my name JEHOVAH was I not known to them.

The name of Jehovah came to be defined by ten redemptive names. One of them has to do with our righteousness, as we saw in the records of the Psalms. The Lord our righteousness is also the red thread in the book of Jeremiah, but there is a Psalm which contains the identity of all ten redemptive names. From there I would like to base our study examining all ten redemptive names of Jehovah. God said that He appeared unto Abraham by the name of God Almighty, but He was not known by the name of Jehovah. This name of Jehovah was built upon and defined through the scriptures as the redemptive names were defined and ultimately fulfilled in Christ. Let us go now to the 23rd Psalm and look at His name.

Psalms 23:1- 6
The LORD *is* my shepherd; I shall not want.
He maketh me to lie down in green pastures: he leadeth me beside the still waters.
He restoreth my soul: he leadeth me in the paths of righteousness for his name's sake.
Yea, though I walk through the valley of the shadow of death, I will fear no evil: for thou *art* with me; thy rod and thy staff they comfort me.
Thou preparest a table before me in the presence of mine enemies: thou anointest my head with oil; my cup runneth over.
Surely goodness and mercy shall follow me all the days of my life: and I will dwell in the house of the LORD for ever.

This Psalm begins with the name of the Lord and ends with the name of the Lord. The Psalm opens with **Jehovah Ro`i**, the Lord my shepherd, but also is filled with His redemptive nature. There are ten names associated

Appendix II

with Jehovah which clarify His redemptive plan:
1) The Lord my shepherd is **Jehovah Ro`i**,
2) The Lord will see and provide is **Jehovah Jireh**,
3) The Lord of the Sabbath is **Jehovah Zeba'oth**,
4) The Lord is my peace is **Jehovah Shalom**,
5) The Lord that heals is **Jehovah Ropheka**,
6) The Lord our righteousness is **Jehovah Zidkenu**,
7) The Lord is there is **Jehovah Shammah**,
8) The Lord our standard is **Jehovah Nissi**,
9) The Lord who sanctifies is **Jehovah Mekaddishkem**, and
10) The Lord most high is **Jehovah Elyon**.

In the 23rd Psalm, the Lord is my shepherd is **Jehovah Ro`i**.

I shall not want, because **Jehovah Jireh** will see and provide.

He makes me to lie down in green pastures, which is rest, for He is **Jehovah Zeba'oth**.

He leads me beside the still waters, which indicates peace, for He is **Jehovah Shalom**.

He restores my soul, because He is **Jehovah Ropheka**, the one who heals.

He leads me in the paths of righteousness for his name's sake, **Jehovah Zidkenu**.

Yea, though I walk through the valley of the shadow of death, I will fear no evil, for thou *art* with me as **Jehovah Shammah**.

Thy rod and thy staff comfort me, because you are **Jehovah Nissi** ; You have prepared a table before me in the presence of mine enemies.

Thou anointed my head with oil; my cup runneth over. You are **Jehovah Mekaddishkem**, the one who sanctifies.

Surely goodness and mercy shall follow me all the days of my life, and I will dwell in the house of the LORD forever. Surely you are **Jehovah Elyon**, the Lord most high.

Let's look at each of these names of Jehovah found here in the 23rd Psalm in light of the other scriptures in God's Word and with regard to Jesus Christ. **Jehovah Ro`i**, which is the Lord my shepherd, occurs here and is also fulfilled in Christ. Jesus has shown us this name experientially in his life.

John 10:11
I am the good shepherd: the good shepherd giveth his life for the sheep.

Appendix II

Hebrews 13:20
Now the God of peace, that brought again from the dead our Lord Jesus, that great shepherd of the sheep.

Jesus showed us in person what was in the name **Jehovah Ro`i.** Jesus was the good shepherd, who gave his life for his sheep. Jesus also knew what was expected of him, because he knew the name of **Jehovah Jireh** .

Genesis 22:7, 8 and 14
And Isaac spake unto Abraham his father, and said, My father: and he said, Here *am* I, my son. And he said, Behold the fire and the wood: but where *is* the lamb for a burnt offering?
And Abraham said, My son, God will provide himself a lamb for a burnt offering: so they went both of them together.
And Abraham called the name of that place Jehovah jireh: as it is said *to* this day, In the mount of the LORD it shall be seen.

God said that He would provide a lamb for a burnt offering. Abraham called the place **Jehovah Jireh,** because God would see and provide. It shall be seen what would follow.

John 1:29
The next day John seeth Jesus coming unto him, and saith, Behold the Lamb of God, which taketh away the sin of the world.

Jesus proved to be the lamb of God, the lamb of God's choosing, and thereby proved the name of **Jehovah Jireh.** Jesus took away the sin which plagued the world. Jesus showed us the name of the Lord and what was in the name of the Lord. He did this in his life by his actions. Next is the name **Jehovah Zeba'oth** for God will make us lie down in green pastures. This is rest. **Jehovah Zeba'oth** is Lord of the Sabbath, because when God finishes a work He rests.

Romans 9:29
And as Esaias [Isaiah] said before, Except the Lord of Sabaoth [Jehovah Zeba'oth] had left us a seed, we had been as Sodoma, and been made like unto Gomorrha.

Appendix II

Isaiah 1:9
Except the LORD of hosts [Jehovah Zeba'oth] **had left unto us a very small remnant, we should have been as Sodom,** *and* **we should have been like unto Gomorrah.**

The Lord of the Sabbath is also referred to as the Lord of hosts in the Old Testament, but always He is, **Jehovah Zeba'oth**. He would have us to rest when our warfare and our work is accomplished.

Exodus 16:23
And he said unto them, This is that which the LORD hath said, To morrow *is* **the rest of the holy Sabbath unto the LORD.**

God set the Sabbath as a day of rest to be a reminder of the covenant that he had with the people in the name of **Jehovah Zeba'oth,** a covenant that would be fulfilled only in Christ and the time appointed by God.

Mark 2:27, 28
And he said unto them, The Sabbath was made for man, and not man for the Sabbath: Therefore the Son of man is Lord also of the Sabbath.

Jesus has also made us to rest in him, being God's finished work and Lord of the Sabbath, although some still await the fulfillment of this promised rest. Then **Jehovah Shalom** speaks of peace, for God will lead us beside the still waters.

Judges 6:23, 24a
And the LORD said unto him, Peace *be* **unto thee; fear not: thou shalt not die.**
Then Gideon built an altar there unto the LORD, and called it Jehovah shalom.

It is this name of **Jehovah Shalom** that sets the peace in the redemptive names of Jehovah. Jesus also sets before us peace through his name.

Ephesians 2:14
For he [Jesus Christ] **is our peace, who hath made both one, and hath broken down the middle wall of partition** *between us*;

Appendix II

John 14:27
Peace I leave with you, my peace I give unto you: not as the world giveth, give I unto you. Let not your heart be troubled, neither let it be afraid.

Jesus established a peace between us and God, allowing us to maintain peace the likes of which the world has not known since Adam. If we desire peace, we can be restored in peace, because Jesus can also be found in the name of **Jehovah Ropheka**, the Lord that healeth thee.

Exodus 15:26
And said, If thou wilt diligently hearken to the voice of the LORD thy God, and wilt do that which is right in his sight, and wilt give ear to his commandments, and keep all his statutes, I will put none of these diseases upon thee [not allow these diseases to be put upon thee], **which I have** [allowed to be] **brought upon the Egyptians: for I** *am* **the LORD that healeth thee.**

It is in the name of **Jehovah Ropheka** that we find the Lord who healeth thee. At times we allow things into our lives that we shouldn't or things we really don't want, but in the face of it all, Jesus ministered the name of **Jehovah Ropheka** to all who wanted to know what was in this name.

Matthew 4:23
And Jesus went about all Galilee, teaching in their synagogues, and preaching the gospel of the kingdom, and healing all manner of sickness and all manner of disease among the people.

I Peter 2:24
Who his own self bare our sins in his own body on the tree, that we, being dead to sins, should live unto righteousness: by whose stripes ye were healed.

Jesus healed all manner of sickness and disease. He took it all upon himself when he was nailed to the tree. Sin, sickness, disease, and death; he took it all out of the way so we could live unto righteousness. This was all in the name of **Jehovah Ropheka**, the Lord that heals. When it comes to doing that which is right, we first had to fix that which was most fundamentally wrong, so Jesus brought the name of **Jehovah Zidkenu** into fruition.

Jeremiah 23:6
In his days Judah shall be saved, and Israel shall dwell safely: and this *is* **his name whereby he shall be called, THE LORD OUR RIGHTEOUSNESS.**

Romans 3:21, 22
But now the righteousness of God without the law is manifested, being witnessed by the law and the prophets;
Even the righteousness of God *which is* **by faith [the believing] of Jesus Christ unto all and upon all them that believe: for there is no difference:**

II Corinthians 5:21
For he hath made him *to be* **sin for us, who knew no sin; that we might be made the righteousness of God in him.**

We have been made the righteousness of God in him, in Christ. We are able to walk even through the valley of the shadow of death and fear no evil for Thou art with us. The Lord our righteousness has done this for us. We stand in the very presence of God without any sense of sin, fear, guilt, or shortcomings, because we are made the righteousness of God in him. You always see the covenant relation of Jehovah fulfilled in Christ, for there isn't any promise given which won't be fulfilled. Israel was also given a promise in the name of **Jehovah Shammah**, for God promised to be there. For us the fulfillment of the name of the Lord being with us is found in the work Christ, completed for us and revealed in the mystery.

Colossians 1:26, 27
***Even* the mystery which hath been hid from ages and from generations, but now is made manifest to his saints:**
To whom God would make known what *is* **the riches of the glory of this mystery among the Gentiles; which is Christ in you, the hope of glory.**

To Israel, also, there was a promise made in the name **Jehovah Shammah** of a future presence where the Lord would be.

Ezekiel 48:31a, 35
And the gates of the city *shall be* **after the names of the tribes of**

Appendix II

Israel:
> *It was* round about eighteen thousand *measures*: and the name of the city from *that* day *shall be*, The LORD *is* there.

Revelation 21:21-23
> And the twelve gates *were* twelve pearls: every several gate was of one pearl: and the street of the city *was* pure gold, as it were transparent glass.
>
> And I saw no temple therein: for the Lord God Almighty and the Lamb are the temple of it.
>
> And the city had no need of the sun, neither of the moon, to shine in it: for the glory of God did lighten it, and the Lamb *is* the light thereof.

Israel will ask, "And how do we know the way to this city of gold?" The answer is the Lord is the way. You will know the way, because Jesus will reveal the name of **Jehovah Nissi**.

Exodus 17:9, 14 and 15
> And Moses said unto Joshua, Choose us out men, and go out, fight with Amalek: to morrow I will stand on the top of the hill with the rod of God in mine hand.
>
> And the LORD said unto Moses, Write this *for* a memorial in a book, and rehearse *it* in the ears of Joshua: for I will utterly put out the remembrance of Amalek from under heaven.
>
> And Moses built an altar, and called the name of it Jehovah nissi.

Jehovah Nissi is our standard or banner. It stands as an ensign to follow, but it also acts as a canopy protecting all who come under the name of **Jehovah Nissi**. The word "standard" is derived from, "a standing place." Moses said, *I will stand on top of the hill with the rod of God in my hand.* The 23rd Psalm reads, "Thy rod and Thy staff comfort me." We are blessed when we come under the protection and comfort of the covering of **Jehovah Nissi**. The 23rd Psalm also states, "Thou preparest a table before me in the presence of mine enemies." This has to do with a wedding or banquet table, which was also covered by a banner when the guests came under it to eat, symbolizing the covering of God on the marriage. To answer the question of how the name of **Jehovah Nissi** reveals the way to the city where the Lord God Almighty and the lamb are, we will look first at how this standard will stand as an ensign to Israel.

Appendix II

Isaiah 49:22, 23b
Thus saith the Lord GOD, Behold, I will lift up mine hand to the Gentiles, and set up my standard to the people: and they shall bring thy sons in *their* arms, and thy daughters shall be carried upon *their* shoulders.

...and thou shalt know that I *am* the LORD: for they shall not be ashamed that wait for me.

Isaiah 11:10-12
And in that day there shall be a root of Jesse, which shall stand for an ensign of the people; to it shall the Gentiles seek: and his rest shall be glorious.

And it shall come to pass in that day, *that* the Lord shall set his hand again the second time to recover the remnant of his people, which shall be left, from Assyria, and from Egypt, and from Pathros, and from Cush, and from Elam, and from Shinar, and from Hamath, and from the islands of the sea.

And he shall set up an ensign for the nations, and shall assemble the outcasts of Israel, and gather together the dispersed of Judah from the four corners of the earth.

Isaiah 18:3
All ye inhabitants of the world, and dwellers on the earth, see ye, when he lifteth up an ensign on the mountains; and when he bloweth a trumpet, hear ye.

Matthew 24:27
For as the lightning cometh out of the east, and shineth even unto the west; so shall also the coming of the Son of man be.

Matthew 24:30, 31
And then shall appear the sign of the Son of man in heaven: and then shall all the tribes of the earth mourn, and they shall see the Son of man coming in the clouds of heaven with power and great glory.

And he shall send his angels with a great sound of a trumpet, and they shall gather together his elect from the four winds, from one end of heaven to the other.

This is what Israel is waiting for. This is their hope. It is in the resurrection that they will see the standard of the Lord. Out of the root of David, Christ will be raised as an ensign for the nations, and all Israel shall

Appendix II

be gathered from wherever they have been scattered. All the inhabitants of the earth shall see when Christ comes to gather Israel. All the dead shall rise and witness the sign of the son of man in heaven coming with power and great glory. There will be things which must occur first. The time for Christ's coming and the mystery which follows must be allowed for, but in the end, the name of **Jehovah Nissi** will be fully known and revealed to all who are called Israel.

I Corinthians 15:21- 25
For since by man *came* death, by man *came* also the resurrection of the dead.
For as in Adam all die, even so in Christ shall all be made alive.
But every man in his own order: Christ the firstfruits; afterward they that are Christ's at his coming.
Then *cometh* the end, when he shall have delivered up the kingdom to God, even the Father; when he shall have put down all rule and all authority and power.
For he must reign, till he hath put all enemies under his feet.

With the resurrection of the dead, all shall be made alive. In the end, Christ will deal with all the nations and tribes of the earth as well as the nation and people of Israel in judgments and righteousness. The 23rd Psalm says, "Thou preparest a table before me in the presence of mine enemies." This speaks of the time when the marriage of the bridegroom, which is Christ and all who belong to the body of Christ, and Israel, which is the bride, are joined.

Revelation 19:1
And after these things I heard a great voice of much people in heaven, saying, Alleluia; Salvation, and glory, and honour, and power, unto the Lord our God:
Revelation 19:7- 11
Let us be glad and rejoice, and give honour to him: for the marriage of the Lamb is come, and his wife hath made herself ready.
And to her was granted that she should be arrayed in fine linen, clean and white: for the fine linen is the righteousness of saints.
And he saith unto me, Write, Blessed *are* they which are called unto the marriage supper of the Lamb. And he saith unto me, These are the true sayings of God.
And I saw heaven opened, and behold a white horse; and he that sat upon him *was* called Faithful and True, and in righteousness he doth

judge and make war.

Revelation 19:14, 19
And the armies *which were* in heaven followed him upon white horses, clothed in fine linen, white and clean.
And I saw the beast, and the kings of the earth, and their armies, gathered together to make war against him that sat on the horse, and against his army.

This speaks of a time yet to come. It will occur after Christ comes back for his saints, which is spoken of in the books of Thessalonians. Christ will come with his saints to gather Israel and deal with the nations in judgment. God will prepare a table in the presence of his enemy. Those who belong to the body of Christ are already covered. Our righteousness will be the covering for the bride who will be joined to us in marriage. There are things available to us today that just weren't available before.

Romans 4:7, 8
Blessed *are* they whose iniquities are forgiven, and whose sins are covered.
Blessed *is* the man to whom the Lord will not impute sin.

Blessed are they whose sins are covered. We enjoy this blessing already in Christ. For those who came before Christ, it remains yet a future blessing. The same is true when it comes to understanding the name of **Jehovah Mekaddishkem**, for our sanctification is already accomplished in Christ. For Israel the sanctification promised is yet in the future.

Exodus 31:12, 13
And the LORD spake unto Moses, saying, Speak thou also unto the children of Israel, saying, Verily my sabbaths ye shall keep: for it *is* a sign between me and you
throughout your generations; that *ye* may know that I *am* the LORD that doth sanctify you.

A sign signifies the work that has been wrought. God was at work in Christ even from the beginning, and the promise of sanctification was set forth even before it was accomplished. But Israel did not like the statutes; they did not want to live in them and wait for the promise of the coming Christ to be fulfilled.

Appendix II

Ezekiel 20:11-13
And I gave them my statutes, and showed them my judgments, which *if* a man do, he shall even live in them.
Moreover also I gave them my sabbaths, to be a sign between me and them, that they might know that I *am* the LORD that sanctify them.
But the house of Israel rebelled against me in the wilderness: they walked not in my statutes, and they despised my judgments, which *if* a man do, he shall even live in them; and my sabbaths they greatly polluted.

The Sabbaths were set forth for rest in order to show the name of **Jehovah Zeba'oth** and to be a reminder of Christ's coming. The Sabbath should be a reminder of the finished work of Christ.

Isaiah 30:1
Woe to the rebellious children, saith the LORD, that take counsel, but not of me; and that cover with a covering, but not of my spirit, that they may add sin to sin.

We have been given a covering in Christ. We have been given the spirit of God in the new birth. We had to believe in Jesus Christ in order to receive this blessing. Israel had to believe as well, but their believing was unto Christ. He had not come at the time of which these things were spoken here in the Old Testament.

Hebrews 3:10, 11
Wherefore I was grieved with that generation, and said, They do alway err in *their* heart; and they have not known my ways.
So I sware in my wrath, They shall not enter into my rest.

God said, "I sware in my wrath." This has to do with a particular time rather than a state of mind. In the time of wrath, they shall not enter into God's rest. God is talking to Israel here. It is Israel's generations with which He is grieved. There will be a day when the wrath of God is revealed against all unrighteousness. As long as it is called today, you and I have the opportunity of believing the truth, receiving the spirit, and being saved from the wrath to come.

II Thessalonians 2:11-13
And for this cause God shall send them strong delusion, that they should believe a lie:

Appendix II

That they all might be damned who believed not the truth, but had pleasure in unrighteousness.

But we are bound to give thanks alway to God for you, brethren beloved of the Lord, because God hath from the beginning chosen you to salvation through sanctification of the Spirit and belief of the truth:

I Thessalonians 5:9
For God hath not appointed us to wrath, but to obtain salvation by our Lord Jesus Christ.

Today we can know the name of **Jehovah Mekaddishkem** because we have salvation and sanctification through Jesus Christ our Lord. Israel also had a promise of sanctification awaiting them in the end if they held fast to their confidence in the name of **Jehovah Mekaddishkem**.

Hebrews 3:14
For we are made partakers of Christ, if we hold the beginning of our confidence stedfast unto the end.

We, meaning Israel, are partakers of Christ if we hold fast to that which was told to us even from the beginning. Many of the children of Israel lived and died before Christ came the first time. Christ had to complete his work before we could believe in him and immediately receive the promise. Yet Israel could still believe in Christ because of what was told to them.

Hebrews 4:1- 3
Let us therefore fear, lest, a promise being left *us* of entering into his rest, any of you should seem to come short of it.
For unto us was the gospel preached, as well as unto them: but the word preached did not profit them, not being mixed with faith in them that heard *it*.
For we which have believed do enter into rest, as he said, As I have sworn in my wrath, if they shall enter into my rest: although the works were finished from the foundation of the world.

Let us fear. Again speaking to Israel. They need to take heed to this, because today their promise is in the Gospel just like everyone else. The last thing they want is to end up in the day of wrath. It is needful to believe in the Lord Jesus Christ today, while it is available to be saved and sanctified and to become a part of the body of Christ. Those of Israel who are alive today have the distinct honor and privilege of becoming members of the

Appendix II

body of Christ, as well as being associated with the bride of Christ.

Hebrews 4:6- 9
Seeing therefore it remaineth that some must enter therein, and they to whom it was first preached entered not in because of unbelief:

Again, he limiteth a certain day, saying in David, To day, after so long a time; as it is said, To day if ye will hear his voice, harden not your hearts.

For if Jesus had given them rest, then would he not afterward have spoken of another day.

There remaineth therefore a rest to the people of God.

The rest which was promised has not yet come for all Israel. There is no need for concern because there remains a rest to the people of God. Israel need not fear because of what is available today. This does not negate what God had previously promised to Israel.

Hebrews 13:10- 14
We have an altar, whereof they have no right to eat which serve the tabernacle.

For the bodies of those beasts, whose blood is brought into the sanctuary by the high priest for sin, are burned without the camp.

Wherefore Jesus also, that he might sanctify the people with his own blood, suffered without the gate.

Let us go forth therefore unto him without the camp, bearing his reproach.

For here have we no continuing city, but we seek one to come.

All of Israel's concerns can be put to rest, because there is a city yet to come. The name of **Jehovah Mekaddishkem** will be known to all those who hold their believing to the end. The book of Hebrews ties the Old Testament with the New for Israel.

Hebrews 11:8- 10
By faith [believing] **Abraham, when he was called to go out into a place which he should after receive for an inheritance, obeyed; and he went out, not knowing whither he went.**

By faith [believing] **he sojourned in the land of promise, as *in* a strange country, dwelling in tabernacles with Isaac and Jacob, the heirs with him of the same promise:**

For he looked for a city which hath foundations, whose builder

and maker *is* God.

Hebrews 11:13
These all died in faith [believing], **not having received the promises, but having seen them afar off, and were persuaded of** *them*, **and embraced** *them*, **and confessed that they were strangers and pilgrims on the earth.**

All these who came before died in believing. They had not received the promise, but they saw it and embraced it. All who are invited to the wedding under the covering of the bride will enjoy the city which God has prepared.

Hebrews 11:16
But now they desire a better *country*, **that is, an heavenly: wherefore God is not ashamed to be called their God: for he hath prepared for them a city.**

Hebrews 11:39, 40
And these all, having obtained a good report through faith [believing], **received not the promise:**
God having provided some better thing for us, that they without us should not be made perfect.

The bride will be made perfect in marriage. Marriage joins two individuals together, and they become as one. All who come under the name of Israel make up the bride. The bride will be joined to the bridegroom. Christ is the bridegroom. All those who now belong to the body of Christ also come under this banner. All that we already have in Christ, belonging to the body of Christ, the bride will also enjoy. However, without us, they could not be made perfect. What a wonderful thing to understand. This is how the name of **Jehovah Mekaddishkem** is made known, in our sanctification. This is why it says in the Psalm, "Surely goodness and mercy shall follow me all the days of my life: and I will dwell in the house of the Lord for ever." The Lord is **Jehovah Elyon**, the Lord most high. Jesus Christ made known the name of **Jehovah Elyon** and then was seated on high awaiting the day when God will send him back to collect his own. **Jehovah Elyon** is the Lord who reigns on high.

Genesis 14:18- 20
And Melchizedek king of Salem brought forth bread and wine:

Appendix II

and he *was* the priest of the most high God.

And he blessed him, and said, Blessed *be* Abram of the most high God, possessor of heaven and earth:

And blessed be the most high God, which hath delivered thine enemies into thy hand.

Psalms 7:17

I will praise the LORD according to his righteousness: and will sing praise to the name of the LORD most high.

The most high God is possessor of heaven and earth. He created it, and He sits as king over a spiritual kingdom. All others who are called gods or who would be king over a kingdom or certain domain still come under the most high God. His name is the Lord most high.

Luke 1:30- 33

And the angel said unto her, Fear not, Mary: for thou hast found favour with God.

And, behold, thou shalt conceive in thy womb, and bring forth a son, and shalt call his name JESUS.

He shall be great, and shall be called the Son of the Highest: and the Lord God shall give unto him the throne of his father David:

And he shall reign over the house of Jacob for ever; and of his kingdom there shall be no end.

Jesus came in the name of the Lord most high, **Jehovah Elyon**. He is the son of the Highest. Jesus came bearing the name of the Lord, and he would show forth all that is in that name. God is a spiritual being, yet Christ is able to show us a clear and distinct image of the person of God through a living expression of His name.

Hebrews 1:3- 5

Who being the brightness of *his* glory, and the express image of his person, and upholding all things by the word of his power, when he had by himself purged our sins, sat down on the right hand of the Majesty on high;

Being made so much better than the angels, as he hath by inheritance obtained a more excellent name than they.

For unto which of the angels said he at any time, Thou art my Son, this day have I begotten thee? And again, I will be to him a Father, and he shall be to me a Son?

Appendix II

Jesus came in the name of **Jehovah Elyon**. What more fitting place for him to be seated once he completed the work he had to do than at the right hand of the Majesty on high, **Jehovah Elyon**. Jesus inherited an excellent name as the son of God. We, too, who believe in Jesus Christ have received an inheritance, for we also take on the name of our Father through the son.

Ephesians 1:5
Having predestinated [foreknown] **us unto the adoption of children** [the adoption of children is one word, sonship] **by Jesus Christ to himself, according to the good pleasure of his will,**

Ephesians 1:10, 11
That in the dispensation [administration] **of the fulness of times he might gather together in one all things in Christ, both which are in heaven, and which are on earth;** *even* **in him:**
In whom also we have obtained an inheritance, being predestinated [foreknown] **according to the purpose of him who worketh all things after the counsel of his own will:**

Ephesians 2:6
And hath raised *us* **up together, and made** *us* **sit together in heavenly** *places* **in Christ Jesus:**

Ephesians 2:18, 19
For through him we both have access by one Spirit unto the Father.
Now therefore ye are no more strangers and foreigners, but fellowcitizens with the saints, and of the household of God.

Surely goodness and mercy shall follow me all the days of my life: and I will dwell in the house of the Lord forever. Now knowing the ten redemptive names of Jehovah, you can see why we can say such a thing as this: Jesus Christ is the fulfillment of the redemptive names of Jehovah and he did it all for us. He did it so you and I could know the name of the Lord. He did it so we could have access by one spirit unto the Father. God is our Father, and we are His sons and daughters. We now belong to the household of God through our Lord and savior, Jesus Christ, whom God raised from the dead and seated at His own right hand. This has been God's plan and good pleasure even from the beginning. The redemptive names of Jehovah

Appendix II

reveal to us God's dealings with man. Jesus Christ shows us in his life, through his life, by his life, and with his life just what is in the name of the Lord. Jesus Christ is God's namesake, and in the name of the Lord, he reveals God's purpose and plan for life.

I am come that they might have life,
and that they might have *it* more abundantly.

www.ingramcontent.com/pod-product-compliance
Lightning Source LLC
Chambersburg PA
CBHW032016230426

43671CB00005B/108